THE HEIBERGS AND THE THEATER
BETWEEN VAUDEVILLE, ROMANTIC
COMEDY AND NATIONAL DRAMA

The Heibergs and the Theater
Between Vaudeville, Romantic Comedy and National Drama

Edited by Jon Stewart

Museum Tusculanum Press
Søren Kierkegaard Research Centre
University of Copenhagen
2012

Jon Stewart (ed.)
The Heibergs and the Theater
Between Vaudeville, Romantic Comedy and National Drama

© Museum Tusculanum Press and Jon Stewart, 2012
Layout and cover design by K.Nun Design, Denmark
Printed in Denmark by AKA-PRINT
ISBN 978-87-635-3897-8
ISSN 1903 3338

Danish Golden Age Studies
vol. 7

General Editor
Jon Stewart

Editorial Board
Finn Gredal Jensen
Mads Sohl Jessen

Cover illustration: *The Royal Theater in Copenhagen*
(Detail from a lithograph, ca. 1860).
Reproduced courtesy of the City Museum of Copenhagen.

This volume is published with financial support from
Aksel Tovborg Jensens Legat
E. Lerager Larsens Fond
Hielmstierne-Rosencroneske Stiftelse
Landsdommer V. Gieses Legat

Museum Tusculanum Press
Birketinget 6
DK-2300 Copenhagen S
Denmark
order@mtp.dk
www.mtp.dk

Mrs. Gyllembourg Reading one of Her Stories aloud for Heiberg and Mrs. Heiberg
(Oil on canvas by Wilhelm Marstrand, 1870,
(Private Collection © The Museum of National History
Frederiksborg Castle / Hans Petersen Foto.)

Table of Contents

List of Contributors

Wolfgang Behschnitt, Universiteit Gent, Vakgroep Scandinavistiek en Noord-Europakunde, Rozier 44, 9000 Gent, Belgium.

Joachim Grage, Albert-Ludwigs-Universität Freiburg im Breisgau, Institut für Vergleichende Germanische Philologie und Skandinavistik, Postfach, 79098 Freiburg, Germany.

Gunilla Hermansson, Göteborgs Universitet, Institutionen för litteratur, idéhistoria och religion, Renströmsgaten 6, Box 200, 405 30 Göteborg, Sweden.

Mads Sohl Jessen, Københavns Universitet, Institut for Nordiske Studier og Sprogvidenskab, Njalsgade 120, 2300 Copenhagen S, Denmark.

Lasse Horne Kjældgaard, Det Danske Sprog- og Litteraturselskab, Christians Brygge 1, 1219 Copenhagen K, Denmark.

Finn Hauberg Mortensen, Københavns Universitet, Institut for Nordiske Studier og Sprogvidenskab, Njalsgade 120, 2300 Copenhagen S, Denmark.

Klaus Müller-Wille, Universität Zürich, Deutsches Seminar, Abteilung für Nordische Philologie, Schönberggasse 9, 8001 Zurich, Switzerland.

Karin Sanders, University of California, Department of Scandinavian Studies, 6303 Dwinelle Hall, Berkeley, CA 94720, USA.

Joachim Schiedermair, Ernst Moritz Arndt Universität, Nordische Abteilung, Hans-Fallada-Str. 20, 17487 Greifswald, Germany.

Jon Stewart, Søren Kierkegaard Forskningscenteret, Københavns Universitet, Farvergade 27D, 1463 Copenhagen K, Denmark.

Acknowledgements

The present volume collects the papers given at the conference "Zwischen Vaudeville, romantischer Komödie und Nationaldrama. Die Heibergs und das Theater," which was held from June 18-20, 2009 at the Deutsches Seminar, Abteilung für Nordische Philologie at the Universität Zürich. This conference, which was organized by Klaus-Müller Wille, Jon Stewart and Kirsten Wechsel, was generously supported by the financial assistance from the Universität Zürich, the Hochschulstiftung der Universität Zürich, the Schweizerische Gesellschaft für Skandinavische Studien, and the Søren Kierkegaard Research Centre.

The writing and scholarly level of this work have been significantly improved by the meticulous corrections and suggestions of Poul Houe. Klaus Müller-Wille played an important role in organizing this volume by, among other things, his frequent correspondence with the authors. I would like to accord a special thanks for Katalin Nun for her outstanding work in typesetting and designing this volume as well as preparing the index. Due to her efforts this work has been made much more aesthetically attractive than it would have otherwise been. The printing costs for the present volume were kindly provided by the following foundations: Aksel Tovborg Jensens Legat, E. Lerager Larsens Fond, Hielmstierne-Rosencroneske Stiftelse, and Landsdommer V. Gieses Legat. I would like to thank these foundations for their invaluable support.

The illustrations appear courtesy of the Department of Maps, Prints and Photographs at The Royal Library, the Copenhagen City Museum, the Theater Museum in Copenhagen, and Thorvaldsen's Museum in Copenhagen.

Introduction:
The Heibergs and the Theater

Not only was Johan Ludvig Heiberg the most famous theater critic of the Danish Golden Age, but he also wrote some of the most important aesthetic essays of his day, in which different theatrical genres played a key role. Some of his dramatic works belong to the most successful plays ever performed at the Royal Theater. Moreover, Heiberg was married to one of the greatest Danish actresses of the nineteenth century. Both his wife Johanne Luise Heiberg and his mother Thomasine Gyllembourg wrote dramatic works that were performed on the stage of the Royal Theater. At the end of his career he became director of that famous cultural institution, a position which he held from 1849 to 1856.

Heiberg dominated theater life in mid-nineteenth century Denmark in an absolutely unique and astonishing way. But it is not only because of this remarkable position in the small literary field of Golden Age Denmark that Heiberg's dramatic works and his theater theory are worthy of study. As the articles in this volume attest, Heiberg's lifelong occupation with theater was closely tied to his far-reaching philosophical and political interests. In this respect his aesthetic essays as well as his plays offer useful material for those hoping to obtain new insight into the cultural life of Golden Age Denmark. His texts should also be considered from an international perspective; Heiberg's somewhat odd attempt to create a new aesthetic hierarchy on the basis of Prussian Hegelian philosophy and Parisian popular theater shows that his works were characterized by paradoxes and contradictions that are of general interest. But before discussing the specific issues we will give a brief survey of Heiberg research that will allow us to frame the specific topic of this volume.

I. Johan Ludvig Heiberg: A Brief History of the Research

Johan Ludvig Heiberg was clearly a major pillar in the Danish Golden Age, authoring a vast array of works on different subjects including lyric poetry, drama, aesthetic treatises, literary criticism, philosophy, natural science, not to mention the numerous translations that he did. Given Heiberg's enormous stature in the period, it is at first glance somewhat surprising that he has not enjoyed a more stable and constant reception on a par with the classics in other languages. While there have been sporadic studies on different aspects of Heiberg's authorship since his death, it is only quite recently that one can with justice talk about a strong and sustained research interest in his varied *oeuvre*. But Heiberg's fate is by no means unique in the Danish context. In fact, many of the leading figures of the Golden Age fell out of the eye of the reading public and became the objects of a collective forgetfulness.

A. After Heiberg's Death

Immediately after Heiberg's death in 1860 his wife Johanne Luise Heiberg (1812-90) in cooperation with Andreas Frederik Krieger (1817-93) put together an ambitious collected works edition of Heiberg's writings. This consisted of 11 volumes of *Prosaiske Skrifter*, 11 volumes of *Poetiske Skrifter*, and one volume of letters.[1] (This replaced an earlier edition that Heiberg published himself from 1833 to 1843 consisting of 7 volumes of *Skuespil*, 2 volumes of *Digte og Fortællinger*, and 3 volumes of *Prosaiske Skrifter*.[2] In 1848-49 Heiberg had also published an eight-

---

[1] Johan Ludvig Heiberg, *Samlede Skrifter, Poetiske Skrifter*, vols. 1-11, Copenhagen: C.A. Reitzels Forlag 1862; *Prosaiske Skrifter*, vols. 1-11, Copenhagen: C.A. Reitzels Forlag 1861-62. *Breve fra og til J.L. Heiberg*, ed. by Andreas Frederik Krieger and Carl Christopher Georg Andræ, Copenhagen: C.A. Reitzels Forlag 1862.
[2] Johan Ludvig Heiberg, *Samlede Skrifter* consisting of *Skuespil*, vols. 1-7, Copenhagen: J.H. Schubothes Boghandling 1833-41. *Digte og Fortællinger*, vols. 1-2, Copenhagen: J.H. Schubothes Boghandling 1834-35. *Prosaiske Skrifter*, vols. 1-3, Copenhagen: J.H. Schubothes Boghandling 1841-43.

volume edition of his poetic works.[1]) Presumably the editors of the 23-volume *Samlede Skrifter*, from 1861-62, would be surprised to learn that theirs remains to this very day the most extensive edition of Heiberg's writings. Although there have been numerous reprints, primarily of Heiberg's poetic or dramatic works, there has been nothing to rival either the *Prosaiske Skrifter* or the *Poetiske Skrifter* from 150 years ago. Only their one-volume edition of letters has been surpassed by subsequent scholarship.

This older edition has several shortcomings, the most serious of which is that it is incomplete. Several of Heiberg's shorter pieces, for example, from his journal *Kjøbenhavns flyvende Post*, have not been included. Similarly, this edition contains changes in orthography and punctuation vis-à-vis the original printings. The texts in this edition are clearly based on some version of the *letzte Hand* principle, with the editors even inserting some of Heiberg's later handwritten notes into the texts. The philological principles for these changes are, however, nowhere outlined or elucidated. Suffice it to say that there is a serious need for a new more complete, scholarly, text-critical edition of Heiberg's works that is in harmony with current philological standards.

B. 1860-1930

In the second half of the nineteenth century there was still a general recognition of Heiberg's status, primarily in the context of the theater. Here one can refer to Arthur Aumont's (1860-1917) monograph *J.L. Heiberg og hans Slægt paa den danske Skueplads* and Julius Clausen's (1868-1951) *Kulturhistoriske Studier over Heibergs Vaudeviller*, both from the year 1891.[2] The great literary critic of the period Georg Brandes (1842-1927) also authored articles on Heiberg during this time.[3]

---

[1] Johan Ludvig Heiberg, *Poetiske Skrifter*, vols. 1-8, Copenhagen: J.H. Schubothes Boghandling 1848-49.

[2] Arthur Aumont, *J.L. Heiberg og hans Slægt paa den danske Skueplads*, Copenhagen: Jørgensen 1891. Julius Clausen, *Kulturhistoriske Studier over Heibergs Vaudeviller*, Copenhagen: V. Pio's Boghandel 1891.

[3] Georg Brandes, "J.L. Heiberg (1791-1860)," in his *Samlede Skrifter*, vols. 1-18, Copenhagen: Gyldendal 1899-1910, vol. 1, pp. 462-512. "Mathilde Fibiger og J.L. Heiberg," in his *Samlede Skrifter*, vol. 15, pp. 298-303.

Mention should likewise be made of the more or less unknown work
by one Peter Hansen, *Om Johan Ludvig Heiberg. Nogle litteraturhistoriske
Oplysninger.*[1] This book consists of two articles previously published
by the author: the first, "J.L. Heibergs første Polemik," which is about
the rich context in which Heiberg's *Christmas Jests and New Year's Fun*
appeared, and the second, "J.L. Heibergs Laterna-magica-Vise," which
is a detailed interpretation of the named poem. Although it can by
no means be regarded as Heiberg research, Johanne Luise Heiberg's
memoirs, published in 1891-92, proved to be an important biographical
source of information about Heiberg.[2]

Amidst this flurry of activity surrounding the literary and biographical
side of Heiberg, the sole sign of interest in Heiberg's philosophy is a brief
chapter by Harald Høffding (1843-1931), "Heiberg og Martensen," in his
Danske Filosofer from 1909.[3] Høffding treats Heiberg and Hans Lassen
Martensen together in a single chapter as representatives of G.W.F.
Hegel's philosophy. Høffding outlines, in an introductory way, Heiberg's
use of this philosophy and its importance in the context primarily of
aesthetics and philosophy of religion.

Starting at around the turn of the century, the literary scholar
Vilhelm Andersen (1864-1953) wrote about Heiberg in a couple of
different contexts.[4] Perhaps most significantly, he canonized Heiberg's

---

[1] P. Hansen, *Om Johan Ludvig Heiberg. Nogle litteraturhistoriske Oplysninger*,
     Copenhagen: Kristian Vissing 1867.
[2] Johanne Luise Heiberg, *Et Liv gjenoplevet i Erindringen*, vols. 1-4, Copenhagen:
     Gyldendalske Boghandel, Nordisk Forlag 1891-92. (Reprinted as Folkeudgave,
     vols. 1-2, 1904. 3rd edition, vols. 1-2, 1913. 4th revised edition, ed. by Aage Friis, vols.
     1-4, 1944. 5th revised edition, by Niels Birger Wamberg, vols. 1-4, Copenhagen:
     Gyldendal 1973-74.)
[3] Harald Høffding, *Danske Filosofer*, Copenhagen: Gyldendalske Boghandel, Nordisk
     Forlag 1909, see pp. 129-137.
[4] See, for example, Vilhelm Andersen, *Tider og Typer af dansk Aands Historie*, Første
     Række: Humanisme. Anden Del: Goethe, vols. 1-2, Copenhagen, Kristiania:
     Gyldendalske Boghandel, Nordisk Forlag 1915-16, vol. 1, "J.L. Heiberg," pp. 219-
     280; vol. 2, "Fra Heiberg til Kierkegaard," pp. 3-64. See also his "J.L. Heiberg," in
     Illustreret dansk Litteraturhistorie, by Carl S. Petersen and Vilhelm Andersen, vols.
     1-4, Copenhagen, Kristiania, London, Berlin: Gyldendalske Boghandel, Nordisk
     Forlag 1924-29, vol. 3, "Det nittende Aarhundredes første Halvdel," pp. 411-434.
     See also his "Den Heibergske Skoles Naturopfattelse," *Danske Studier*, Copenhagen:
     Gad 1893, pp. 96-171.

place in Danish literary history by devoting extensive chapters to him in his two-volume work, *Tider og Typer af dansk Aands Historie* (1915-16), and later in a four-volume work, coauthored with Carl S. Petersen (1873-1958), *Illustreret dansk Litteraturhistorie* (1924-29).

Along the same lines is Paul V. Rubow's (1896-1972) *Dansk litterær Kritik i det nittende Aarhundrede indtil 1870*, which was first published in 1921.[1] While this work gives an overview of literary criticism in Denmark from Adam Oehlenschläger (1779-1850) to Georg Brandes, it is Heiberg who plays the central role. Indeed, when Rubow reworked the text for a new edition, he effectively turned it into a book on Heiberg with the new title *Heiberg og hans Skole i Kritiken*.[2] While Rubow discusses some aspects of Heiberg's Hegelian philosophy, his main focus is clearly on Heiberg as critic and theorist of aesthetics.

C. The 1930s-1940s

Perhaps the strongest period of research came in the 1930s and 1940s. This period was marked by a decided biographical interest in Heiberg and his family and was crowned by the work of the literary scholar Morten Borup (1894-1989). An important forerunner to Borup's biographical work was Julius Clausen's *Omkring det Heibergske Hus* from 1934.[3] This highly readable book begins with the story of Heiberg's parents, Peter Andreas Heiberg (1758-1841) and Thomasine Gyllembourg (1773-1856) and ends with the death of Johanne Luise Heiberg in 1890. Unlike Borup's later work, Clausen keeps primarily to the biographical dimension of the Heiberg family and does not enter into detailed discussions of their actual works. In 1940 Aage Friis (1870-1949) edited a volume of correspondence between Johan Ludvig Heiberg and his wife under the title *Fra det Heibergske Hjem*.[4] Three years later Morten Borup

[1] Paul V. Rubow, *Dansk litterær Kritik i det nittende Aarhundrede indtil 1870*, Copenhagen: Levin & Munksgaard 1921.
[2] Paul V. Rubow, *Heiberg og hans Skole i Kritiken*, Copenhagen: Gyldendal 1953.
[3] Julius Clausen, *Omkring det Heibergske Hus*, Copenhagen: Bianco Lunos Bogtrykkeri Aktieselskab 1934.
[4] *Fra det Heibergske Hjem. Johan Ludvig og Johanne Luise Heibergs indbyrdes Brevveksling*, ed. by Aage Friis, Copenhagen: J.H. Schultz Forlag 1940.

published a volume of correspondence, entitled *Heibergske Familiebreve*.[1] This collection contains, among other things, letters from Heiberg to his exiled father in Paris and letters from Thomasine Gyllembourg to her son and daughter-in-law. This edition clearly represents the preliminary work to Borup's later more extensive collection of Heiberg's letters. At roughly the same time as Borup's work there appeared Torben Krogh's (1895-1970) *Heibergs Vaudeviller. Studier over Motiver og Melodier.*[2]

The definitive edition of Heiberg's letters was edited by Morten Borup and appeared in five volumes from 1946-50.[3] This work was a vast improvement over both the previous one-volume edition that was published as a part of Heiberg's *Samlede Skrifter* and the abovementioned editions. Work on the letters supplied Borup with a wealth of information that he used for his landmark three-volume biography of Heiberg, which appeared from 1947-49.[4] Known for its thoroughness and accuracy, this outstanding piece of scholarship remains a profoundly useful resource even to this day. Many later biographical accounts are virtually paraphrases of it.

D. The Late 1960s, 1970s and 1980s

After this high watermark in the research in the 1940s, little happened in Heiberg research over the next two decades. It was only with the work of Henning Fenger (1921-85) in the 1970s that Heiberg again became a topic among literary scholars.[5] Of particular importance was his very readable monograph *The Heibergs*, which first appeared in English translation in 1971 and oddly two decades later in the Danish

[1] *Heibergske Familiebreve*, ed. by Morten Borup, Copenhagen: Gyldendal 1943.
[2] Torben Krogh, *Heibergs Vaudeviller. Studier over Motiver og Melodier*, Copenhagen: Povl Branner 1942.
[3] *Breve og Aktstykker vedrørende Johan Ludvig Heiberg*, vols. 1-5, ed. by Morten Borup, Copenhagen: Gyldendal 1946-50.
[4] Morten Borup, *Johan Ludvig Heiberg*, vols. 1-3, Copenhagen: Gyldendal 1947-49.
[5] See Fenger's "Jean-Louis Heiberg et son premier séjour à Paris," in *Rencontres et courants littéraires franco-scandinaves, Actes du 7e Congrès International d'Historie des Littératures Scandinaves (Paris 7-12 juillet 1968)*, Paris: Lettres Modernes Minard 1972, pp. 129-143.

original as *Familien Heiberg*.[1] This was a highly significant work since it brought Heiberg to an international audience for the first time. Taking Clausen's abovementioned *Omkring det Heibergske Hus* as his model, Fenger attempts to see the Heiberg family as an organic unit and to present the contributions of its individual members as a part of a larger continuous whole.

From this same period comes the work of the Kierkegaard scholar Niels Thulstrup (1924-88). In particular his *Kierkegaards Forhold til Hegel og til den spekulative Idealisme indtil 1846*, translated into English as *Kierkegaard's Relation to Hegel*, attempts to demonize Heiberg, along Kierkegaardian lines, as a simple-minded Hegelian.[2] This work touches briefly on some of Heiberg's most important philosophical texts but is not interested in the other aspects of his authorship. Heiberg is portrayed here solely as the deserving target of Kierkegaard's sarcastic pen.

From this period also stems Niels Birger Wamberg's (1930-) *H.C. Andersen og Heiberg*.[3] This book carefully traces the complex relation between the hopeful young author and playwright Hans Christian Andersen (1805-75) and the critic Heiberg. During this period Hans Hertel (1939-) edited a useful paperback collection of Heiberg's prose works under the title, *Om Vaudevillen og andre kritiske Artikler*.[4] This work, which appeared in 1968 and contained primarily articles from Heiberg's dramatic criticism, was widely read by students and scholars alike.

---

[1] Henning Fenger, *The Heibergs*, trans. by Frederick J. Marker, New York: Twayne Publishers 1971. *Familien Heiberg*, Copenhagen: Museum Tusculanum 1992.

[2] Niels Thulstrup, *Kierkegaards Forhold til Hegel og til den spekulative Idealisme indtil 1846*, Copenhagen: Gyldendal 1967. In English as *Kierkegaard's Relation to Hegel*, trans. by George L. Stengren, Princeton: Princeton University Press 1980. See also his "Situationen i Danmark og Kierkegaards Reaktion," in *Afsluttende uvidenskabelig Efterskrift*, ed. with Introduction and Commentary by Niels Thulstrup, vols. 1-2, Copenhagen: Gyldendal 1962, vol. 2, pp. 79-102. In English as "The Situation in Denmark and Kierkegaard's Reaction," in Thulstrup's *Commentary on Kierkegaard's Concluding Unscientific Postscript*, trans. by Robert J. Widenmann, Princeton: Princeton University Press 1984, pp. 70-90.

[3] Niels Birger Wamberg, *H.C. Andersen og Heiberg*, Copenhagen: Politikens Forlag 1971.

[4] Johan Ludvig Heiberg, *Om Vaudevillen og andre kritiske Artikler*, ed. by Hans Hertel, Copenhagen: Gyldendal 1968.

The most important event in the research in this field in the 1980s was certainly the publication of the photomechanical reproduction of Heiberg's journal *Kjøbenhavns flyvende Post*.[1] This project was carried out by Uffe Andreasen (1943-) under the auspices of the Society for Danish Language and Literature. Previously, access to this journal had been limited since copies of the original printings of *Kjøbenhavns flyvende Post* were rare and expensive. Most scholars could only read them at the Royal Library in Copenhagen. With this facsimile edition, Andreasen opened up this rich body of material more widely for students and researchers.

E. 1990s to the Present

It can be said that since the 1990s there has been a Heiberg renaissance. This claim can be justified by both the number of scholars writing about Heiberg and the different dimensions of Heiberg's thought that are attracting them. While Heiberg scholarship has traditionally been a solely Danish affair, it has now for the first time become something truly international, involving scholars primarily from the Anglophone and Germanophone world. Some of this international interest has been an offshoot of international Kierkegaard scholarship. Here one need only mention names such as Bruce H. Kirmmse,[2] George Pattison[3] and Alastair Hannay[4] in order to see how Heiberg has come to be regarded

[1] *Kjøbenhavns flyvende Post*, ed. by Uffe Andreasen, vols. 1-4, Copenhagen: Det Danske Sprog- og Litteraturselskab 1980-84.

[2] See, for example, Bruce H. Kirmmse, "Johan Ludvig Heiberg," in his *Kierkegaard in Golden Age Denmark*, Bloomington and Indianapolis: Indiana University Press 1990, pp. 136-168.

[3] See, for example, George Pattison, "Søren Kierkegaard: A Theatre Critic of the Heiberg School," *The British Journal of Aesthetics*, vol. 23, 1983, pp. 25-33. Reprinted in *Kierkegaard and His Contemporaries: The Culture of Golden Age Denmark*, ed. by Jon Stewart, Berlin and New York: Walter de Gruyter 2003 (*Kierkegaard Studies Monograph Series*, vol. 10), pp. 319-329. *Kierkegaard: The Aesthetic and the Religious*, 2nd ed., London: SCM Press 1999 [1992]. *'Poor Paris!' Kierkegaard's Critique of the Spectacular City*, Berlin, New York: Walter de Gruyter 1999 (*Kierkegaard Studies Monograph Series*, vol. 2). *Kierkegaard, Religion and the Nineteenth-Century Crisis of Culture*, Cambridge: Cambridge University Press 2002.

[4] Heiberg plays an important role in Hannay's *Kierkegaard: A Biography*, Cambridge: Cambridge University Press 2001.

as an important object of both Kierkegaard's criticism and respect. The Anglophone scholarship has also been interested in Heiberg's relation to Hans Lassen Martensen.[1]

This international interest has been facilitated by new English translations of Heiberg's prose works in the series *Texts from Golden Age Denmark*.[2] While the translations in this series tend to focus on Heiberg's contributions to the philosophical discussions of the age, there have also been useful translations of some of Heiberg's literary and dramatic works such as "A Soul After Death," *No*, and *The April Fools*.[3]

The Danish scholarship has also of course continued as well. Here one can mention the names of scholars such as Finn Hauberg Mortensen and Lasse Horne Kjældgaard.[4] The biographical research on Heiberg also continues to this day.[5] In 2009 Klaus P. Mortensen published his *Stjernekiggeren. Johan Ludvig Heibergs 'sande Biographie.'*[6] This intriguing

[1] See Robert Leslie Horn, *Positivity and Dialectic: A Study of the Theological Method of Hans Lassen Martensen*, Copenhagen: C.A. Reitzel 2007 (*Danish Golden Age Studies*, vol. 2). Curtis L. Thompson, *Following the Cultured Public's Chosen One: Why Martensen Mattered to Kierkegaard*, Copenhagen: C.A. Reitzel 2008 (*Danish Golden Age Studies*, vol. 4). *Hans Lassen Martensen: Theologian, Philosopher and Social Critic*, ed. by Jon Stewart, Copenhagen: Museum Tusculanum Press 2012 (*Danish Golden Age Studies*, vol. 6).

[2] *Heiberg's On the Significance of Philosophy for the Present Age and Other Texts*, ed. and trans. by Jon Stewart, Copenhagen: C.A. Reitzel 2005 (*Texts from Golden Age Denmark*, vol. 1). *Heiberg's Speculative Logic and Other Works*, ed. and trans. by Jon Stewart, Copenhagen: C.A. Reitzel 2006 (*Texts from Golden Age Denmark*, vol. 2). *Heiberg's Introductory Lecture to the Logic Course and Other Texts*, ed. and trans. by Jon Stewart, Copenhagen: C.A. Reitzel 2007 (*Texts from Golden Age Denmark*, vol. 3). *Heiberg's Contingency Regarded from the Point of View of Logic and Other Texts*, ed. and trans. by Jon Stewart, Copenhagen: C.A. Reitzel 2008 (*Texts from Golden Age Denmark*, vol. 4). *Heiberg's Perseus and Other Texts*, ed. and trans. by Jon Stewart, Copenhagen: Museum Tusculanum Press 2011 (*Texts from Golden Age Denmark*, vol. 6).

[3] Johan Ludvig Heiberg, *A Soul After Death*, trans. by Henry Meyer, Seattle: Mermaid Press 1991. *No*, in *Three Danish Comedies*, trans. by Michael Meyer, London: Oberon Books 1999. *The April Fools or An Intrigue at School*, trans. by Peter Vinten-Johansen, Madison: Wisconsin Introductions to Scandinavia 1999.

[4] See, for example, Lasse Horne Kjældgaard, *Mellem hverandre. Tableau og fortælling i Søren Kierkegaards pseudonyme skrifter*, Hellerup: Forlaget Spring 2001. *Sjælen efter døden. Guldalderens moderne gennembrud*, Copenhagen: Gyldendal 2007.

[5] See, for example, Vibeke Schrøder, *Tankens Våben. Johan Ludvig Heiberg*, Copenhagen: Gyldendal 2001.

[6] Klaus P. Mortensen, *Stjernekiggeren. Johan Ludvig Heibergs 'sande Biographie,'* Copenhagen: Gyldendal 2009.

book examines Heiberg's biography and work in connection with the leading women in his life. But one should not forget to mention the interest in Heiberg's philosophical production by figures such as Carl Henrik Koch, who dedicates a chapter to Heiberg in his history of Danish philosophy.[1]

An absolutely invaluable resource for Heiberg research is C.J. Ballhausen's Heiberg bibliography, which was published in the year 2000.[2] New editions of some of Heiberg's works have also appeared in recent decades. In 1990 Klaus P. Mortensen edited a new edition of *Nye Digte*, in the series of Danish classics published by the Society for Danish Language and Literature.[3] A decade later Jens Kristian Andersen published a collection of Heiberg's dramatic works in the same series.[4] Both of these editions are useful not only for making these texts more generally available to the modern reader but also for the new explanatory notes and materials that they include.

At present there are scholars interested in many different aspects of Heiberg's works, indeed, far more than ever before. While the traditional fields of interest are still represented, that is, his poetry, drama, criticism and aesthetics, other areas of his genius are now also being explored, especially his philosophy and his social-political views. Only his works in the natural sciences seem to remain in obscurity to modern research. In any case Heiberg research can truly be said to be an interdisciplinary matter. Moreover, there is recognition that Heiberg must be understood in the larger context of his literary family.

The time has passed when Heiberg was a mere footnote to Kierkegaard or Hans Christian Andersen. Celebrated in Denmark and internationally, he is now rightfully regarded as a major figure of the Golden Age in his own right.

---

[1] Carl Henrik Koch, "Johan Ludvig Heiberg" in his *Den danske idealisme. 1800-1880*, Copenhagen: Gyldendal 2004, pp. 225-248. See also his "Heiberg's 'Hegelian' Solution to the Free Will Problem," in *Johan Ludvig Heiberg: Philosopher, Littérateur, Dramaturge, and Political Thinker*, ed. by Jon Stewart, Copenhagen: Museum Tusculanum Press 2008 (*Danish Golden Age Studies*, vol. 5), pp. 5-36.

[2] C.J. Ballhausen, *Peter Andreas og Johan Ludvig Heiberg. En annoteret bibliografi*, Copenhagen: Dansk Bibliofil-Klub and C.A. Reitzel 2000.

[3] Johan Ludvig Heiberg, *Nye Digte*, ed. by Klaus P. Mortensen, Copenhagen: Det Danske Sprog- og Litteraturselskab, Valby: Borgen 1990.

[4] Johan Ludvig Heiberg, *Dramatik i udvalg*, ed. by Jens Kristian Andersen, Copenhagen: Det Danske Sprog- og Litteraturselskab, Valby: Borgen 2000.

II. Politics, Philosophy and Aesthetic Morality:
The Omnipresence of Theater in Golden Age Denmark

As the survey has shown, Heiberg research has gained momentum during the last decades. While there are some works on Heiberg that contain individual articles about some of his dramaturgical essays or some of his plays, there is to date still no single monograph or anthology that deals exclusively with Heiberg's relation to theater.

In the first article of this volume *Finn Hauberg Mortensen* shows how central this relation is to understanding Heiberg's work as a whole. Hauberg Mortensen offers a bio-bibliographical survey of Heiberg's *oeuvre* with emphasis on his relation to the theater. The article presents a remarkable panorama of Heiberg's critical articles and theoretical studies as well as his most important dramatic works. In unfolding this survey, Hauberg Mortensen stresses Heiberg's lifelong relation to the most important writer of dramatic works during the earlier period of Danish romanticism—Adam Oehlenschläger.

Because of his critique of Oehlenschläger's romantic drama *Varangians in Constantinople* that was based on a pure genre-theoretical argumentation, Heiberg has often been designated as a representative of a formalist aesthetics. This assumption has even led to the description of Heiberg as an author typical of the apolitical or conservative Danish Biedermeier culture. In his article *Lasse Horne Kjældgaard* polemizes against this interpretation of Denmark in the 1830s-40s. With reference to works of Poul Martin Møller, Henrik Hertz and Heiberg, he is able to show that Heiberg's contemporaries described the 1840s as a distinctive political age. Furthermore, he shows that this new political consciousness produced some new concepts for art theory that were based on a critique of pure aestheticization.

Also *Klaus Müller-Wille* is interested in the political dimension of Heiberg's literary works. With reference to Heiberg's royal dramas he tries to show that the author's concept of vaudeville from the beginning was based on a political reflection on the theater's function in a modern state. Already in *Elves' Hill* Heiberg delivers a very subtle defense of the king's role in the nation state. Like the other royal dramas, *Elves' Hill* makes frequent use of intertextual references to Hegel's philosophy of the state. But by using Hegel's philosophy in a dramatic setting, Heiberg changes

the central assumptions of Hegel: the function of the "real" king as the corporal representative of the nation is supplemented by the kingdom and the kings of the national theater. In his late play *Day of the Seven Sleepers* Heiberg deconstructs this pure aesthetic apology of monarchy.

The central question of the aesthetic and political representation of the national body is also discussed in *Wolfgang Behschnitt's* article. In focusing on Thorvaldsen's glamorous return to Denmark, he asks the question of how far the role of the king as the representative of the nation was supplemented by the performance of a "royal" artist. Moreover, the reaction of the chaotic riot of the mob during the welcome ceremony as well as the unloading of Thorvaldsen's classical sculptures raises the central question of the popularity of art. On the one hand, Heiberg is well aware of the problem that Thorvaldsen's classical style is a bad example for national art. But, on the other hand, he uses just the chaotic excesses of the public festival during Thorvaldsen's return to illustrate the danger of an uneducated popular form of art consumption. The real popularity of art should combine national popular elements with ideals of a classical culture.

The question of the popularity of art also stands at the center of Heiberg's famous vaudeville essay that *Joachim Grage* examines in his article. Grage delivers a precise description of the complex genre architecture that Heiberg unfolds in his essay. He shows that the essay certainly presents a new philosophically inspired way of dealing with art in a systematic theoretical frame. But since Grage places the delicate question of the status of the opera in this theory at the center of his own examination, he is able to present a new interpretation of Heiberg's argumentation. First of all he shows that Heiberg's polemical reaction against the Italian opera rests on his general system of aesthetics, where vaudeville is placed between opera and theater. At its core Heiberg's genre theory was based on the concept of a national *Bildungstheater*, where popular and elitist elements were blended. Even if Heiberg was not the convinced opera hater that he has been described to be in the research, he could not appreciate newer forms of opera due to the commitments of his aesthetic system.

Whereas Grage's article circles around the phenomenon of a new form of philosophy of the theater, *Jon Stewart* examines Heiberg's theater of philosophy. The article deals with Heiberg's famous flop at the Royal

Theater—the play *Fata Morgana*. Stewart unfolds the contemporary Danish discussions about the possibility of a speculative drama that brings philosophy to the stage. His survey illustrates the skepticism towards this kind of philosophical approach to art that was formulated by Poul Martin Møller. He also proves the fundamental role of Hans Lassen Martensen, who not only anticipated the concept of a speculative drama but even wrote a long review of *Fata Morgana* where he defends the philosophical conception of the play. The focus on Martensen also helps to illustrate Heiberg's attempt to react to a fundamental cultural crisis of the age that both he and Martensen diagnosed.

The new interest in Heiberg's writings has, as noted, often been motivated by studies on Søren Kierkegaard. *Mads Sohl Jessen* also focuses on the relation between the two Danish philosophers. But in contrast to earlier studies he shows the fundamental role of theater and dramatic theory in the critical dialogue that the two writers established. In his survey of Heiberg's and Kierkegaard's dramaturgical writings especially dealing with the aesthetics of vaudeville, Sohl Jessen uncovers the hidden polemics with which the two authors constantly mocked each other.

Around 1830 Heiberg published a series of articles that were later collected under the heading "Bidrag til en æsthetisk Moral" in which he developed the concept of an aesthetic morality.[1] These articles help to illustrate the range of Heiberg's theories of theater with which he even aimed to influence common behavior. Among other things, Heiberg discusses the relevance of courtesy and *bon ton* in private societies, while he rebukes the bad manners of people who attend certain folk festivities and the theater. In other words, Heiberg discusses the relevance of a performance culture in everyday life. It is clear that this attention to a general role-playing even includes attention to the different rules of behavior for men and women. The last three articles of the present volume deal with this specific aspect of Heiberg's theater theory. All three articles try to explore the relevance of an ethics of performance and focus on the different aspects of ethics as relevant for gender. Perhaps it is not astonishing that two of these articles deal with writings of Heiberg's mother and wife.

---

[1] See Heiberg, *Prosaiske Skrifter*, vols. 1-11, Copenhagen: C.A. Reitzels Forlag 1861-62, vol. 8, pp. 441-509.

Heiberg's play *Nina* belongs to the large number of his dramatic works that has not attracted attention in the research. *Gunilla Hermansson's* argumentation starts with the astonishing notion that the play *Nina*, with its focus on excessive feelings, represents much of what Heiberg was eager to distance himself from in his other writings. Hermansson uses the play to explore the ethics of feeling that Heiberg develops. She stresses his ambivalent concept of love that reveals both a deep fascination with the destructive power of eros and the attempt to regulate these powers. At first glance Heiberg's play seems to be an heir of the typical paradoxes and ambivalences that accompanied the rise of a middle-class understanding of family, virtue and love. But the fact that Heiberg rewrote the play several times shows that his interests in the dark sides of human emotions and his attempt to tame these emotions with the help of a theatrical economy did not cease after his famous philosophical initiation.

Heiberg shares the interest in excessive emotions with his mother Thomasine Gyllembourg. In his examination of Gyllembourg's novel, *Near and Far, Joachim Schiedermair* stresses Gyllembourg's astonishing critical reflections on theater. The critique moves from a reproof of pathetic-theatrical behavior of women in private everyday life to an accusation of an exaggerated passion for the illusory world of theater. On the one hand, theater is criticized for not being authentic, while, on the other hand, it is reproached for being old-fashioned because the longing for meaningful stories and representations of a metaphysical order is inadequate in a world that is ruled by contingent economic transactions.

Both Schiedermair and Hermansson touch upon the criticism of female role-playing in everyday life that Heiberg and Gyllembourg develop in their texts. *Karin Sanders'* article deals with the specific ethics of a female performance. But in this case it is again the performance on stage that is discussed. In the fourth and final volume of her posthumously published autobiography *A Life Relived in Memory*, Johanne Luise Heiberg inserts a theoretical essay about the question of whether the art of acting can be described as a morally justified art form. In her examination of this essay Sanders not only develops Johanne Luise's quasi-religious conception of the art of acting but also uses a comparison of Johan Ludvig's corresponding ideas to illustrate the theoretical

similarities and differences between the two. Both Johan Ludvig and Johanne Luise condemn the idea of acting as a naive and nonreflective art form. But whereas Johan Ludvig's conception of theater and acting rests on the philosophical conception of theater as a state, Johanne Luise persists in an idealistic approach where art is defined by its relation to religion.

In presenting the present volume to the readers, we hope to make a small contribution to the growing international interest in Heiberg, the Danish theater and the Danish Golden Age. The various issues and themes treated in the articles here will, it is hoped, serve to stimulate future research in this rich interdisciplinary field.

Klaus Müller-Wille (Zurich) and Jon Stewart (Copenhagen)

Johan Ludvig Heiberg and the Theater: In Oehlenschläger's Limelight

Finn Hauberg Mortensen

In between Ludvig Holberg's Enlightenment and the Modern Breakthrough two authors exerted pivotal influence on the Danish theater: Adam Oehlenschläger (1779-1850) and Johan Ludvig Heiberg (1791-1860). Their significance generated from both their dramatic texts and their drama criticism. Each engendered a public debate and a legitimization of aesthetic reflections on theater and criticism. When Heiberg stepped onto the stage, Oehlenschläger still owned the limelight. In the twentieth century Tom Kristensen reflected that "The limelight elevates the actors' masks into a higher sphere,"[1] and in the case of Oehlenschläger and Heiberg we clearly detect a competition for the center stage spotlight. On a personal-historical level, during his formative years, Heiberg had a close relationship to the "king of the poets"; on an aesthetic-historical level, Heiberg and his cohorts positioned themselves in opposition to Oehlenschläger and those who shared Oehlenschläger's aesthetic convictions; on a reception-historical level, the scholarly and professional study of Danish literature throughout the twentieth century developed from these two disparate roots—Oehlenschläger and Heiberg.

The present article is a revised version of my "Johan Ludvig Heiberg," in *Danish Writers from the Reformation to Decadence, 1550-1900*, ed. by Marianne Stecher Hansen, Detroit: Thomson/Gale 2004 (*Dictionary of Literary Biography*, vol. 300), pp. 220-227.

[1] Tom Kristensen, *Livets Arabesk*, Copenhagen: Gyldendal/Det Danske Sprog- og Litteraturselskab 2010, p. 66.

Johan Ludvig Heiberg lived in a Copenhagen that was still under the influence of the so-called Florissant period's elegant theater and salon life. Heiberg's taste, more cosmopolitan than the national romantics, was in line with the new classicists, who were making their mark on the Danish capital's reconstruction around 1830 and whose leading architect was C.F. Hansen. During the following twenty years Heiberg exerted a dominating influence on the formation of taste in Denmark via his periodicals, his aesthetic criticism and, perhaps most significantly, his contributions to the Royal Theater, where he reshaped the repertoire from heavy Oehlenschlägerian tragedies to lighter genres, not the least of which was vaudeville. As a playwright, Heiberg was influenced by French theater, and the model for his style-conscious adaptations and translations was first and foremost Eugène Scribe. Philosophically, however, Heiberg's aesthetics was inspired by Hegel's dialectic and Hegel's considerations of genre questions. By way of his aesthetics in general and his theater criticism in particular, Hegel's influence spread throughout Danish cultural life through Heiberg with a force that neither before nor after has been surpassed by any philosopher, Danish or otherwise.

When Heiberg's father P.A. Heiberg (1758-1841) was exiled from Denmark after being censured for his political satires, his son Johan Ludvig was taken away from his mother Thomasine (1773-1856) and placed in foster care with Thomasine's sister. Although P.A. Heiberg made this decision, in May 1802 he arranged to have his son moved into the care of his friends Knud Lyne Rahbek (1760-1830) and Kamma Rahbek (1775-1830). Although the Rahbeks lived in the so-called Bakkehus, outside of the city walls in Frederiksberg, Johan Ludvig could not have grown up any closer to the heart of the literary establishment. He studied Latin with Knud Lyne and modern language with Kamma, and they took in a young theologian, Peter Hansen, who was in charge of young Heiberg's education for the subsequent six years. Hansen was followed by yet another theologian, who, in 1809, recommended Johan Ludvig for acceptance at the university. None other than the famous H.C. Ørsted taught the young boy mathematics until the completion of his exams. Johan Ludvig enjoyed visiting the Rahbeks, who were childless, but already after two years, he stopped living with his foster parents. The Bakkehus had many guests, and some of them made

remarks about Thomasine's divorce from P.A. Heiberg that hurt the boy's feelings. In 1804 he moved in again with his aunt, Thomasine's sister, and spent more and more time with his mother and her new husband, the Swedish Baron Gyllembourg-Ehrensvärd. In reality, starting in 1811, he lived in a beautifully furnished room in their apartment on the corner of Amaliegade and Fredericiagade with a fine view of the ships in the harbor. Here too there was a great deal of high society as well as emotional entanglements across family ties. Consider how H.C. Ørsted proposed to Oehlenschläger's celebrated sister Sophie immediately after she had given her consent to his brother, Anders Sandøe who, as a jurist, was almost as highly regarded as Hans Christian himself. Or consider how Oehlenschläger married Christiane, who was Kamma Rahbek's sister at the Bakkehus, a woman who managed to hold several platonic love triangles going all at once. All this was in the spirit of the times.

While the revolutionary writers of the Florissant period and the new romanticists flocked to the Bakkehus, nobility and diplomats hovered around the Gyllembourgs. Johan Ludvig was also a frequent guest at Sophienholm and in Dronningens Tværgade—in the salon of the German-born, wealthy grocer, Consular Advisor Constantin Brun (1746-1836) and his wife Frederike (1765-1835). She was the daughter of the priest at the German church, St. Petri, and already in her younger years she was actively writing literature in German. Their marriage was based on a mixture of common sense and freethinking, which was in fashion amongst the Florissant trade aristocracy. Brun was somewhat older than Frederike, and he accepted that she took long trips through Europe with her lover and the youngest of their five children, Ida, whom Frederike had chosen to give a free and sensitive upbringing inspired by Rousseau and fashionable amongst the aristocracy. At one point, though, this became too much for Brun. Frederike chose the marriage and the child, who then became the celebrated centerpiece in the day's most prominent salon for artists and intellectuals. Everyone admired Ida's beauty and talent, and it was not surprising that Johan Ludvig too fell in love with her—albeit unrequited.

At the Bruns' Heiberg was called "*l'enfant*"—in the sense that in his youthful innocence, Johan Ludvig was allowed to come and go, visiting the many celebrities who contributed to his education. As a boy, he was once bedridden, and composer C.E.F. Weyse (1774-1842) and author

Laurids Kruse (1778-1839) built a puppet theater for him. Johan Ludvig wrote his first plays for this puppet theater, with rhyming dialogue and in the style of Holberg. In 1812 he wrote *Don Juan*, a four-act play based on Molière's original, for a birthday party celebrating the young Swedish countess Anna Taube, to whom the young aesthete had lost his heart. Johan Ludvig was applauded and indeed from all directions. His youth and upbringing unfolded in social circles that were frequented either by Jens Baggesen or Adam Oehlenschläger—or by both alternatively. Baggesen and Oehlenschläger were the two main players in the new century's major literary feud. At the birthday performance of *Don Juan* Heiberg received a fraternal embrace from an enthusiastic Oehlenschläger, who by doing so repeated Baggesen's behavior at Oehlenschläger's own departure from Copenhagen in 1800 when Baggesen acknowledged Adam's genius and welcomed *him* to Parnassus. Baggesen was also inspired by the young rising star and predicted, with great precision, that Heiberg would one day "pass poetic judgment on the feud between Baggesen and Oehlenschläger."[1]

The Taube family invited young Johan Ludvig to travel with them home to Stockholm in 1812. The fashion-dandy lived with them for three months. He was introduced into the highest social circles, partied, went to the theater and became acquainted with Carl Michael Bellman's melodies, which he later utilized in his vaudevilles. He was living the good life, which fit him perfectly. His mother wrote angry letters to the countess, whom she believed was about to seduce him. Without basis, because her son's desire had evaporated when the countess told him she was pregnant with another man's child. Back in Copenhagen Johan Ludvig published his debut, *Marionette Theater* (1814), which in addition to the romantic-mystic drama *Don Juan* also included the comedy, *The Potter Walter*, which was inspired by Ludwig Tieck's literary comedies.[2] In 1815 Heiberg's life became more economically difficult after his stepfather's death. Together with his mother, he moved out to

[1] Baggesen's eulogy was originally printed in the journal *Skuddag*. Here quoted from *Breve og Aktstykker vedrørende Johan Ludvig Heiberg*, vols. 1-5, ed. by Morten Borup, Copenhagen: Gyldendal 1946-50, vol. 1, p. 50.
[2] Johan Ludvig Heiberg, *Marionettheater*, Copenhagen: Fr. Brummer 1814.

his cousin, Andreas Buntzen, who was married to the beautiful Camilla. Camilla later gave birth to Johan Ludvig's illegitimate son in 1816.

I. Early Works

Heiberg's literary breakthrough took place in 1817 when, in a continuation of Oehlenschläger's *Midsummer Night's Play* from *Poems* (1803), he wrote his most original work, the literary revue *Christmas Jests and New Year's Fun* (1817).[1] It was irresistible for Heiberg not to poke fun at the sentimental and gothic early poetry written by B.S. Ingemann (1789-1862). But he paid a price when N.F.S. Grundtvig (1783-1872) rose to his colleague's defense. This led to more glee from Heiberg who countered with the flippantly titled: *New A-B-C Book in one Hour's Instruction, in Honor and for the Use and Enjoyment of the Young Grundtvig: A Pedagogical Essay* (1817).[2] It all ended as festively as it started with Heiberg's poem to peace: "Springtime and Peace."[3] Heiberg managed to publish three more books that year. He defended his dissertation in Latin on the Spanish dramatist Pedro Calderón de la Barca (1600-81).[4] This short thesis attempted to demonstrate how Calderón's drama was typically Spanish, in the sense that it argued that the formal aesthetics of Spanish poetry was typically romantic. It follows that Calderón, in Heiberg's optic, was the most markedly romantic of all poets, and this contention was at odds with Oehlenschläger, who by far preferred Shakespeare over the anemic Spaniard. Heiberg's treatise was built on the Schlegelian concept of a special connection between certain types of literature and nationality, written even before Heiberg became acquainted with Hegel. Nevertheless the chain of arguments in his treatise was clearly ready to

---

[1] Johan Ludvig Heiberg, *Julespøg og Nytaarslöier*, Copenhagen: Hofbogtrykker Christensen 1817.

[2] Johan Ludvig Heiberg, *Ny A-B-C-Bog i en Times Underviisning til Ære, Nytte og Fornøielse for den unge Grundtvig. Et pædagogisk Forsøg*, Copenhagen: Thieles Bogtrykkerie 1817.

[3] Johan Ludvig Heiberg, "Vaaren og Freden," *Athene, et Maanedsskrift*, vol. 8, May 1817, pp. 494-496. (Reprinted in Heiberg's *Digte*, Copenhagen: Bröderne Thiele 1819, pp. 13-15.)

[4] [Johannes Ludovicus Heiberg], *De poëseos dramaticae genere hispanico, et praesertim de Petro Calderone de la Barca, principe dramaticorum*, Copenhagen: Typis Hartv. Frid. Popp 1817.

be incorporated into a dialectical construction, in which Heiberg's own aesthetic criticism had its roots. Heiberg also applies this construction to a number of his dramatic works that were tied to Nordic folk poetry. In 1817 Heiberg also published the romantic drama *Well Begun is Half Won*, which was Calderónian both in language and content.[1] Finally, in 1817, he published the mythological drama *Psyche*,[2] where the materials of antiquity received a romantic treatment with a Nordic tone and where he used Ida Brun's bodily expression, the so-called plastic "attitudes," so admired in the milieu. From this point on, no one could be in doubt of the young poet's energy and sense of form.

Encouraged by the Brun family, Heiberg imagined himself having a future in diplomacy, with his dissertation as a kind of letter of introduction. Instead, he received a travel stipend from the king and in 1819 traveled via London to Paris where he moved in with his father for three years, bringing along his many talents: natural science, mathematics, writing and aesthetics. But a great deal of his attention was still directed towards high society festivities. Prince Christian and Princess Caroline Amalie had established a salon in Paris where he met many soon-to-be politicians as well as many other budding literary talents like himself, such as Christian Molbech (1783-1857), Carsten Hauch (1790-1872) and Peder Hjort (1793-1851). Hjort would later become Heiberg's opponent in the ongoing feud regarding Oehlenschlägerian views on literature and theater. More importantly than anything else, however, was Heiberg's frequent visits to the theater, which inspired his only literary endeavor during this period, the drama *Nina, or the Madness of Love* (1823).[3] His stay in Paris did not provide Johan Ludvig with any more clarity about his future, but it was quite expensive for his father who, after his son's visit, had to live frugally until his death in 1841.

Johan Ludvig, who was sent home in 1822, paid for by the prince, then tried in vain to obtain employment at the Sorø Academy. Instead he was obliged to accept the outcome of a successful application, fashioned

---

[1] Johan Ludvig Heiberg, *Dristig vovet halv er vundet*, Copenhagen: Boas Brünnich 1817.

[2] Johan Ludvig Heiberg, *Psyche*, Copenhagen: Boas Brünnich 1817.

[3] Johan Ludvig Heiberg, *Nina, eller den Vanvittige af Kierlighed*, Copenhagen: Andreas Seidelin 1823.

by his mother, for the Danish lectureship at the university in Kiel starting in the fall semester of 1822. The transition from the good life in Paris to the role as breadwinner with a poorly paid position in Danish language and literature was severe. But Heiberg learned to concentrate. If his natural science interests had been the center of his focus during his Paris sojourn, philology was now prioritized. On the basis of his lectures at Kiel, Heiberg published *Formenlehre der dänischen Sprache* (1823) and *Nordische Mythologie* (1827).[1] In his morphology, the author's lack of historical sense is apparent when, without reference to philologists such as Rasmus Rask (1787-1832) and Jacob Grimm (1785-1863), he portrays the Icelandic language's endings as a deviation from and not a basis of the Danish language, which he labels as an ideal type.

II. Hegel on His Mind: Faith, Knowledge, and Education

When Heiberg embraced Hegelian thought in 1824, it had significant consequences for Danish cultural and intellectual life for the rest of the century. On this basis, we must clarify how Heiberg understood his own breakthrough, and in what sense it altered the germination of this young intellectual author.

In May 1824, with support from the Danish king, Heiberg traveled from Kiel to Berlin, leaving behind the lectureship that he had accepted without enthusiasm. As before, he divided his time between pleasures that chewed away at his already perilous economic situation (business endeavors, where he futilely attempted to place his dramatic efforts with publishers) and superficial studies. Nonetheless, already after a week in the Prussian capital he was able to make personal contact with G.W.F. Hegel himself, due to a letter of introduction from a colleague at Kiel, who furthermore had lent him a copy of Hegel's *Science of Logic*. During his long stay in Berlin, Heiberg tried to delve into the philosopher's dialectical system of thought, partly by talking to Hegel and his students, partly by reading his writings, among others *Elements of the Philosophy of*

---

[1] Johan Ludvig Heiberg, *Formenlehre der dänischen Sprache*, Altona: Johann Friedrich Hammerich 1823. *Nordische Mythologie*, Schleswig: Gedruckt und verlegt im Königlichen Taubstummen-Institut 1827.

Right. By the time Heiberg returned home to Kiel he was hungry for, yet not in a position to fully comprehend, the new epistemology. Precisely in this over-determined situation, the system manifested itself for him in an image that, in a single moment, allowed for total comprehension. It happened in Hamburg, on his way home to his everyday grind in Kiel, while mulling over Hegel's philosophy in the Hotel König von England. Let me cite Heiberg's own description:

> ...suddenly, in a way which I have experienced neither before nor since, I was gripped by a momentary inner vision, as if a flash of lightning had illuminated the whole region for me and awakened in me the theretofore hidden central thought. From this moment the system in its broad outline was clear to me, and I was completely convinced that I had grasped it in its innermost core, regardless of however much there might be in the details which I still had not made my own and perhaps never will. I can say, in truth, that that strange moment was just about the most important juncture in my life, for it gave me a peace, a security, a self-confidence which I had never known theretofore.[1]

With precision and in concurrence with his scientific background, Heiberg dissects his momentous personal-intellectual breakthrough. During his previous pondering, leading up to the epiphany, he was evidently energized by listening to "beautiful hymns, which sounded almost without pause from the bells of Petri's Church."[2] Perhaps the music of the bells opened up his mind to a higher power. Yet he does not draw such a conclusion; neither does he use religious vocabulary when describing the experience. Indeed, one should not expect a religious word choice, partly because Heiberg, along with his interest in French theater, used his time in Paris to study the natural sciences, and partly because Hegelianism must have appealed to him as a philosophy that attempted

[1] Heiberg, "Autobiographiske Fragmenter," in Heiberg's *Prosaiske Skrifter*, vols. 1-11, Copenhagen: C.A. Reitzel 1861-62, vol. 11, pp. 500f. This passage is translated by Jon Stewart in *On the Significance of Philosophy for the Present Age and Other Texts*, ed. and trans. by Jon Stewart, Copenhagen: C.A. Reitzel 2005 (*Texts from Golden Age Denmark*, vol. 1), p. 65.
[2] Heiberg, "Autobiographiske Fragmenter," in Heiberg's *Prosaiske Skrifter*, vol. 11, p. 500. *On the Significance of Philosophy for the Present Age and Other Texts*, p. 65.

not only to bring order to a confused world of data, but also promised to elevate itself above religion and position itself for the historical forward-leaning realization of "absolute common sense" through human liberation.

Despite Heiberg's lack of explicit religious references, it is nevertheless clear that the word choice he uses to describe his situation comes out of a pious Christian tradition that depicts how true faith is revealed to an individual: as a sudden breakthrough that opens the way to both God and "a better self." We recognize comparable descriptions from contemporary intellectuals who similarly, and after much soul-searching, attempted to document their religious breakthroughs in sharply annotated narratives fixed in time and place. I name in passing Søren Kierkegaard, who in this regard seems to resemble one of his main adversaries, Bishop Mynster, who later became the leader of the State Church. Following tradition, Heiberg points to the irreversible difference between life before and after the decisive experience: "It is certain that the new light which dawned on me has had a definite influence on all my subsequent undertakings, even those where one would not suspect a connection."[1]

In 1824 J.L. Heiberg was confronted with something new. In this sense the term "breakthrough" is appropriate. The depiction of this breakthrough, however, is from 1839. That is to say, it was written down long after he had stepped into character as a Hegelian, while in his diary from 1824 not a trace of a critical personal and intellectual breakthrough is to be found. Even though Heiberg's word choice leads one to think of a religious awakening, one still might question if he is not using the breakthrough as a device to meld previously prepared ideas into a structured way of thinking. If this is the case, then we are not talking about a contradictory or an antagonistic break, but a deliberate configuration of a continuing, already established, perhaps spiraling process of culturization.

It seems that Heiberg constructed his own breakthrough in such a way that he over-emphasized the difference between "before" and "after," and despite his scientific and non-religious attitude, helped himself to a piously oriented presentation of a breakthrough to a philosophy that

---

[1] Heiberg, "Autobiographiske Fragmenter," in Heiberg's *Prosaiske Skrifter*, vol. 11, p. 501. *On the Significance of Philosophy for the Present Age and Other Texts*, p. 66.

he himself believed was elevated above Christianity and other religions. Arguments for this understanding can, among other places, be found in Heiberg's sense for systems and structures that existed long before his encounter with Hegel, a sense that manifested itself in both his scientific and linguistic efforts. Add to this Heiberg's superior gift for abstract, philosophical thought which, when combined with his refined sense of aesthetics, allowed him to rise above Hegel by using the philosopher's aesthetic classification system so freely that he could accentuate his own favorite author, Calderón, above Hegel's favorite author, Shakespeare. Finally, on the personal level, there was the not insignificant fact that through the years Heiberg had futilely sought a fitting profession, position and financial security. Necessity was banging on the door, as was the reality that he had used more years bumbling about than needed.

After returning home to his debts and the poorly paid lectureship in Kiel, Heiberg busied himself with a production based on his new realization. In the fall of 1824—before Hegel's aesthetics had reached any further than his students' lecture notes—Heiberg made a draft of his "Grundlinien zum System der Aesthetik als speculative Wissenschaft," which he chose to leave unpublished. Aside from this, he contributed to the day's great debate (the Howitz controversy) with his book *On Human Freedom* in 1824.[1] Finally, he sent proposals to patrons in Copenhagen about several Hegelian publications along with applications for higher compensation for his position in Kiel or—preferably—a position as professor at the University of Copenhagen. It was all in vain. On the 17th of April 1825, he took the matter into his own hands and traveled to the capital city—without sabbatical permission and with no intention of returning to his position in Kiel. After two years of neglecting his obligations in Kiel, Heiberg was dismissed, honorably but with neither pension nor severance pay. Heiberg even compelled his successor to pay him 300 Rigsdaler a year from the lectureship salary until our newly converted Hegelian managed to find a permanent position. In the meantime, he positioned himself at the center of everything. With Hegel's system he had found the Archimedes point from which he could

---

[1] Johan Ludvig Heiberg, *Om den menneskelige Frihed. I Anledning af de nyeste Stridigheder over denne Gjenstand*, Kiel: Universitets-Boghandling 1824.

turn everything on its head in the king's Copenhagen—as the arbiter of taste above all others.

III. Life and Work after the Breakthrough

With the premiere of his first theater piece *King Solomon and Jørgen the Hatter* on November 28, 1825, Heiberg's success was ensured.[1] Both actors and audience subscribed to this alternative to the many tragedies, dressed up in medieval costumes that had characterized the previous generation's national romanticism. At this point one new play followed another. After noticing the 13-year-old Johanne Pätges, who together with C.N. Rosenkilde performed Poul Martin Møller's dialogue piece *Hans and Trine*, he wrote *The April Fools* for the pair.[2] The play had its premiere on April 22, 1826, and like *An Adventure in Rosenborg Garden* and *The Inseparables* it was fashioned to serve Johanne's special talent.[3] After having been criticized for *The Reviewer and the Animal*,[4] Heiberg took the play off the bill and crafted his principal statement on the new dramaturgy, partly for the general audience and partly aimed directly at K.L. Rahbek and others who did not find vaudeville's tomfoolery fitting for the Royal Theater: *On Vaudeville as Dramatic Genre and its Significance for the Danish Stage: A Dramaturgic Investigation* (1826).[5] The play was then restaged in a revised version and became a success.

Heiberg's connection with the general public continued with *Kjøbenhavns flyvende Post*; the first edition hit the streets on January 1, 1827 and then was published twice a week. After a pause in 1829 the popular journal came out three times a week until the end of 1830. From

---

[1] Johan Ludvig Heiberg, *Kong Salomon og Jørgen Hattemager*, Copenhagen: C.A. Reitzel 1825.

[2] Johan Ludvig Heiberg, *Aprilsnarrene eller Intriguen i Skolen*, Copenhagen: Ferdinand Printzlau 1826.

[3] Johan Ludvig Heiberg, *Et Eventyr i Rosenborg Have*, Copenhagen: Ferdinand Printzlau 1827. *De Uadskillelige*, Copenhagen: Ferdinand Printzlau 1827.

[4] Johan Ludvig Heiberg, *Recensenten og Dyret*, Copenhagen: Ferdinand Printzlau 1827.

[5] Johan Ludvig Heiberg, *Om Vaudevillen, som dramatisk Digtart, og om dens Betydning paa den danske Skueplads. En dramaturgisk Undersøgelse*, Copenhagen: Ferdinand Printzlau 1826.

Johan Ludvig Heiberg (1791-1860)
(After a drawing by D. Monie, Em. Bærentzen & Co. lithographiske Institut, 1842,
Department of Maps, Prints and Photographs, The Royal Library, Copenhagen.)

January 1834 through December 1837 it was succeeded by *Kjøbenhavns flyvende Post. Interimsblade*, which came out intermittently in 235 editions. With the *Flyve-Post* Heiberg revived the publicist role that was characteristic of the generation directly before the romantics, not least that of P.A. Heiberg and K.L. Rahbek. A new group of writers were offered a chance for a first appearance in print; among others Christian Winther and Hans Christian Andersen had their debuts as lyricists in this journal. A new prose authorship arose in its pages in the form of Carl Bernhard, a pen name invented by Heiberg for Andreas Nicolai de Saint-Aubain (1798-1865), and Heiberg's mother Thomasine Gyllembourg produced not only an authorship, but also a new genre under her pen name: "Author of 'A Story from Everyday Life.'"

In *Kjøbenhavns flyvende Post* the educated public could acquaint themselves with the reevaluation of the aesthetic form in the shape of the very judgment that Baggesen had foreseen that Heiberg would pronounce between Oehlenschläger and himself. In his critique of Oehlenschläger's

drama *Varangians in Constantinople* Heiberg chose Baggesen's point of view,[1] that is to say: form is more important than content. With this, the stage was set for the next round of literary feuding, with Heiberg in the lead along with formal aestheticians against the supporters of Shakespeare and Oehlenschläger's life-poetry.

As something never before seen in Denmark, Heiberg established a comprehensive aesthetic point of view that placed the concept of genre at its core. He positioned the main genres—the lyric, the epic and the dramatic—in a triad, and further placed a triadic development within the dramatic genre—from immediate drama via tragedy to comedy—thus enabling him to elevate his vaudevilles above the traditional tragic Nordic medieval costume dramas. While he was willing to allow the audience to evaluate the "poetic" quality of a literary work, he reserved "technical" criticism for the professionals. The goal of this criticism was to assess the individual work in the context of its genre ideal. Oehlenschläger—whom Heiberg regarded as an epic-lyrical poet—should stick to the romances that he was best at, while Heiberg himself was allowed to ponder more reflective dramatics within a genre hierarchy where the new lighter pieces obtained an elevated position.

Elves' Hill was written as a celebratory performance for a royal wedding in November 1828 and has Christian IV as its main character.[2] All theatrical art forms are utilized in this offering of folk ballads and—via Friedrich Kuhlau's music—folk melodies. The work became a national *Festspiel* and remains the most frequently performed play at the Royal Theater. Its characters are thinly drawn, following a script that declares that form is more important than content. Toward the end of the premiere month, as appreciation for the play, Heiberg was promoted to writer in residence with a steady salary and duties to translate a fixed number of plays per year as well as writing prologues and other occasional writings. One of the first results of his own theatrical efforts was *Princess Isabella, or the Three Evenings at the Court* (1829), which in October 1829

---

[1] Johan Ludvig Heiberg, "Svar paa Hr. Oehlenschlägers Skrift: 'Om Kritiken i *Kjøbenhavns flyvende Post*, over Væringerne i Miklagard,'" in *Kjøbenhavns flyvende Post*, 1828, (I, no. 7; II, no. 8; III, no. 10; IV, no. 11; V, no. 12; VI, no. 13; VII, no. 14; VIII, no. 15; IX, no. 16).

[2] Johan Ludvig Heiberg, *Elverhöi*, Copenhagen: Ferdinand Printzlau 1828.

was performed for the first and last time.[1] More successfully, Heiberg undertook dramaturgical arrangements and translated a large portion of Eugène Scribe's enormous repertoire of plays and vaudevilles.

In 1829 Heiberg received the title of Professor, and in the following year he was hired as lecturer of Logic, Aesthetics and Danish Literature at the establishment of the Royal Military College. During his tenure as a teacher, which continued until 1836, he published lectures which had a comprehensive character and were important for testing his Hegelian thinking: *Overview of the Danish Belles Lettres* (1831),[2] *Outline of the Philosophy of Philosophy or Speculative Logic* (1832),[3] *On the Significance of Philosophy for the Present Age* (1833),[4] and *Introductory Lecture to the Logic Course at the Royal Military College* (1835).[5]

On July 31, 1831 Heiberg married Johanne Luise Pätges (1812-90) in Slangerup Church, where his former teacher, Peter Hansen, was pastor. After her success in 1826 with the leading female part in *The April Fools*, Johanne Luise was released from her obligations as a dancer and was admitted as a drama student. She had already inspired a number of poets to write roles for her, and several young men had proposed, including Johan Ludvig. He was refused the first time around and, with P.A. Heiberg's encouragement, became interested in the daughter of a very wealthy Norwegian grocer, who lived in Paris. But Thomasine took the young actress into her home, and she was soon secretly engaged to the son of the house. Returning the favor, as newlyweds, the couple took Thomasine Gyllembourg into their home at Søkvæsthuset in Christianshavn.

After her marriage at the age of 19, a "Mrs." would precede Johanne Luise's name on the theater bill. Her husband zealously kept a close watch

---

[1] Johan Ludvig Heiberg, *Prindsesse Isabella, eller de Tre Aftner ved Hoffet*, Copenhagen: Ferdinand Printzlau 1829.

[2] Johan Ludvig Heiberg, *Udsigt over den danske skjønne Litteratur. Som Ledetraad ved Forelæsninger paa den kongelige militaire Høiskole*, Copenhagen: Andreas Seidelin 1831.

[3] Johan Ludvig Heiberg, *Grundtræk til Philosophiens Philosophie eller den speculative Logik. Som Ledetraad ved Forelæsninger paa den kongelige militaire Høiskole*, Copenhagen: Andreas Seidelin 1832.

[4] Johan Ludvig Heiberg, *Om Philosophiens Betydning for den nuværende Tid*, Copenhagen: C.A. Reitzel 1833.

[5] Johan Ludvig Heiberg, *Indlednings-Foredrag til det i November 1834 begyndte logiske Cursus paa den kongelige militaire Høiskole*, Copenhagen: J.H. Schubothe 1835.

on the gossipmongers; it was far from acceptable for the wife of a person of high standing to appear on stage. In the following year he continued his tireless dramaturgical efforts, and a number of his occasional writings were collected in *A Half Dozen Selected New Year's Verses from the Theater to the Public* (1832).[1] In addition he wrote the vaudevilles *A Domestic Nuisance in Køge* (1831), *The Danes in Paris* (1833) and *No* (1836),[2] as well as several monologues, such as *Yes!* (1839), and *The Fairies* (1835)—a fairy tale comedy in the spirit of Tieck.[3]

During 1837-38, after taking a trip with his wife to Berlin and Paris where they visited his father, Heiberg's authorship grew from vaudeville to speculative writing, whose distinctive character Heiberg discussed in his new periodical, *Perseus, Journal for the Speculative Idea*. With the fairy tale comedy *Fata Morgana* (1838) about false appearances and reality,[4] Heiberg again offers an example of the genre he defined—in this case speculative comedy, which he now placed at the top of his genre hierarchy. Instead of using the concrete (material) to lead the way to ideas, the speculative writings led the way from ideas to even higher ideas. The same gesturing towards a meta-level of ideas can be seen in the title of one of his course descriptions from the Military College from 1832: *Outline of the Philosophy of Philosophy or Speculative Logic*. Heiberg's idealism now became objective in that ideas were perceived as the controlling force not only in relationship to phenomena but also in relationship to individuals. Neither *Fata Morgana* nor the equivalent *Festspiel*, *Day of Seven Sleepers* (1840) was successful on the stage,[5] and in 1839 Heiberg was relieved of a portion of his translation work so he could perform the function of theater censor.

Heiberg's popularity was waning, not least because he had made several conservative comments in *Kjøbenhavns flyvende Post. Interimsblade* about the fragile democratic development in connection with the establishment of the

---

[1] Johan Ludvig Heiberg, *Et halvt Dusin udvalgte Nytaarsvers fra Theatret til Publicum*, Copenhagen: Ferdinand Printzlau 1832.

[2] Johan Ludvig Heiberg, *Kjøge-Huuskors*, Copenhagen: Ferdinand Printzlau 1831. *De Danske i Paris*, Copenhagen: J.H. Schubothe 1833. *Nei*, Copenhagen: J.H. Schubothe 1836.

[3] Johan Ludvig Heiberg, *Ja*, Copenhagen: C.C. Lose & Olsen 1839. *Alferne*, Copenhagen: J.H. Schubothe 1835.

[4] Johan Ludvig Heiberg, *Fata Morgana*, Copenhagen: J.H. Schubothe 1838.

[5] Johan Ludvig Heiberg, *Syvsoverdag*, Copenhagen: J.H. Schubothe 1840.

Provincial Assemblies in 1834. His *New Poems* (1841) was based on the German model,[1] adopted in both Oehlenschläger's and Staffeldt's *Digte*, an arrangement with a lyric, an epic, and a dramatic section. The latter consisted of the apocalyptic comedy "A Soul after Death," where new liberal politicians were grouped in a hell of triviality, a terrible infinity where the dialectical movement had not yet begun and where everything therefore ceaselessly repeated itself. As hell is on earth, so also is heaven, which Heiberg wrote about in the collection's lyric poetry. He now perceived Protestantism as a religion where thought and God were one.

In the journal *Intelligensblade* (1842-44) readers were informed that the masses lacked the ability, even the right, to pass judgments on intellectual issues. Thus the audience's sudden change of interest from literature and philosophy to the political and concrete became an object of Heiberg's disdain and the target of his satire in *Denmark: A Painter's Atlas* (1841-42) and in the satyric play *The Nutcrackers* (1841-42).[2] On a personal level, there was a rekindling of his natural scientific interests, which now focused on astronomy. He shared a birth date with his role model Tycho Brahe, and he published a three-volume yearbook *Urania* with articles about astronomy as well as longer articles about Hven and Brahe's sister Sophie. In *Valgerda* (1847),[3] which was staged anonymously but was his only modern comedy, he held himself above the political conflicts between liberal and conservative. Here, women's rights were debated, and Heiberg caused a bit of commotion when, in 1851, he supported those rights by publishing Mathilde Fibiger's *Clara Raphael: Twelve Letters*.

IV. Monopoly Stories: Democracy's Kiss of Death

On July 23, 1849 Johan Ludvig and Johanne Luise Heiberg were passengers in Titular Councilor of State J.T. Suhr's coach. When it stopped

---

[1] Johan Ludvig Heiberg, *Nye Digte*, Copenhagen: C.A. Reitzel 1841.
[2] Johan Ludvig Heiberg, *Danmark, et malerisk Atlas*, vols. 1-2, Copenhagen: H.I. Bing og Söns 1841-42. *Nøddeknækkerne, et Satyrspil*, in Heiberg's *Urania*, Copenhagen: H.I. Bing og Söns 1845, pp. 143-208.
[3] Johan Ludvig Heiberg, *Valgerda*, Copenhagen: J.H. Schubothe 1847.

in front of Minister of Culture J.N. Madvig's home on Nørrevold they were informed that Heiberg had been named to the coveted position of Director for the Royal Theater, which he would go on to hold for seven turbulent years. Heiberg considered the appointment to be a well-earned feather in his cap after a long career. But Johanne Luise foresaw the problems that might arise, not only for herself, as the theater's leading actress, but for her husband. The appointment came 25 years too late. Heiberg's taste was not that of the people, and similarly, his sense for the new dramatics was miniscule at best. In addition to this, Heiberg had even less respect for the press—especially when it placed demands on the theater. It was clearly a problem for the fledgling democracy whose primary cultural institution Heiberg would now lead.[1] Not least because, concurrent with his appointment, the Royal Theater was released from the royal court and placed under the auspices of the parliament.

Since the end of the 1820s Heiberg had been his predecessor's sharpest critic. Now he had a hard time honoring his own demands concerning the repertoire; he had difficulties in cooperating with the actors, and even more so living up to the audience's demands. Oehlenschläger died on January 20, 1850, and on his deathbed he asked that *Socrates* be performed in its entirety. That Heiberg did not piously follow the dying poet's wishes—and instead allowed *Hakon Jarl* to be staged followed by a mere fragment of *Socrates* (a play that had bored the audience in earlier performances) was amongst the lesser squabbles during his first year as director. Although Heiberg took into consideration the public taste and exhibited *decorum* by closing the theater the day after Oehlenschläger's death and also by draping the balustrades and proscenium in black during memorial tributes, he was reproached, even by people who felt that the abbreviated version of *Socrates* ruined the atmosphere that *Hakon Jarl* had created. His dramaturgical judgment was clearly in line with the spectators', but the audience took offense nevertheless at his inability to judge the situation. The evening was not intended to be about *good* theater but about following the will of the "king of poets." A monument should have been erected, and, if necessary, raised with the support of the failed drama.

---

[1] See Jens Engberg, *Dansk guldalder eller Oprøret i tugt-, rasp- og forbedringshuset i 1817*, Copenhagen: Rhodos 1973.

New media forms have long since taken over the function of the Royal Theater as the central producer of national ideology and information. It is not immediately obvious to draw contemporary parallels, but the TV-theater during the period of Danmarks Radio's monopoly is probably the contemporary institution that comes closest. Unlike the 1800s proscenium stage, the electronic media could count on a large portion of the nation as its actual audience whenever Danish drama was projected from the screen. Before the break-up of DR's monopoly, the press kept a watchful eye on the TV-theater, which was comparable to its interest in the Royal Theater during Heiberg's time.

In mid-November 1979, a short-lived uproar erupted in the press about rumors that DR was contemplating a repeat broadcasting of *A Midsummer Night's Play* in honor of Oehlenschläger's 200th birthday. Instead, the press demanded direct transmission of the Royal Theater's gala performance of the tragic drama *Dina* to be staged in honor of the same occasion. In their belated ritual tribute to the bard, the TV leadership had less backbone than Heiberg as they succumbed to the pressure to show the aging poet's effort.

In a feature article in the newspaper *Information* Hans Hertel found that the transmission "with royal incense and wreath laying at the literary institution"[1] was a question of cultural politics: under the guise of dissemination of literature, the only thing disseminated was "the concept of our literary heritage as an embalmed corpse that on special occasions is to be exhumed from the opened burial mound for viewing, then quickly reinterred. Not directly foul-smelling, but inescapably deceased."[2]

At the same time a representative for the younger generation, the student of journalism Anja Westphal from *Politiken*, was given the task of finding out if the corpse had anything at all to say to a generation which "in greatest disrespect sat knitting or furtively completed English exercises while the teacher, in a two hour one-man-show, lectured on 'The Golden Horns.'"[3] The immediate background for this was probably that Hertel—referring to the pedagogically tenacious tradition from Vilhelm

[1] Hans Hertel, "Qvirilit! Qvirilit! nyudgaver op til Oehlenschlägers 200-årsdag i dag," *Information*, November 14, 1979.

[2] Ibid.

[3] Anja Westphal, "Hvil i fred gamle gulddreng," *Politiken*, November 18, 1979.

Andersen's thesis on "The Golden Horns"—had written in his editorial that " 'The Golden Horns' is one of Danish literature's most brilliant poems, but try to find a Danish literature student from before 1960 who does not become nauseous from even hearing its title."[1] This diagnosis was confirmed when the representative of the "knitting" generation after being force-fed with Oehlenschläger exclaimed: "Congratulations, Adam, and rest in peace—both in your grave and in the chair in front of the Royal Theater."[2]

Bissen's statue of the king of poets sitting in a chair was unveiled in 1861 on Sct. Annæ Plads, a few steps from Oehlenschläger's home on Amaliegade. Then in 1874 the statue was moved to its current position in front of the Royal Theater in connection with the inauguration of the new building. One year after Johan Ludvig's death in 1860, a man of letters from the younger generation sought to rehabilitate Oehlenschläger with a biographical work.[3] The biography is worthy of attention because it was the first to reevaluate the authorship after Heiberg's lengthy and fervent criticism. The work can be seen as a break from Heiberg and from his school, in regard to taste, methods and judgment. The author was Peder Ludvig Møller, who at that point in time was forced to live by his pen in Paris after being ostracized by the Copenhagen Parnassus in connection with the so-called *Corsair* affair with Kierkegaard; Møller became an exiled intellectual like Heiberg's father, Peter Andreas Heiberg. While Oehlenschläger and Heiberg both wrote their way into good positions and into the center of the cultural power elite, Møller's life and talented pen brought him nothing but sickness, poverty and loneliness. He died in a hospital in Rouen in 1865 after feeling sick at the train station, never managing to claim the position, rightfully his, as Heiberg's successor. Møller was far closer to an actual understanding of Romanticism than the two Biedermeier poets in respectively *Dina* and *New Poems*. He had found it both in the great European literature and in Danish literature, where he was the first critic who had an informed understanding of Blicher, Winther, Aarestrup and Kierkegaard.

---

[1] Ibid.

[2] Ibid.

[3] P.L. Møller's work was originally printed as an article in the newspaper *Berlingske Tidende* (November 21-27, 1861) and then later as a book. See P.L. Møller, *Adam Oehlenschläger. Et Erindringsblad*, Copenhagen: Otto B. Wroblewskys 1876.

V. The Oehlenschläger School and the Heiberg School

The main lines of Danish literary critical history in the 1800s can more or less be divided in two, depending on critical attitudes to Oehlenschläger. By way of the poet feuds, with Oehlenschläger and his followers on one side, and Baggesen and Heiberg on the other, the literary establishment was delimited during the same period that democracy slowly took over from the absolute monarchy. On the one side was the Oehlenschläger school, including, among others, literary thinkers from the Sorø Academy like Carsten Hauch and pre-Hegelian aesthetes like Frederik Christian Sibbern. On the other side were the Heibergians, who served to give literary criticism a systematic, perhaps even a scientific, foundation. In this group we find, among others, Henrik Hertz, Johan Nicolai Madvig and the theologian Hans Lassen Martensen.

VI. Exit Heiberg: A Love Story

Heiberg left the public scene with a poem to "Adelaide the Countess of Bombelles," alias Ida, the love of his youth, who in 1816 married the aristocratic Austrian ambassador in Copenhagen. Her death in 1857 brought Heiberg back to Frederiksdal, where he had swooned over her loveliness, and, apparently in an effort to aggravate the political press, he allowed his beautiful stanzas to be printed in the *Adresseavis*, a modest neighborhood paper consisting largely of advertisements. With her talent for plastic-mimicry, Ida inspired a circle of devotees, both at home and abroad, which could still appreciate the unity of the good, the beautiful and the true. Among her admirers were Goethe, Wieland, A.W. Schlegel, Canova, Thorvaldsen and Mme. de Staël Holstein. On the Danish Parnassus she could bring together Baggesen and Oehlenschläger in shared admiration. Both wrote poems in her honor. In Heiberg's portrayal of the two feuding poets' tributes we glean a portrait of Heiberg himself. Thoughts of the beautiful Ida formed his memories, so that the news of her death brought him strength. Without being sentimental, he could embrace his own feelings, while at the same time emotionally preserve her in her youth:

They gather, as wonderful dreams,
Those rich memories from a vanished spring,
As golden clouds swimming in the sky,
Though the sun sits beneath the horizon.

I wonder if Phantasus will empty his horn of plenty
In the magic circle his scepter makes?
They gather in strong, closed clusters,
And death's message rejuvenates their lives.

De samle sig, lig underfulde Drømme,
De rige Minder fra en svunden Vaar,
Lig gyldne Skyer, som paa Himlen svømme,
Skjøndt Solen under Horizonten staaer.

Mon Phantasus sit Fyldehorn vil tømme
I Tryllekredsen, som hans Scepter slaaer?
De samle sig i stærke, tætte Klynger,
Og Dødens Budskab deres Liv forynger.[1]

The stanza is a portrait and a self-portrait, but in addition to this, there is also a connection to Oehlenschläger's breakthrough romanticist poem "The Golden Horns." Several words are borrowed from this poem, but also the entirety of its Golden Age construction, which makes Ida identical to Oehlenschläger's "vanished days." When examining the genre of death poetry, one finds a striking lack of Christianity in Heiberg's work. In *Poems* (1803) Oehlenschläger used strong colors, and in "Harald in Offerlunden" he used sound effects, so that the "forest howled, and the rooster crowed" when Harald dreams of paganism:

Here in the dark shadows of the grove
My last tears ran down,
Onto these alter stones
Puddled blood of my veins!

---

[1] Johan Ludvig Heiberg, "Adelaide Grevinde af Bombelles," in *Poetiske Skrifter*, vols. 1-11, Copenhagen: C.A. Reitzel 1861-62, vol. 8, p. 394.

Blood spattered sacrificial priests
Ferociously crushed my forehead,
Plunged a dagger into my heart,
Intoxicated with wild rage.

Her i Lundens skumle Skygger
nedrandt mine sidste Taarer,
her paa disse Alterstene
sprudled Blod af mine Aarer!

Blodbestænkte Offerpræster
grumt min Pande sønderknuste,
joge Dolken i mit Hjerte,
Vildt af Raserie beruste.[1]

Up against this kind of dynamic and plasticity Heiberg's poem shows classic restraint and calm. In it he seeks to position himself between Enlightenment and Romanticism in relationship to literary ancestors such as Holberg, Baggesen, Oehlenschläger and Staffeldt, and contemporaries such as Scribe, Winther and Møller. If one is to believe the text, Pan does not lose his way in dark woods, but remains in Frederiksdal where nature and culture is in balance:

Where can a wandering thought best find foothold?
In your woods, dark Frederiksdal,
Where groups used to meet to visit the house,
That beckoned from the lake, clear and cool.

Hvor skal en vildsom Tanke helst sig fæste?
I dine Skove, dunkle Frederiksdal,
Hvor Skarer mødtes, for det Huus at gjæste,
Der vinkede fra Søen klar og sval.[2]

---

[1] Adam Oehlenschläger, *Digte*, ed. by Povl Ingerslev-Jensen, Copenhagen: Oehlenschläger Selskabet 1979, p. 60.
[2] Heiberg, "Adelaide Grevinde af Bombelles," in *Poetiske Skrifter*, vol. 8, p. 394.

After his departure in June 1856 as director of the Royal Theater, Heiberg once again became theater censor, and he used his last years traveling as well as exploring his scientific interests. As a natural scientist he would remain an amateur. As a philosopher his great contribution grew out of his use of the Hegelian system to establish a genre-oriented aesthetic, which made it possible to make systematic analyses and evaluations of literary texts. This occurred before Hegel himself adapted his own theories to this particular subject, and resulted in clear differences between the two aesthetics since Heiberg's and Hegel's literary tastes were quite different.

Heiberg's second great contribution, as author, translator, dramaturge, censor and director, was to develop the Royal Theater in such a way that an elegant comedy could carry on the tradition from Holberg. Lack of content became Heiberg's signature and, to a certain degree, his strength. It also became his weakness, because Heiberg's interest in psychology and history remained undeveloped, so that his evaluation of literary works could seem unreasonable. A third contribution is that Heiberg's fine taste and structural sense in combination with Hegel's dialectic became the standard-bearer of Danish right-Hegelianism, which gained supporters among writers and poets, but also among influential theologians, humanists and jurists during Denmark's transition from monarchy to democracy. Heiberg's fourth great contribution issued from these points as he, with his wife Johanne Luise, offered his contemporaries an ideal image of what a tasteful prosaic life should look like. Kierkegaard called their circle "the family" and found it more intimate than the salon life Heiberg had grown up with.

VII. Epilogue

This epilogue deals with the question of why Heiberg's breakthrough, despite its significance, did not receive the same prominent status in traditional Danish literary history as the Romantic Breakthrough and the Modern Breakthrough.

Debate about and inspiration from Hegelianism dominates Danish aesthetics, literature, and theater history from the middle of the 1820s until approximately 1850. It involved the movement of public interest

away from literary writings towards philosophy, theology and politics right up to 1849 when the Hegelian-inspired Constitution was approved. For the entire second half of the nineteenth century—in the now legitimized centralized state with its institutions and influential bourgeois representation—there were enormous debates about science and faith, philosophy and theology, based on the contradictions between the Hegelians and the anti-Hegelians, as well as the right and left Hegelians. Kierkegaard and many others who eagerly fought against the Hegelian dialectic were in fact profoundly dependent on it. Brandes, Jacobsen and many others who, with their left Hegelianism, fought for modernity and science against faith-based belief systems also used the Hegelian dialectic as a discursive strategy. Well up into the 1900s the development of ethics in Denmark was marked by the opposition between Hans Lassen Martensen's Hegelian shoring up of Christianity and Harald Høffding's development of human-based moral teaching on behalf of the Modern Breakthrough.

Heiberg's Hegel-inspired breakthrough from 1824 was, in short, disseminated and had decisive influence on Danish intellectual history for three quarters of a century. Even though Paul V. Rubow, among others, emphasized this breakthrough's significance, it has not attained the status that it deserves.[1] That the dominating Danish literary tradition, in line with Vilhelm Andersen, has not emphasized this breakthrough may be due to the fact that the Hegel-influenced Heibergian breakthrough stresses a German influence that cannot be dismissed in favor of Danishness, such as the two other breakthroughs were able to do.

The first breakthrough was the Romantic Breakthrough, which grew out of young Oehlenschläger's moment of inspiration in 1802 during his famous stroll with Heinrich Steffens after the latter's lecture at Ehler's Collegium about German Romanticism. The second breakthrough was the Modern Breakthrough that, in 1872, manifested itself in the aftermath of Georg Brandes' lectures at the University of Copenhagen about the main currents of European literature. These breakthroughs were epoch-making for Vilhelm Andersen's understanding of the history of

---

[1] See Paul V. Rubow's main works *Dansk litterær Kritik i det 19. Aarhundrede*, Copenhagen: Levin & Munksgaard 1921 and *Saga og Pastiche*, Copenhagen: Levin & Munksgaard 1923.

Danish literature. They both combined, pedagogically and rhetorically, a comprehensive breakthrough for an individual author and allowed major mental shifts to define an epoch. Descriptions of these two paradigm breakthroughs are repeated in literary history after literary history, where they pedagogically and rhetorically emphasize the importance of the breakthroughs and underplay the continuity of the authorships.

Paul V. Rubow and Henning Fenger's examination of Brandes' deep anchoring in Danish and European Romanticism could have given the tradition of literary history a more complex portrait of the Modern Breakthrough.[1] The mainstream tradition of literary history would then present European modernity as radically different from the backwards Danish 1800s, a view which Vilhelm Andersen inherited from Brandes himself. Andersen, however, uses rhetoric along these lines together with the underlying supposition that the breakthrough was a radical change, in order to hold firmly onto the national opposition between Danish and foreign, echoed in the understanding of Brandes as a foreign Jew. The Modern Breakthrough could thus be seen as a period of foreign influence, which imploded already when Brandes himself left his youthful ideals behind, and was replaced by the "Danish" new millennium generation, which Vilhelm Andersen considered himself to be part of.

Regarding the Romantic Breakthrough, Vilhelm Andersen wanted to focus on how Oehlenschläger, with his healthy Danish common sense, returned home from abroad and distanced himself from the German Romantic swooning, which Steffens tried to get him to accept. Here it is emphasized how the radical breakthrough is followed by a continual process of culturization, away from youth and what is foreign. Ejnar Thomsen objected that the young Adam never rejected his relationship to the Germans because he never actually embraced them.[2] While Vilhelm Andersen works with a concept of inspiration from the outside world, which only after a personal breakthrough became epoch-making for a

---

[1] See Paul V. Rubow, "Georg Brandes' Forhold til Taine og St. Beuve," in *Edda*, vol. 6, 1916, pp. 249-301; *Georg Brandes og hans Lærere*, Copenhagen: Povl Branner 1927 (*Studier fra Sprog- og Oldtidsforskning*, vol. 127); as well as *Georg Brandes' Briller*, Copenhagen: Levin & Munksgaard 1932. See also Henning Fenger, *Georg Brandes' læreår*, Copenhagen: Gyldendal 1955.

[2] Ejnar Thomsen, *Omkring Oehlenschlägers tyske Quijotiade*, Copenhagen: Bianco Luno 1950.

"Danish" Romanticism, Thomsen emphasizes continuity in the poet, thus making the breakthrough far less dramatic. With this he modifies Andersen's national angle, which, in light of the Danish defeat in 1864, sees Danish Romanticism as a victory over the German. Thomsen's skepticism was not a well-placed contribution to the confirmation of tradition in the same way that, in 1950, he did not contribute to the still necessary postwar Danish "nation building." Even though he was a professor of Nordic literature, he positioned himself, along with comparative literature professors Fenger and Rubow, outside the mainstream of Danish/Nordic literary history, whose leading proponent was Vilhelm Andersen, who dominated the field until approximately 1975.[1] Not surprisingly Thomsen's contributions have largely been forgotten.

The conclusion for the history of reception seems to be that Heiberg's Hegelian breakthrough, despite its significance in subsequent Danish social and cultural life, became marginalized by a tradition of literary history that favored other breakthroughs seemingly better suited for the national literary-historic line, breakthroughs preferred by Vilhelm Andersen and usable for "nation building" efforts. Oehlenschläger's breakthrough is the most prominent of these. Similarly, the aesthetic battle between Heiberg and Oehlenschläger, and with it their divergent inspirations from German writing and aesthetics, was decided *post festum*, based on the Danish defeat by the Germans on the battlefield in 1864. A hundred years later "the battle fever from Dybbøl," which Herman Bang put on the agenda in his novel *Tine*, 1889, was still a proviso for the understanding of Danish literature.

---

[1] F.J. Billeskov Jansen established an alternative with his genre-oriented literary history *Danmarks Digtekunst*, vols. 1-2, Copenhagen: Munksgaard 1944-47, 2nd ed. 1964. But it was only after the collective, reflective social history, *Dansk litteraturhistorie* (vols. 1-9, Copenhagen: Gyldendal 1983-85) that a decisively different paradigm was worked through.

I. Theater and Politics

An Artist Among Rebels?
Johan Ludvig Heiberg and the Political Turn of the Public Sphere

Lasse Horne Kjældgaard

"The Artist Among the Rebels" is the title of a famous poem by Poul Martin Møller, called "Kunstneren mellem Oprørerne" in the original Danish.[1] It was published for the first time in the year of Møller's death, 1838, as a poetical commentary on current political affairs. The artist referred to in the title, and the protagonist of the poem, is a sculptor, working in his studio, surrounded by sculptures and apprentices. The silent and dedicated atmosphere of the studio is contrasted with the noise and unrest in the street, where a mob is shouting and cheering. The eighth stanza of the poem vividly evokes the situation on the street:

> The magnificent banner of rebellion
> In the air proudly flies:
> Our tyrants are being overthrown,
> Bond and bolt are being broken.
> The heroes of freedom are already approaching
> With guns, clubs and spears.
> Listen how the brave hordes
> Are singing songs of joy.[2]

---

[1] Poul Martin Møller, "Kunstneren mellem Oprørerne," in *Nytaarsgave fra danske Digtere*, vols. 1-4, ed. by H.P. Holst and Christian Winther, vol. 4, 1838, pp. 82-94. Unless otherwise noted, all translations are my own.

[2] Ibid., p. 85.

Outside of the studio, revolution is in the air, and the conflict cannot be kept out. Suddenly, some of the armed "heroes of freedom" enter the studio in order to confront the master with his lack of political commitment. They scorn him for his artistic trade, which they see as a cowardly, unmanly escape from reality and mere flattering of the rich and powerful. The rebels give the artist a chance to make amends, if he commits himself to their fight for freedom. When he declines, the rebels begin to vandalize his studio, leading to fatal consequences. Anger strikes the artist, who begins to froth and fight back. He seizes a club and beats the rebels in the studio. He chases them out and ends up driving the entire rebellious crowd out of town, together with the King's soldiers.

In the aftermath of the confrontation, the Samsonesque artist is greeted by the King, who offers to decorate him for his heroic deed. But the artist declines; he will have none of the royal bling-bling and recognition offered—and, once again, he does not allow himself to be enlisted in the King's service: "In my studio, the silent, / I bid the world goodbye. / I will never play the judge, / Nor people kill."[1] The artist does not wish to ally himself either with the established order or with those wishing to overthrow this order. With his double rejection, he attempts to steer around the political traps waiting for him, but without success. This is the point of Møller's poem: it is impossible to remain uninvolved when things become politicized. And, indeed, the artist gets himself involved by launching his vigilante counterattack on the rebels—in order to save his artworks. Circumstances draw him into the battlefield in a situation where passivity would only lead to further damage, and where the autonomy of art and the artist can only be maintained at the expense of the destruction of art.

Nothing in the poem suggests that it takes place in Denmark, while nothing in it suggests that it does not. However, if one only knows the standard descriptions of the age of the poem from Danish literary history, it will be difficult to grasp what the poem can be said to comment upon. Civil unrest, uproar and uprising in the street, vandalizing thugs, coercive demands for political commitment in art—what is the poem talking about?

---

[1] Ibid., p. 94.

The 1830s was an unpolitical Biedermeier age where everybody was cultivating "the serene, the quiet and refined," as Erik Lunding stated in his very influential article about "Danish Biedermeier" in 1968.[1] The conventional characterization of the age, handed down in Danish literary history under this concept, emphasizes the static and politically laid back condition of Danish literary and intellectual life of the time. "The political interests, which in the 1840s under the reign of Christian VIII assumed power from the aesthetic [interests], manifested themselves only weakly in the poetical literature of the 1830s, in the last decade of the paternal [*landsfaderlige*] rule of Frederik VI," Vilhelm Andersen has claimed.[2] Andersen, endorsing the King's own rhetoric by reiterating the regal keyword "*landsfaderlige*," was adamant in his insistence that the 1830s was "the real aesthetic age of Danish literature."[3]

This depiction of the age needs to be adjusted, particularly in order to analyze the polemical context of some of the literary maneuvers of Johan Ludvig Heiberg and his apprentice Søren Kierkegaard in the 1830s and '40s. What I would like to do in this article is to present some historical correlates to the revolutionary atmosphere in Møller's poem—that is, the rapid politicization of the Danish public sphere in the 1830s—and Johan Ludvig Heiberg's strategic reaction to this change. In 1833, Heiberg observed, "it is the very political character of the age which constitutes its crisis."[4] Unrest was the keyword of Heiberg's characterization of his contemporary moment, and this unrest chiefly manifested itself in the political commotion. The following year, Heiberg noted that "our entire European unrest is a spiritual battle between two parties: the conservative and their opposites (whom I will not label out of fear of not finding the right name), but, consequently, every government does *eo ipso* take part in the battle."[5] So did Heiberg, and he initiated, as we shall see, several

---

[1] Erik Lunding, "Biedermeier og romantismen," *Kritik*, vol. 7, 1968, p. 47.

[2] Vilhelm Andersen, *Illustreret dansk Litteraturhistorie*, vols. 1-4, Copenhagen: Gyldendal 1934, vol. 3, p. 585.

[3] Ibid.

[4] Johan Ludvig Heiberg, *On the Significance of Philosophy for the Present Age and Other Texts*, ed. and trans. by Jon Stewart, Copenhagen: C.A. Reitzel 2005 (*Texts from Golden Age Denmark*, vol. 1), p. 95.

[5] Johan Ludvig Heiberg, "Christensens Skrift om Trykkefriheden," *Kjøbenhavns flyvende Post*, ed. by Uffe Andreasen, vols. 1-4, Copenhagen: Det Danske Sprog- og Litteraturselskab/C.A. Reitzel 1981, vol. 4, *Interimsblad*, no. 16, 1834, p. 72.

campaigns in his poetry as well as in his journalistic enterprises in order both to defy and to comply with this political turn.

The situation was, on a biographical note, particularly precarious for Heiberg. He was the son of a rebel, Peter Andreas Heiberg, who had been banished from Denmark, in 1799, due to his satirical authorship attacking specific Danish authorities as well as absolutism in general.[1] Johan Ludvig Heiberg's childhood had been uprooted as a result of his father's interference in politics, and it is possible to argue that the banishment of the father—when the son was only eight years old—was the singularly most influential event in his life.

As the son of a rebel, Johan Ludvig Heiberg was put in a situation comparable to that of the artist of Poul Martin Møller's poem: he could not, by any means, escape politics. He was confronted with the forced choice of rebelling, thus imitating the father, or refusing to rebel, which can be understood as another kind of revolt, against the authority of the father. No matter what he did, Johan Ludvig Heiberg's political behavior was prone to be analyzed in relation to his paternal origin. Also for this reason, it is interesting to see how he reacted when the dismantling of absolutism, which his father had supported in the wake of the French Revolution, gained new momentum in the 1830s in the aftermath of another French Revolution, the July Revolution of 1830.

I. Young Denmark

Now, were there any political rebels in Danish literature and intellectual life in the late Golden Age? The standard answer to this question would be no. There is, instead, a rather obvious lack of "youth" in Danish literature in this period, comparatively speaking. It is commonplace in literary history to talk about *Young Germany*—with Heine, Börne, and Feuerbach—and *Young France*, including Stendhal, Hugo, and Lamartine. A somewhat similar blend of romanticism and political radicalism can be found earlier in English literature in the art of the trio: Keats, Shelley, and Lord Byron. But no equivalent can be detected in Danish literature.

---

[1] Further biographical information about Peter Andreas Heiberg can be found in Henning Fenger, *The Heibergs*, New York: Twayne Publishers 1971, pp. 23-37.

There is no literary formation known as "young Denmark" in the history of Danish literature, not in this period, at least, no united group of hotspurs using their eminent literary powers to advocate political reform, or, indeed, revolution.

I am not going to argue here that Johan Ludvig Heiberg, who was born in 1791, represents an unrecognized young Denmark. Although leaning toward the Hegelian Left in matters of aesthetics and religion,[1] Heiberg was close to the Hegelian Right and rather conservative in political questions. He was, for instance, a staunch supporter of state absolutism and liked to compare the state to an artwork, since they were both ends in themselves and not a means to something else. He even turned this principle into an aphorism: "the state does not exist for the sake of the citizens, but the citizens for the sake of the state."[2] One should certainly not ask what the state could do for you, but what you could do for the state, Heiberg contended.

Subscribing to such views, Heiberg was not disposed to embrace either liberalism or natural law, invoked by the political reformists in his time. Indeed, formulations like these place him in direct opposition to them. Still, one should not neglect that the role of the King was also subordinated to the superiority of the state, according to Heiberg's political views.[3] Heiberg's Hegelian separation of the state—as an independent concept, from, say, the Kingdom or the Throne—can even be seen as a subversive act in itself, due to its immanent downgrading of the King's role.

Heiberg did, furthermore, pay heed to the growing political movement, and he did not always refrain from labeling it. He referred to the liberal political movement, at least once, with the term "young Denmark." He did so in a remark to the journal *Fædrelandet* in his own journal *Kjøbenhavns flyvende Post*, in 1836. Heiberg's intervention was

---

[1] See Lasse Horne Kjældgaard, *Sjælen efter døden. Guldalderens moderne gennembrud*, Copenhagen: Gyldendal 2007.

[2] Johan Ludvig Heiberg, "Autoritet," *Intelligensblade*, no. 7, 1842, p. 165.

[3] Studies in Heiberg's political philosophy include Aage Kabell, "J.L. Heiberg og Hegels retsfilosofi," *Danske Studier*, 1944, pp. 110-28, and Leonardo F. Lisi, "Heiberg and the Drama of Modernity," in *Johan Ludvig Heiberg: Philosopher, Littérateur, Dramaturge, and Political Thinker*, ed. by Jon Stewart, Copenhagen: Museum Tusculanum Press 2008 (*Danish Golden Age Studies*, vol. 5), pp. 421-448.

a reply to a call that had been made by Johannes Hage for a so-called "contra-opposition literature," aimed at the oppositional literature said to be flourishing at the time. The contention, to which Heiberg responded, was that the new political voices made a deafening noise, while receiving no reply from the literary establishment—from the defenders of the old regime, the despotism of King Frederik VI. Heiberg deployed the term "young Denmark" ironically about these voices, pointing to a purely political movement with no evident literary allies.[1]

That does not mean, however, that the political movement was of no consequence to contemporary literature. In this article, I will suggest that "young Denmark" might, indeed, be a useful concept to deploy in order to understand the antagonistic—yet also, in some respects, politically converging—literary enterprises of Johan Ludvig Heiberg and Søren Kierkegaard. What is interesting about Heiberg's use of the phrase, and the exchange that he engaged in, back in 1836, is that it provides a rather different picture of the situation than the one that has been transmitted in Danish literary history. It suggests that there was, indeed, a Young Denmark, which was of importance to the literature of the period, although the movement did not manifest itself, at least not primarily, in imaginative literature.

I will argue for this view by looking at three mutually related tendencies in the 1830s, which challenge the depiction of the age as "the real aesthetic age of Danish literature": the critique of aestheticization, the pitting of politics against aesthetics (and vice versa) and, finally, the fast politicization of the press taking place during the decade. These

---

[1] Some decades later, the term was picked up by Heiberg's wife, Johanne Luise Heiberg, who used it in the same context in her memoirs, *A Life Relived in Memory* (1891-92), see Johanne Luise Heiberg, *Et Liv gjenoplevet i Erindringen*, vols. 1-4, ed. by Aage Friis, Copenhagen: Gyldendal 1944, vol. 1, p. 258 and vol. 2, p. 177. Earlier, it had been used as a title for the novel *Det unge Danmark* (Copenhagen: C.A. Reitzels Forlag 1879) by the Danish author and later Nobel Laureate Karl Gjellerup. This novel incited Sophus Claussen to write an unpublished poem with the same title. But to Gjellerup and Claussen, the term "young Denmark" would refer to the later movement in Danish literature normally labeled "the Modern Breakthrough." It had nothing to do with the 1830s and '40s. Yet, in spite of the fact that the term has been employed occasionally, it has never become a household word in Danish literary historiography, with reference to currents or movements during either the Golden Age or the Modern Breakthrough.

three trends are important to bear in mind when considering Heiberg's literary and polemical tactics in those years.

II. The Critique of Aestheticization

One of the ironical aspects of the afterlife of the 1830s in Danish literary history is that the interpretation that has made "young Denmark" invisible was, actually, introduced by the foremost representative of this movement, Orla Lehmann. As a concept, Biedermeier was first successfully introduced by Erik Lunding in 1968 (who offered a sympathetic re-evaluation of Georg Brandes' negative depiction of the period), but as an epochal self-characterization it was circulating in the age itself, as a biased contribution to the political discussion.[1] The young Orla Lehmann, who was leading the liberal faction, and who later became a key figure in the development of Denmark's first parliamentary government, launched it on February 12, 1836, in the liberal journal *Kjøbenhavnsposten*.

Commenting upon what he saw as the motionless state of the Danish general public since the Censorship Act of 1799 and since the disastrous Napoleonic Wars, Lehmann noted that these events had served to scare the public away from politics and left them "aestheticizing," as he said. For too long, his countrymen had been playing with "Old Denmark and the Dannebrog" and other "jingling" while "forgetting or lacking the courage to begin briskly on what was to be done: to reestablish, with force and prudence, what had been destroyed by all the tempests playing havoc with Denmark."[2] Lehmann here delivered the basis for that interpretation of the period, for which Georg Brandes became famous, and which lives on today in Lunding's more positive Biedermeier characterization of the age. He did so with a bold gesture with obvious political motives,

---

[1] A historical account of the Biedermeier concept in Danish literary historiography can be found in Lasse Horne Kjældgaard, "Kultur i et snævert rum. Biedermeiers begrebshistorie," *Kritik*, no. 167, 2004, pp. 8-18.

[2] Orla Lehmann "Trykkefrihedssagen," *Kjøbenhavnsposten*, February 12, 1836, p. 169.

fashioning himself as a "man of movement" in contrast to the stagnation he ascribed to his opponents and to the preceding age.[1] Lehmann considered the great interest in art and aesthetics, for which the 1830s are known, as a childish kind of escapism and compensation for historical defeat. Lehmann's accusations echo the words of the rebels confronting the artist in Møller's poem. Or vice versa, Lehmann's critique of the aesthetical apathy of the nation provides a historical correlate to the accusations made by the vandalizing radicals evoked by Møller. Lehmann expounded the "aestheticizing" as a collective withdrawal from the unbearable political reality to the private sphere, where one could indulge in sentimental idylls and avoid the present by escaping into glorious fictions about the past.

The Danish *Restaurationszeit* had, indeed, manifested itself aesthetically in poetic glorifications of the past: Adam Oehlenschläger's and N.F.S. Grundtvig's rediscovery of Nordic mythology, B.S. Ingemann's historical novels and his song "Paa Sjølunds fagre Sletter" are seen in this light—as cultural reverberations of the nation's traumatic defeats. It was this political attack on Romantic escapism by Orla Lehmann— strongly influenced by Heinrich Heine—which paved the way for the interpretation of the age now known under the rubric of Biedermeier.

III. Politics versus Aesthetics

The Biedermeier characterization of the age is quite simply inadequate. It was certainly not an apolitical age but, on the contrary, a time in which an array of issues was becoming highly politicized. This is attested to by the word I have just used: politicize or, in Danish, "*politisere.*" "Politicize" was a verb frequently used by the defenders of the old order, and it has an equivalent in the conversion of the noun "aesthetics" into the verb "aestheticize," which was employed by Young Denmark when advocating political reforms. Orla Lehmann, for instance, repeatedly used it. Both

---

[1] For an account of this antithesis in the intellectual and political life of the time, see the chapter "Stillestandsmændene i Fyrrerne" in Otto Borchsenius' book *Fra Fyrrerne. Litterære Skizzer*, vols. 1-2, Copenhagen: C.A. Reitzels Forlag and Otto B. Wroblewskys Forlag 1878, vol. 1, pp. 246-308.

of these linguistic innovations ascribe a bad habit to the opponent of wanting to extend his or her perspective on the world—aesthetic or political—way beyond its limits. The words were weapons in the ongoing battle between aesthetics and politics that took place in the 1830s—a clash that can even be traced to a philological level.

A vivid impression of the conflict between aesthetics and politics can be found in Henrik Hertz's long forgotten roman à clef *Moods and Conditions*, from 1839.[1] It provides a kind of literary report on the moods and conditions among the intellectuals in Copenhagen in the 1830s. One of the novel's most interesting figures is the so-called translator, "*Translatøren*," who is allegedly based upon the young Søren Kierkegaard, portrayed some years before his pseudonymous frenzy. The translator is a fiery character, who talks a lot, and his favorite topic is how political everything had recently turned: "At the time, when the King gave the decree on the establishment of the Assemblies, people here in Copenhagen gave little thought to politics. We were, so to speak, all aesthetical. Every single one of us aestheticized, at all parties people aestheticized, and all the journals aestheticized."[2]

But that had come to an end. The epoch-making event that the translator is referring to here is the establishment by law of four Advisory Provincial Assemblies. The assemblies had defined a new era—that is what the translator says while showing his scorn by placing the concept of "era" in quotation marks.

The assemblies were established in 1834, and they provided a vital step towards the constitution of 1849, replacing absolute monarchy with representative democracy. The obligation to establish the four assemblies was an old one. It was one that Frederik VI had brought upon himself during the Congress of Vienna in 1815. But he had only been compelled to comply with his promise in 1831, under German pressure. Political unrest in the wake of the July Revolution made it expedient to do so. So, the political revival in Denmark, registered in Henrik Hertz's novel, had

---

[1] Henrik Hertz, *Stemninger og Tilstande. Scener og Skildringer af et Ophold i Kjøbenhavn*, Copenhagen: C.A. Reitzel 1839. For Henrik Hertz's role in the contemporary critique of the politicization, see Bertel Nygaard, "Fremmedgørende politik. Henrik Hertz og kritikken af 1830'ernes politisering," *Fortid og Nutid*, no. 3, 2010, pp. 163-188.

[2] Ibid., p. 219.

its impetus in the exact same event as the one that had given rise to Young Germany and Young France, namely, the July Revolution in France in 1830. This event paved the way for new demands for political reforms in Denmark, which the King sought to play down by establishing the four Advisory Provincial Assemblies.

To many contemporary observers, this event marked a turning point and the beginning of a new age, a political age. The political movement began as an elite phenomenon and only slowly evolved into mass movements, but, from the beginning, it counted a high number of press entrepreneurs and gifted writers on contemporary public issues. Due to their intervention, the public sphere underwent not a structural but a thematic transformation: as questions about constitutionalism, civil rights, and freedom of the press were raised, the agenda changed from aesthetics to politics. The press turned political and imported, again according to Hertz's translator, a "language of opposition" ("*et Oppositions-Sprog*"), which had hitherto been unheard in little peaceful Denmark, where conflict of interests, allegedly, had not emerged until then. A new factionalism had set in, due to the influx of foreign ideas, the translator asserts.

This notion was widespread: the political enthusiasts were only imitating new fashionable trends that they had picked up in France, in particular. "If a political spirit were to rush into us Danes, then we would do well to put on the same political clothes which are worn in England and France," Heiberg sarcastically remarked in his pseudonymous "Letters to a Village Pastor" from 1834, using indirect communication in order to chastise what he saw as political fanaticism brewing.[1] The political zeal was not homegrown, so to speak. This was, of course, a way of opposing the nationalist rhetoric often used by those advocating political reforms.

---

[1] Johan Ludvig Heiberg, "Letters to a Village Pastor," in *Contingency Regarded from the Point of View of Logic and Other Texts*, ed. and trans. by Jon Stewart, Copenhagen: Museum Tusculanum Press 2008 (*Texts from Golden Age Denmark*, vol. 4), p. 204.

IV. The Politicization of the Press

The transformation of the press was even investigated empirically at the time. The media researcher who did so was an apprentice of Heiberg and a young student of theology by the name of Søren Kierkegaard. He studied the change of agenda in the periodical literature towards political matters and gave a talk about his results in the Students' Association on November 28, 1835 with the title "Our Journalistic Literature: A Study from Nature in Noonday Light," that is, "Vor Journallitteratur. Studium efter Naturen i Middagsbelysning."[1] It is probably due to this very early intervention that the largely unknown Søren Kierkegaard appears in Henrik Hertz's novel, from 1839, drawing similar conclusions about the political turn.[2]

The change of agenda in the newspapers and journals appeared to Kierkegaard as striking. In the introduction to the second volume of *Kjøbenhavns flyvende Post* in 1828, Heiberg had celebrated the great importance of art in his age, to which his new journal was meant to bear witness.[3] This is the great interest in art and aesthetics for which the period is reputed—as "the real aesthetic age of Danish literature," in Vilhelm Andersen's words. But it did not last long; interest in art was in decline in the early 1830s, and it had almost vanished ten years later, when all the great journals concerned with aesthetics and literature— *Maanedsskrift for Litteratur*, *Tidsskrift for Litteratur og Kritik*, and *Journal for Litteratur og Kunst*—had been closed down. The times seemed to have changed.

Kjøbenhavnsposten, the foremost liberal newspaper, started as an aesthetic journal, but its agenda shifted over into politics in 1834. So also, although to a lesser degree, the agenda of Heiberg's journal *Kjøbenhavns flyvende Post* upon its third launch, in 1834, shifted. "The new version

---

[1] See Søren Kierkegaard, "Our Journalistic Literature: A Study from Nature in Noonday Light," in *Early Polemical Writings*, ed. and trans. by Julia Watkin, Princeton: Princeton University Press 1990, pp. 35-52.

[2] See also Teddy Petersen, *Kierkegaards polemiske debut. Artikler 1834-36 i historisk sammenhæng*, Odense: Odense Universitetsforlag 1977 (*Odense Studies in Scandinavian Languages and Literatures*, vol. 9).

[3] Johan Ludvig Heiberg, "Til Læserne ved den nye Aargangs Begyndelse," *Kjøbenhavns Flyvende Post*, ed. by Uffe Andreasen, vol. 2, p. 14.

of the *Flyvende Post* had a decidedly political bent, thus diverging from
its original profile as a journal primarily for literature and aesthetics,"
Jon Stewart has recently observed, thus backing up Kierkegaard's
conclusions about the political turn of the press.[1] One may note that
the politicization of the press to a high degree follows the historical
pattern of the 1789 Revolution, upon which Jürgen Habermas based his
classic study on the *Structural Transformation of the Public Sphere*. The
infrastructure of the public sphere—such as the journals and private
parties referred to in Hertz's novel—had been aesthetically oriented,
and yet full of antagonisms, and gradually, or rather quite suddenly, the
conflicts became framed as political. The aesthetic debates may thus
be seen as a kind of *Vorschule*—or "a training ground," with Habermas'
phrase—to the democratic debates that followed.[2]

To the young Kierkegaard, this turn towards politics was a regrettable
change. His overwhelming literary enterprise became devoted to the
task of turning the attention of his readers "back" to the things that really
mattered—and that also meant away from politics. He complained that
people had lost interest in what he then called "aesthetics and in the
higher purposes of life," while immersing themselves totally in politics.[3]
This was not an original insight attained by the young Kierkegaard. His
mentor, Johan Ludvig Heiberg, had registered this change of interest
back in 1833.

---

[1] Jon Stewart, *A History of Hegelianism in Golden Age Denmark*, Tome I, *The Heiberg Period: 1824-1836*, Copenhagen: C.A. Reitzel 2007 (*Danish Golden Age Studies*, vol. 3), p. 474.

[2] Jürgen Habermas, *The Structural Transformation of the Public Sphere: An Inquiry into a Category of Bourgeois Society*, trans. by Thomas Burger, Cambridge, Massachusetts: MIT Press 1989, p. 29: "Even before the control over the public sphere by public authority was contested and finally wrested away by the critical reasoning of private persons on political issues, there evolved under its cover a public sphere in apolitical form—the literary precursor of the public sphere operative in the public domain. It provided the training ground for critical public reflection still preoccupied with itself—a process of self-clarification of private people focusing on the genuine experiences of their novel privateness."

[3] Søren Kierkegaard, "On the Polemic of *Fædrelandet*," in *Early Polemical Writings*, ed. and trans. by Julia Watkin, p. 16.

V. The Directions and Distractions of the Age

Johan Ludvig Heiberg grasped, from early on, the scale of the change that was happening: an epoch was swiftly closing, and a new one slowly dawning. That was how Heiberg characterized the age in a short prospectus that he issued in 1833, in order to advertise for a private course of lectures on modern philosophy that he offered—*On the Significance of Philosophy for the Present Age*. The present age was, according to Heiberg, a time of transition and turmoil, with many forces working in many directions:

> Anyone who, with an attentive eye, has observed the present generation... will without doubt have found that [it] strives powerfully forward in manifold new directions. However, it does not itself know where many of these directions will lead it and thus does not know whether they all lead to a common goal or what that might be....A condition of this kind is actually no condition; it is only a transition from a previous condition to one that is yet to come. It is not a fixed existence but only a becoming, in which what is old ends and what is new begins, an appearance of existence, destined to take the place of a real condition; in other words, it is a crisis.[1]

With the concept of crisis, Heiberg closed the chain of predicates that he used, periphrastically, to characterize "the present age" as a transitional period. According to him, unrest was the defining feature of the efforts of "the present generation," seeking peace without knowing how to attain it. Restlessly, they were moving in many directions, but they did not know which way "the cunning of reason" would eventually take them.

But Heiberg knew. Heiberg used the crisis of the "present age" as an occasion to retell Hegel's grand narrative of how the history of the different symbolic forms, in which Spirit—"humanity," in Heiberg's vocabulary—has manifested itself, had culminated now with the appointment of philosophy as the purveyor of the highest truth. In the prospectus, he made a strong claim for the supremacy of philosophy over lower forms of knowledge such as religion and poetry and art, importing to Denmark

---

[1] Heiberg, *On the Significance of Philosophy for the Present Age*, p. 87.

Hegel's rumor of the death of art,[1] known to him from *Kollegieheften* collected in Berlin.[2] In the current situation, religion had a choice between either merging with philosophy or maintaining independence, which would, in either case, result in its inevitable downfall. Poetry, still, was able to blend with philosophy and benefit from the alliance, making it possible and theoretically justifiable for Heiberg to sustain his primary occupation as a dramatist and poet.

The epochal characterization, put forth by Heiberg in the prospectus, is remarkably similar to the one Hegel had casually advanced in his famous preface to the *Phenomenology of Spirit* from 1807.[3] And yet, the acuteness of the crisis, as Heiberg presents it, seems to have increased dramatically. Something was threatening art and poetry very imminently, according to Heiberg. What was it? What were the signs—or rather the symptoms—of the disorder he sought to explain?

Heiberg mentions two recent developments in the prospectus. The first was the growing interest in the natural sciences, and the consequent loss of domain that the arts and the humanities suffered. The second trend that Heiberg points to is the political revival taking place in Denmark at the time: "Politics is indeed in our time the present in which the cultured world lives."[4] This is the turn—not only towards politics, but also against art and aesthetics—that Heiberg registered in the prospectus. It put the diagnosis in rather direct terms: "it is the very political character of the age which constitutes its crisis," Heiberg wrote.[5]

Heiberg's significant statement establishes both that there was a crisis, and that this unfolding crisis manifested itself in the fact that things had turned political. Politics had superseded religion as the final

---

[1] The notion of addressing Hegel's influential thesis of the death of art as a "rumor" is derived from Eva Geulen, *Das Ende der Kunst. Lesarten eines Gerüchts nach Hegel*, Frankfurt am Main: Suhrkamp 2002.

[2] As documented by Heiberg's letter to Hegel in February 1825: Johan Ludvig Heiberg, *Breve og Aktstykker vedrørende Johan Ludvig Heiberg*, vols. 1-5, ed. by Morten Borup, Copenhagen: Gyldendal/Det Danske Sprog- og Litteraturselskab 1946, vol. 1, p. 162.

[3] G.W.F. Hegel, *Phenomenology of Spirit*, trans. by A.V. Miller, Oxford: Oxford University Press 1977, p. 6: "Besides, it is not difficult to see that ours is a birth-time and a period of transition to a new era."

[4] Heiberg, *On the Significance of Philosophy for the Present Age*, p. 95.

[5] Ibid.

vocabulary, which people used to make sense of the world and their lives. The "cultured [*de Dannede*] are in recent times the people engaged in politics,"[1] Heiberg contended, and to this newly emerged social class, politics was even regarded as the new eschatology: "the cultured...have their heaven and hell in the ferment of politics."[2] The very ideal of salvation had been secularized and politicized.

The dethronement of religion was not bemoaned by Heiberg. But he objected to the idea that political aspirations could provide that "real condition" which everybody was longing for. Only philosophy could supply such serenity, according to Heiberg, and that was a good reason for signing up for a seat in his philosophy class. Since too few did so, the course was cancelled.

Heiberg's invitation to the philosophical lecture series—and its diagnosis of the age—exerted, however, a long and profound influence upon the entire intellectual life in Copenhagen. It is a text of modest appearance but with an enormous influence. The description of the age, offered by Heiberg in *On the Significance of Philosophy for the Present Age*, was of vital importance to Søren Kierkegaard as a continued source of provocation and inspiration. Kierkegaard eagerly offered alternatives to Heiberg's description of the "present age," while heavily depending upon it.

This is evident from Kierkegaard's first book, his critique of Hans Christian Andersen, *From the Papers of One Still Living*, from 1838. The review reiterates Heiberg's definition of the age as a transitional period—"a period of fermentation" in Kierkegaard's words—while also noting that the "main trend of the age" is "in the political sphere."[3] Kierkegaard's bizarre review attacks Andersen on a number of accounts, one of them being his political inclinations. Indeed, one may see Kierkegaard's critique as a warning to Andersen (who had avidly read Heine in the company of Orla Lehmann).[4] "With his critique, Kierkegaard wants to tell Andersen that he is about to take a dangerous and damaging course,"

---

[1] Ibid., p. 95.
[2] Ibid., p. 94.
[3] Søren Kierkegaard, *From the Papers of One Still Living*, in *Early Polemical Writings*, ed. and trans. by Julia Watkin, p. 63.
[4] H.C. Andersen, *Mit Livs Eventyr*, vols. 1-2, ed. by Helge Topsøe-Jensen, Copenhagen: Gyldendal 1996, vol. 1, p. 109.

Johan de Mylius has observed.[1] Do not turn political, was the implicit admonition, and, according to the conventional wisdom of Andersen scholarship, Andersen followed it.[2]

By warning—or, perhaps, threatening—Andersen, Kierkegaard was paying lip service not only to Heiberg in *From the Papers of One Still Living* but also to Poul Martin Møller, his honored teacher of philosophy at the University of Copenhagen. The year before he wrote "The Artist Among the Rebels," Møller had, in 1836, published an extensive review of Thomasine Gyllembourg's (Johan Ludvig Heiberg's mother) story of everyday life, *The Extremes*, in which he had held up Gyllembourg as a contrast to the political literature thriving on the continent—as does Kierkegaard in *From the Papers of One Still Living*. Møller deplored what he called the "constantly repeated call for literature to enter more than it had done into the service of politics, a thought which must be considered a big mistake."[3] Møller's intervention here supports the ample evidence that the possible emergence of a Young literary Denmark was the specter that the literary establishment, revolving around Heiberg, was fighting against. They would not allow it to happen.

VI. *The Resurgence of Poetry*

This was the political condition that Johan Ludvig Heiberg put into words in 1833, and through which he maneuvered with his theoretical and poetical writings of the 1830s and '40s. Art and poetry had, under the present circumstances, been "relegated to a simple recreation amidst

---

[1] Johan de Mylius, "Af en endnu Levendes Papirer," in *Den udødelige. Kierkegaard læst værk for værk*, ed. by Tonny Aagaard Olesen and Pia Søltoft, Copenhagen: C.A. Reitzel 2005, p. 32.

[2] Again, it is tempting to quote Vilhelm Andersen, whose words have been repeated over and over again in Andersen scholarship: "There is not a single political motif in Andersen's fairy tales, not a single political thought in his collected works" (Vilhelm Andersen, *Illustreret dansk Litteraturhistorie*, vols. 1-4, Copenhagen: Gyldendal 1934, vol. 3, p. 586).

[3] Poul Martin Møller, "Nye Fortællinger af Forfatteren til en Hverdagshistorie. Udgivne af Johan Ludvig Heiberg. Andet Bind: Extremerne," *Maanedsskrift for Litteratur*, vol. 15, 1836, p. 138.

the seriousness of political life"[1]—and were badly in need of someone who could restore them to their rightful place. This was the role Heiberg designed for himself and tried to fulfill. Already in 1833, Heiberg had prophesied a resurgence of poetry: "Let the serious, politically reasoning and politically acting citizen remain unaware that his actual life lies in what he considers mere amusement. The time will come when he will have his eyes opened."[2] What the political minds would discover was the salving powers of poetry—its ability to provide that tranquility they were striving for. This was the goal Heiberg subsequently worked towards, opening the eyes of the philistines to the powers of poetry.

Heiberg's venture to restore the prominence of poetry included his attempts to create a new kind of poetry after the death of art, "speculative poetry." Regarded in the context that I have tried to establish here, speculative poetry may indeed be regarded as a kind of "contra-opposition literature," to recycle Heiberg's phrase from 1836. Along similar lines, but with a very different output, Kierkegaard launched his pseudonymous enterprise in the 1840s. This enterprise was (also) intended as art against politics, which may serve to explain the curious dual position towards issues of art and aesthetics in Kierkegaard's authorship: on the one hand, it defends them, and, on the other, it critiques the aestheticizing tendencies of Heiberg, thus providing what we may call—and now it is beginning to sound like something from a Monty Python movie—an "anti-contra-opposition literature."[3] In terms of political aversions, Heiberg and Kierkegaard were, nevertheless, two of a kind.

The most successful speculative drama Heiberg wrote might also be considered his most efficacious attack on the political tendencies of the age, that is, his 1840 closet drama, "A Soul after Death," labeled by Heiberg as an "apocalyptic comedy." The comedy contains a soft

---

[1] Heiberg, *On the Significance of Philosophy for the Present Age*, p. 98.
[2] Ibid.
[3] In *Prefaces* (1844), for instance, Søren Kierkegaard associates Heiberg with his political antagonist, the liberal editor of *Kjøbenhavnsposten*, Andreas Peter Liunge, by hinting that their literary entrepreneurships served similar objectives, to simulate movement. See Lasse Horne Kjældgaard, "The Age of Miscellaneous Announcements: Paratextualism in Kierkegaard's *Prefaces* and Contemporary Literary Culture," in *Prefaces and Writing Sampler and Three Discourses on Imagined Occasions*, ed. by Robert L. Perkins, Macon, Georgia: Mercer University Press 2006 (*International Kierkegaard Commentary*, vols. 9-10), pp. 7-28.

condemnation of exactly that "serious, politically reasoning and politically acting citizen," whom he had addressed in the 1833 pamphlet. Although often wallowing in philosophical pathos, Heiberg repeatedly teased the political minds for their pathos and seriousness, which he perceived as a kind of fanaticism.

Indeed, one of the faults of the soul of "A Soul after Death" is his lack of self-irony and inability to look upon himself from the outside. The deceased protagonist of the poem is a liberally minded soul, who admires America—"the country where one dwells upon the soil of freedom"[1]—and who had avidly been reading the new political press in Denmark. The soul, finally, finds employment and a home in Hell as one who tries to fill the bottomless barrel of the Danaids, implying that his idea of progress, as a "man of movement," amounts to nothing but endless repetition. The poem ridicules the soul for his insipidness, thus returning a verdict upon the continued political aspirations of the age. But, interestingly, the poem does so by deploying a literary mode considered political *par excellence*: satire. Heiberg was, in this regard, infected by that disease which he actively tried to cure with literary means: the political mobilization of art. Like the poor artist in Møller's poem, Heiberg had to imitate the opponents in his counterattack. In this sense, Heiberg was an artist among the rebels, but without self-pity or scruples about playing the judge.

VII. A New Waker

A similar attack on the political turn can be found in Heiberg's new publicistic enterprise of the 1840s, the journal *Intelligensblade*. Heiberg had, in his journal *Kjøbenhavns flyvende Post*, accommodated for the emerging political debate and also taken part in it. But this appeasement was replaced with confrontation, when he, in 1842, launched the *Intelligensblade*. The preface, which clearly admonishes the dominance of the political in the public sphere, sets out explicitly Heiberg's wish to lead the audience ("*Publicum*") back from the political paths it had been straying upon—"back" to literature and aesthetics:

[1]   Johan Ludvig Heiberg, *Nye Digte*, ed. by Klaus P. Mortensen, Copenhagen: Borgen/ Det Danske Sprog- og Litteraturselskab 1990, p. 29.

We Danes have been blamed that we, until a few years ago, have been so absorbed in literary and chiefly aesthetic interests that we had become blind to the great political endeavors of the age, and somewhat deaf to the call to orient ourselves in our own civil and constitutional conditions that are contained in these efforts. But by continually debating these issues for a long time, the press has remedied this lack, and the time has come when the opposite one-sidedness is thriving, so that the literary and especially aesthetic interests could need if not a new waker (for they could not possibly slumber when once awakened)—then rather a regulator, so that the public [*Publicum*], which has for too long been walking on its own, may be led back from the wrong ways, which it so easily treads upon when left to its own guidance.[1]

The preface reiterates the key metaphor of the 1833 prospectus *On the Significance of Philosophy for the Present Age*, depicting history as a journey with many distractions but with only one right direction. But it also introduced a more active role of the journal, as a kind of shepherd leading the flock back to the right path—back to "the literary and especially aesthetic interests." Curiously enough, Heiberg and Kierkegaard shared this desire to turn the interest of the public away from the political with the aesthete Georg Carstensen, the founder of Tivoli, who, according to an unverified anecdote, in an 1842 audience with the King, offered this explanation of his amusement park: "When the people have fun, they forget to politicize."[2]

Tivoli's achievement in this respect was probably bigger than Heiberg's, and, yet, neither succeeded with their attempts to change the interests of the public. The politicization continued to escalate up through the 1840s, culminating with the Constitution of 1849. We get, however, an impression of the consequences of Heiberg's campaign from the critic P.L. Møller, who—without naming him—repeated, and subtly modified, Heiberg's epochal characterization in 1843:

Our age is a crisis, a transition, a period of unrest and fermentation. This must be true, at least it has been repeated until tedium. But the movement

---

[1] Johan Ludvig Heiberg, "Til Læserne," *Intelligensblade*, no. 1, 1842, p. 1.
[2] Alfred Jeppesen, *Kjøbenhavns Sommer-Tivoli 1843-1968*, Copenhagen: Aschehoug Dansk Forlag 1968, p. 31.

is not, as the philosophers think, a merely philosophical urge, nor, as the politicians think, a merely political one. It is a generally emerging tendency of emancipation, a desire to break loose, in many directions, from the bolt of a civilization, which in many regards is outdated, over-refined and fallen from nature. This longing for emancipation is felt in all national, religious and social affairs, as well as in philosophy and politics. Philosophers and politicians only represent the extreme Right and Left of the general movement. As poetry is a popular and pleasing means of communication, all the struggling parties seek to take possession of it, and as drama is the fattest province in the kingdom of poetry, they fight over it....On the one side, it has turned into a matter of honor for poetry to personally participate in the political fights; on the other side, it is threatened with death and destruction if it does not immediately trade its earlier content for the philosophical ideas.[1]

It was Heiberg who had "threatened" poetry with "death and destruction" if it did not enter into the service of philosophy. He is, here, exposed by P.L. Møller as a participant in the ongoing fights, which poetry could hardly stay out of—as an artistic rebel among rebels.

P.L. Møller blamed the politicians and philosophers, to whom Heiberg belonged, for being wrong about the encompassing nature of the "generally emerging tendency of emancipation." This expression elaborates upon Heiberg's significant essay on "Authority" from the year before, but it also anticipates that revolt against the "authority principle," which later became a leitmotif in Georg Brandes' *Main Currents in Nineteenth Century Literature*. But, considered in the contemporary context, P.L. Møller's diagnosis differs from Heiberg's due to its orientation toward the past rather than the end toward which all historical processes are tending. On a more Rousseauean note, Møller believed that the contemporary turmoil should be considered a reaction, a move away from a corrupt civilization rather than a confused step forward, in a direction that eventually would turn out to be right.

[1] P.L. Møller, "Om Poesi og Drama, med Hensyn til Prof. Heiberg, Ørkenens Søn og Fr. Hebbels Tragedier," *Arena, et polemisk-æsthetisk Blad*, 1843, pp. 95-96.

VIII. An Artist Among Rebels?

With critical detachment, P.L. Møller analyzed the condition of art and poetry in this era of unrest, where attempts were made to mobilize them from both political and philosophical sides. It was in many ways the same situation as that which Poul Martin Møller had staged with his poem "The Artist Among the Rebels," about the artist going berserk. Poul Martin Møller himself fought against the political turn, while admitting, in "The Artist Among the Rebels," the impossibility of maintaining artistic autonomy in the heat of the battle. Five years later, P.L. Møller added, with his observations, to the impression that the "aesthetic age" was long gone in the early 1840s. In 1842, Heiberg conceded that it was "impossible to separate the political trend from the literary," since "the relation of poetry to politics manifests itself in something much deeper than the direct use of political matters."[1]

In the wake of the July Revolution, the demands for political reform had intensified in Denmark, and an irreversible politicization of the public sphere had begun. Young Denmark existed as a political formation that called all non-committed aesthetic activities into question. I believe this political turn, or the actual scope of it, has been underestimated in the literary historiography of the period. Even though works of art and poetry were not intended as political messages, they were, nevertheless, easily politicized due to the trends I have outlined in this article. The tension between aesthetics and politics structured the thinking and writing of Heiberg but also of Kierkegaard and other Danish intellectuals of the time. The pseudonymous missile battery, which Søren Kierkegaard launched the year after, was—among other things—targeted against the political turn of the age. Heiberg regarded this turn as a crisis, and he handled it as a crisis in poetical and polemical writings from the period. He may have been an artist among the rebels, but he was also opposing the rebels in a number of politically and aesthetically interesting ways.

---

[1] Johan Ludvig Heiberg, "Folk og Publicum," *Intelligensblade*, no. 6, 1842, pp. 136-137.

Ghostly Monarchies—Paradoxical Constitutions of the Political in Johan Ludvig Heiberg's Royal Dramas

Klaus Müller-Wille

I. *Theatrical Politics*

On the 1st and 2nd of November 1828 a royal wedding, more extravagant than any other ever before, was staged in Copenhagen. The marriage between the Danish Prince Frederik and the Danish Princess Wilhelmine Marie was celebrated as a public wedding parade in which the absolutist court presented themselves to its citizens in a number of magnificent processions through Copenhagen.[1] The city itself had been illuminated just for this occasion. The wedding cost an at the time unimaginable sum of 312,043 *Rigsbanksdaler*.

The festivities took place during the reign of Frederik VI (1768-1839, King from 1808 to 1839), who had assumed power as the crown prince at the end of the eighteenth century and whose accession to power awoke hope of extensive liberal reforms. This hope, however, was dashed early on since, in reaction to the French Revolution, Frederik VI pursued a distinct conservative policy. Above all he opposed every attempt to question his absolutist position of power. This manifested itself in, among other things, harsher censorship laws which remained in force until 1848.

---

[1] A richly illustrated presentation of this occasion with many peculiar detailed observations is offered in Ole Villumsen Krog, "Århundredets bryllup," *Siden Saxo*, no. 4, 2004, pp. 4-18.

Also in 1828, in the Swedish governed Drammen (Norway), the most prominent victim of this *Trykkefrihedsforordningen*, Peter Andreas Heiberg (1758-1841), managed to publish a monograph, *Enevoldsmagtens Indførelse i Dannemark i Aaret 1660* or *The Introduction of Absolutism in Denmark in 1600*, which was advertised as a "historical and critical inquiry."[1] Behind the harmless title was a sharp reckoning with the antiquated absolutist constitution of Denmark. The work, which was based on Heiberg's studies during his exile in France, had already been published in 1820 under the appropriate title "Prècis historique et critique de la Constitution du royaume de Danemark" in the *Journal général de Législation et de Jurisprudence*.[2] Heiberg's work signaled the callous political tone that was to shape the Danish press in the 1830s and onward. Especially within the ambit of the journal *Fædrelandet* (1834-82) a national liberal opposition formed which—with recourse to the idea of national thought—addressed the question of the political representation of the people (*Folket*) time and time again. The political debates were also reflected in moderate and conservative organs such as *Kjøbenhavns flyvende Post* (1827-30), *Kjøbenhavns flyvende Post. Interimsblade* (1834-37) and *Berlingske Tidende* (1749-).[3] The opposition was able to register their first success in 1831 when the king summoned the Advisory Assembly of the Provincial Estates. Despite this, in many ways unsatisfactory, solution, Christian VIII (1786-1848, King from 1839 to 1848), Frederik VI's successor, also managed to prevent crucial constitutional reforms, which in turn caused the political debates to intensify once again. Following his death though, Denmark received one of the most advanced constitutions in Europe, decisively restricting the King's sphere of power.

With this historical excursus in mind, let us return to the pompous royal wedding in 1828. As took place elsewhere, the Danish court tried to meet the growing political pressure with new forms of self-glorification. The restrictions of the civil public due to the censorship went hand-

---

[1] Peter Andreas Heiberg, *Enevoldsmagtens Indførelse i Dannemark i Aaret 1660. Historisk og kritisk Undersøgelse*, Drammen: C.F. Rode 1828.

[2] Peter Andreas Heiberg, *Prècis historique et critique de la Constitution du royaume de Danemark. Extrait du Journal général de Législation et de Jurisprudence*, Paris: Imprimerie de Madame Jeunehomme-Crémière 1820.

[3] With regards to the changed political climate in Denmark during the 1830s see the contribution by Lasse Horne Kjældgaard in this volume.

in-hand with an opening of the court for the civil audience, who were integrated into the festivities of the crown in a new manner. Even the Royal Theater was used in this sense as a type of interface between the civil and court public. On November 6, 1828, the façade of the Theater was richly decorated in order to celebrate the premiere of a play that was written for the royal wedding.[1] With its novel fusion of vaudeville, folk song and historical drama, Johan Ludvig Heiberg's *Elves' Hill* seems to be well suited in every aspect to the new type of liaison between the court and civil public. Without a doubt, the play struck the nerve of the time. With its 155 performances between 1828 and 1867, *Elves' Hill* belonged not only to the most successful plays of the Golden Age, but with over 1000 performances, it also is among the most successful plays ever performed at the Royal Theater.

II. Political Theater

When one considers the success of *Elves' Hill* it is perhaps not surprising that Heiberg was contractually engaged by the Royal Theater as a poet.[2] Included among the manifold of activities linked to this position was the task of writing songs, poems and dramatic plays for the court's festivities. If one traces the commissioned works which Heiberg wrote in this capacity, then the series of three (or four) royal dramas that the author created for birthdays and weddings in the royal family catch one's eye. In 1829, that is, directly following the success of *Elves' Hill*, Heiberg worked on the draft for his play *King Valdemar Atterdag*, which he intended to be performed on occasion of the King's 62nd birthday. But due to the objections of the court's censor, the play had to be withdrawn. Only one draft of it remains which was published posthumously in *Prosaiske Skrifter* in 1862. In contrast to *King Valdemar Atterdag* the play *Fata Morgana*, written by Heiberg for the King's 70th birthday, was performed in 1838. Nonetheless, just like *Day of the Seven Sleepers*, which Heiberg wrote for the crowning of Christian VIII and had its premiere on the 1st of July 1840 at the Royal Theater, *Fata Morgana* was a public flop.

---

[1] See Morten Borup, *Johan Ludvig Heiberg*, vols. 1-3, Copenhagen: Gyldendal 1947-49, vol. 2, pp. 146f.

[2] Ibid., pp. 148f.

In the research on Heiberg, *Day of the Seven Sleepers* is seen as a counterpart to *Elves' Hill* for good reasons.[1] Both plays struggle with the previously mentioned fusion of vaudeville, folk song and historical drama. In each case, Heiberg also collaborated closely with prominent contemporary composers—Friedrich Kuhlau and Johan Peter Emilius Hartmann. Moreover, in both dramas Heiberg makes use of a similar double-layered structure built on a clear dichotomy of historical reality and a fantastical dream world, whereby the climax of each of the plays is comprised of a dream sequence in which these two spheres meet. In both plays kings and symbolic rings serve in different ways as mediators between the two worlds. Finally, the close relationship between the two plays can also be proven historically since the abovementioned 1829 draft of the play *King Valdemar Atterdag* anticipates at least one essential plotline for the later realized play *Day of the Seven Sleepers*.

Nevertheless, the similarities mentioned here between *Elves' Hill* and *Day of the Seven Sleepers* should not obscure the equally distinct differences that separate the two plays from one another. One of these disparities—as already noted—is the completely divergent receptions of the plays. In later remarks, Heiberg still behaves skeptically with regard to a re-staging of *Day of the Seven Sleepers*, which he—with reference to Goethe—tries to classify as occasional poetry for a specific event:

> In its entire structure, this play is so tightly bound to the occasion which created it that it is totally unnecessary to throw a veil over it by changing the conclusion in any manner. However, I also do not see any problem in the occasion being disclosed. On that score, the audience finds itself in a strange intellectual confusion; it has the prejudice that the poetic and especially the sublime do not tolerate any contact with an externally given occasion. Goethe, however, said that every work was more or less an occasional work.[2]

It is highly questionable whether Heiberg would have also characterized *Elves' Hill* as occasional poetry. All the same, I do not want to pursue

---

[1]   Borup, *Johan Ludvig Heiberg*, vol. 3, pp. 10-15.
[2]   *Breve og Aktstykker vedrørende Johan Ludvig Heiberg*, vols. 1-5, ed. by Morten Borup, Copenhagen: Gyldendal 1946-50, vol. 4, p. 305.

further the thus implied question about the aesthetic appraisal of *Elves' Hill* and *Day of the Seven Sleepers* in this context. Rather, my aim is to carve out the striking structural differences between the two texts in order to expose the extensive political implications of the plays. Both dramas are involved—at least according to the central thesis that this article is based on—with the delicate questions of representation theory linked with the relationship between monarchies and theatrality.[1] In this sense, both plays can truly be understood in the sense outlined by Heiberg himself as occasional poetry in that they are very closely connected to the previously unknown form of a public, festive-pompous staging of the royal power by means of which the Royal Theater (and thus also Heiberg) take part in the wedding and royal festivities of the court. In my opinion, Heiberg exploits the opportunity of the publicly staged court wedding and crowning to reflect critically and philosophically about the specific function of the monarchy in a state of the early and mid-nineteenth century.

In this article, I would like, on the one hand, to draw attention to the plays' level of political-aesthetic reflection, which in my opinion can be revealed quite well by falling back on the comments about the specific functions of the king in the modern state which were developed by Georg Wilhelm Friedrich Hegel (1779-1831) in his *Elements of the Philosophy of Right* (1821).[2] On the other hand, I would like to explore

---

[1] This essay is decisively inspired by two studies which, based on Cornelius Castoriadis' concept of the political imaginary, explore the reciprocal relation between imagination and politics or more concretely between theater theory and the political debate of the 1830s and 1840s. See Cornelius Castoriadis, *Gesellschaft als imaginäre Institution. Entwurf einer politischen Philosophie*, Frankfurt a.M.: Suhrkamp 1990; Jörg Wiesel, *Zwischen König und Konstitution. Der Körper der Monarchie vor dem Gesetz des Theaters*, Vienna: Passagen 2001; and Thomas Frank, Albrecht Koschorke, Susanne Lüdemann, and Ethel Matala de Mazza, *Des Kaisers neue Kleider. Über das Imaginäre politischer Herrschaft*, Frankfurt a.M.: Fischer 2002. The last two treatises are primarily interesting in the context of this study because with Hans Christian Andersen and Heinrich Theodor Rötscher they draw attention to two authors whose writings Heiberg knew intimately.

[2] The reference to *Elements of the Philosophy of Right* seems obvious, since—at least according to Paul Rubow—of all Hegel's writings this book had made the deepest impression on Heiberg because of its relation to reality. See Paul V. Rubow, *Heiberg og hans Skole i Kritiken*, Copenhagen: Gyldendal 1953, p. 35. See also Aage Kabell, "J.L. Heiberg og Hegels retsfilosofi," *Danske Studier*, 1944, pp. 110-128.

the pronounced differences that separate *Elves' Hill* in this perspective
from *Day of the Seven Sleepers*. In order to understand the development
from *Elves' Hill* to *Day of the Seven Sleepers* references will also be made
to the draft of *King Valdemar Atterdag* and the play *Fata Morgana*.

III. The King's Two Bodies: Elves' Hill (1828)

The vaudeville *Elves' Hill* stands in direct relation to the theoretical
foundation of the vaudeville genre published by Heiberg in 1826.[1] In
this context, I am interested not in the extremely interesting conceptual
contradictions and inconsistencies that characterize *On Vaudeville
as a Dramatic Genre* as a treatise on genre theory,[2] but rather only in
the function that Heiberg ascribes to vaudeville within the context of
Danish theater life. The idea of a national drama forms the basis of his
related comments developed in recourse to Ludvig Holberg's (1684-
1754) comedies. According to Heiberg, these in no way serve to convey
moral dogma, but instead serve to develop a national self-image: "The
moral benefit of the play is therefore only *indirect*, insofar as it fuels
the poetic disposition of the individual and the nation as well as the
development of these poetic dispositions, like every other ability which
is a part of a moral totality."[3] The manner with which Heiberg tries to
incorporate Holberg's comedies into a national aesthetic of the early
nineteenth century also defines his approach to other forms of popular
theater. Thus Parisian vaudeville was consciously taken up by him as a

[1] See Johan Ludvig Heiberg, *Om Vaudevillen som dramatisk Digtart og om dens
Betydning paa den danske Skueplads. En dramaturgisk Undersøgelse*, in *Prosaiske
Skrifter*, vols. 1-11, Copenhagen: C.A. Reitzel 1861-62, vol. 6, pp. 1-111.

[2] For more on this point, I refer to a fine article by Kirsten Wechsel, in which she
precisely reveals the breaks and hybrid nature of Heiberg's genre concept. See
Kirsten Wechsel, "Herkunftstheater. Zur Regulierung von Legitimität im Streit um
die Gattung Vaudeville," in *Faszination des Illegitimen. Alterität in Konstruktionen
von Genealogie, Herkunft und Ursprünglichkeit in den skandinavischen Literaturen seit
1800*, ed. by Constanze Gestrich and Thomas Mohnike, Würzburg: Ergon 2007, pp.
39-60.

[3] Heiberg, *Om Vaudevillen som dramatisk Digtart og om dens Betydning paa den danske
Skueplads. En dramaturgisk Undersøgelse*, in *Prosaiske Skrifter*, vol. 6, p. 79.

popular and contemporary genre. Nonetheless, it was not his aim to copy this genre. Quite the contrary, he strived to give vaudeville a completely new function in the context of the Danish theater. Since vaudeville, as a type of theater aimed at creating a diversion and entertaining the public, appealed to a broad audience, it was particularly well suited to fostering a national culture. In order to underline this concern of a national *Bildung* (culture), the poet, however, cannot bend to the poor taste of the masses. He has to learn how to use the genre strategically in order to create the public's hidden poetic disposition and thus unite it into a cultured national sentiment.

Elves' Hill is suitable for this program in a number of respects. On the one hand, the play, with its mistaken identity and unveiling story, serves the expectations of a simply structured melodrama. On the other hand, the vaudeville with its allusions to Danish folk songs and Christian IV as its central historical figure should awaken national sentiment. This intention is strengthened by the character inventory of the historical narrative, which in no way contains only nobles, but rather represents all levels of the social strata and in particular the Danish farmers in an extremely conflict-free plot.

The corresponding strategy of Heiberg is in the meantime well documented in the research.[1] In this context, I want to concentrate only on the role of the king in the play. Early on it is clear that the king functions as a type of detective, who reveals the basic story of the mistaken identity and with that contributes to the lovers being able to unite at the end of the play.

Even when he appears as a type of Enlightenment philosopher, he distinguishes himself—in contrast to the representatives of the aristocracy—through the especially gentle manner with which he faces the superstitions and the corresponding folk songs and tales of the farmers: "King: And I relish these tales and songs. A coin, no longer of value, but which is still collected by the peasantry with the hope that one

---

[1] See, for example, Hans Kuhn, "*Elverhøi*: The Making of a National Musical," in *Nordisk litteratur og mentalitet*, ed. by Malan Manersdóttir and Jens Cramer, Tórshavn: Føroya Fróðskaparfelag 2000, pp. 294-298.

day it will be of worth, is also a part of the fatherland's treasure."[1] Within the context of the massive economic turmoil that Denmark was exposed to in the early nineteenth century, the metaphor of money that became worthless and could again gain value after a period of inflation, does not seem to be randomly selected. Apart from the far-reaching implications of the metaphor though, the remarks made by the Christian IV character can be set in direct correlation to Heiberg's poetic technique. The King's comment that the old folk tales will one day regain value is fulfilled not least in the vaudeville *Elves' Hill* itself, in that the old semiotic material of the folk tales is integrated into a new context and therefore appreciates in value.

A similar conversion of folk tales can naturally be illustrated best by the king of the elves' saga, which is already alluded to in the title of the play. The play uses the tales about the king of the elves in order to blend them with the image of Christian IV, who is thus mythologized and revalued as a component of Danish folk culture.

The close relationship between the ghostly and real king reaches its climax in the fourth act. After Agnete has dreamt of the king of the elves and searches for him, she meets Christian IV, whom she nonetheless does not recognize as the king:

> King: Upon my life! This is a peculiar turn of events: You seek the king and stand before him.
> Agnete: I beg your pardon?
> King: As I have said.
> Agnete: No master! You are breaking your promise and are mocking me.
> King: I speak the truth; is it so difficult to believe?
> Agnete: You are like one of us, from flesh and blood?
> King: My child! Is the king not made of flesh and blood?
> Agnete: No, Master, no! He is a passing mist, a breath is enough to make him float in the evening air; his heart has no blood, his bones no marrow, he is nothing like you.

---

[1] Johan Ludvig Heiberg, *Elverhøi. Drama i fem Acter*, in *Poetiske Skrifter*, vols. 1-11, Copenhagen: C.A. Reitzel 1862, vol. 3, p. 368: "*Kongen: Og mig behage disse Sagn og Viser. / En Skillemynt, som ikke meer har Cours, / Men som dog Bondestanden samler paa, / I Haabet om, at den engang vil gjælde, / Er og en Deel af Fædrelandets Skat.*"

King: In God's name! That is what I call a wonderful concept of a king! ... You know no other king here than that which your imagination has created. It is time that I depose him and show you fools who reigns here. You believe in someone who is only a figment of your imagination; and with me, who stands before your own eyes, with me you dare to negate life and truth? Let these foolish thoughts be gone![1]

The humorous dialogue contains a highly explosive political potential, since the question of whether or not the king is actually to be understood as an illusion, as a type of fleeting mist or delusion, is in no way irrelevant in the era following the French Revolution. It is no wonder that Heiberg's king pushes to raise awareness that the king is not an abstract idea that one can get rid of, but rather that the monarchy is, more or less, embodied in a person made of flesh and blood. Perhaps it is symptomatic of this context that in one of his lines Christian IV draws attention to the "concept of a king" ("*Begreb om Kongen*") and with that—at least according to my thesis—indirectly to Hegel's comments about the "concept of the monarch" ("*Begriff des Monarchen*") in *Elements of the Philosophy of Right*.

Hegel was probably one of the last great political theorists who stood up for the untouched position of the monarch in a modern state. In doing so his surprisingly conservative plea is based on the concept of the king's physicality:

Without its monarch and that articulation of the whole which is necessarily and immediately associated with monarchy, the people is a formless mass. The latter is no longer a state, and none of these determinations which are

---

[1] Ibid., pp. 478f. and p. 481: "*Kongen: Saa sandt jeg lever! det sig selsomt føier: / Du søger Kongen, og for ham du staaer. / Agnete: Hvorledes? / Kongen: Som jeg siger. / Agnete: Nei, o Herre! / I har jert Løfte brudt, I spotter mig! / Kongen: Jeg taler Sandhed; er den saa utrolig? / Agnete: I er som En af os, af Kjød og Blod? / Kongen: Mit Barn! er Kongen ei af Kjød og Blod? / Agnete: Nei, Herre, nei! Han er en flygtig Taage, / som svæver for et Pust i Aftenluften; / Hans Hjerte har ei Blod, hans Been ei Marv, / Han ingen Lighed har med jer. / Kongen: Guds Død! / Det kalder jeg et smukt Begreb om Kongen! ...I kjende her ei nogen anden Konge, / End den som eders Indbildning har skabt. / Det er paa Tiden jeg afsætter ham, / Og viser jer, I Daarer, hvo der hersker. / Du troer paa hiin, som kun er Hjernespind; / Og mig, der synlig for dit Øie staaer, / Hos mig du tør benægte Liv og Sandhed? / Lad fare denne taabelige Tanke!*"

encountered only in an internally organized whole (such as sovereignty, government, courts of law, public authorities, estates, etc.) is applicable to it….If a people is represented neither as a patriarchal *tribe*, nor as existing in an undeveloped condition in which democratic or aristocratic forms are possible…or indeed in any other arbitrary and inorganic condition—but is envisaged as an internally developed and truly organic totality, its sovereignty will consist in the personality of the whole, which will in turn consist in the reality appropriate to its concept, i.e., the *person of the monarch*.[1]

In this passage, Hegel clearly falls back on the medieval theory of the king's two bodies, according to which the king unifies the biological body and the state body in one person.[2] This idea is so central to Hegel because the king then becomes an example for a general theory of signs in which the universal is amalgamated with the particular. In contrast to the imaginations or delusions with which democracies or aristocracies attempt to give an image of the state as a whole, the coincidentally given king's real body should guarantee that this image is formed through a biological organism's quasi-natural laws.

Although Heiberg oriented himself on questions related to theories of representations, on which Hegel's political speculation is based, the reference to *Elements of the Philosophy of Right* within the context of the passages cited from *Elves' Hill* seems problematic. In no way does the king in the play appear as a synthesis of two bodies; rather he appears to be reduced to just his material physicality. That means he seems to lose every representative function because the idea of the immaterial body of the king is linked to the silly imagination and delusions of the people. In my opinion, this clearly staged separation between Christian IV's pure material body and the purely imagined, ghostly body of the king of the elves are part of a specific dialectical strategy of Heiberg, with which he

---

[1] Hegel, *Sämtliche Werke. Jubiläumsausgabe*, vols. 1-20, ed. by Hermann Glockner, Stuttgart: Friedrich Frommann Verlag 1928-41, vol. 7, § 279, pp. 383f. (English translation: *Elements of the Philosophy of Right*, trans. by H.B. Nisbet, ed. by Allen Wood, Cambridge and New York: Cambridge University Press 1991, § 279, p. 319.)

[2] With regard to this see also the now classic study by Ernst Hartwig Kantorowicz, *Die zwei Körper des Königs. Ein Studie zur politischen Theorie des Mittelalters*, Munich: Deutscher Taschenbuch-Verlag 1990.

prepares the synthesis of matter and spirit in the body of the king. This synthesis finds its conclusion in the figure of Christian IV, generated by the play itself. On stage, this character functions simultaneously as a real person as well as an image of the Danish spirit. Moreover, as such the figure succeeds in embodying the organic totality of the Danish nation.

The interpretation suggested here can be considerably extended if one refers to the only conflict that is dealt with in the play. When, during the course of the play, Christian IV takes possession of the imaginary body of the king of the elves and thus the Danes' folklore, he is only able to do so in that he symbolically appropriates it from the old farmer Karen.[1] Karen, who at the start of the text is introduced as a type of personification of folk poetry,[2] is tellingly missing at the harmonic double wedding that concludes the text. Her function as a "living archive"[3] of folk poetry is then adopted by the figures of the play acting on the stage. This may indicate that the constitution of the Danish body of people, for which the monarch is here claimed, is accompanied by specific exclusions, which not without reason an old female character from the lower class is subjected to.

IV. Demonical Possession and Sovereignty of the King: King Valdemar Atterdag *(1829)*

The extensive reference to Hegel's theoretical writings in association with a reading of *Elves' Hill* may seem forced. However, the extent to which Heiberg explored the difficult passages concerning the person of the monarchy in Hegel's *Elements of the Philosophy of Right* in the late 1820s becomes clear in my opinion in the draft of the play *King Valdemar Atterdag* written by Heiberg directly following *Elves' Hill* in 1829. Similar to *Elves' Hill*, this play also builds on the difference between

---

[1] The final interpretation suggested here is essentially based on an idea from Kirsten Wechsel.

[2] Heiberg, *Elverhøi. Drama i fem Acter*, in *Poetiske Skrifter*, vol. 3, p. 365: "*Naar hun engang døer, saa er det forbi med vor Folkepoesi.*" With this description Karen is presented to the King, who at the end of the piece steps in with his own person for the survival of folk poetry.

[3] Ibid., vol. 3, p. 365: "*[E]t levende Arkiv.*"

two levels of reality: "The subject of this play has both a fantastical and a historical component, of which the first is consciously emphasized because the writer here, as in *Elves' Hill*, was anxious to gain a musical aspect from the subject."[1] In the play, Heiberg processes the later well-known "Gurre material," that is, the story of the extravagant love of King Valdemar for the maid Tove. According to a legend, this love was created by a magical ring which enchanted the King. Since the dead Tove still wears the ring, the King refuses to let her be buried. Only when the poet Thorstein takes the ring does the King transfer his love to the poet. Thorstein passes the ring onto the lady's maid Anna. The King's desire wanders with the ring from the poet to the lady's maid. Since the ring is finally lost to the servant Balthasar, the King falls subject to a homosexual desire. Only when the King's advisor casts the ring into Lake Gurre does the King then project his love to the Danish landscape. The national sentiment created by this brings him to reconcile with his wife Helvig at the end of the play. On the whole we are dealing with a fantastical plot that confronts the Biedermeier audience with the phenomena of necrophilia, pederasty and homosexuality, which had to be perceived by contemporaries as sexual perversions.

This fantastical plot is combined with a sober, traditional political story of intrigues. Together with his advisor, the King skillfully succeeds in speeding up the wedding of the Danish Princess Margareta to King Hakon from Norway, who was originally engaged to Elisabeth von Holstein. This wedding is politically motivated and serves primarily to ensure Danish supremacy in the Baltic Sea realm.

Heiberg himself draws attention to the difficulties related to the conspicuous division of the material:

> The greatest difficulty of this subject is not so much that it contains a double plot as it is that King Valdemar turns out to be a double character. In the fantastical part of the subject he is restricted, bound to a dark magic; however, in the historical part he has all the freedom in his judgment, all the independence in his actions without which one would not recognize the portrait of this king.[2]

---

[1] Johan Ludvig Heiberg, "Plan til Kong Valdemar Atterdag. Skuespil i 5 Acter," in *Prosaiske Skrifter*, vol. 11, pp. 468f.
[2] Ibid., vol. 11, p. 484.

The estimated danger of such political content emphasized in a play becomes clear in the reaction of the theater's director who expressed concerns about the objectionable topic of the play and did not allow its performance. By examining the demonic desires of the king embodied by the ring, Heiberg does indeed involve himself in a tricky venture. The contemporary critique of the absolutist monarch's great power is indeed directed again and again against the idea of a king, controlled by drives, who sets his personal desires above the good of the state. Peter Andreas Heiberg bases his critique of *Kongeloven* on an objectionable legal article that guarantees the king absolute sovereignty:

> The result of this article and all of the other comments that I have previously made is that if a king of Denmark was to be a tyrant, if one ever came to the throne, then he would be infallible in all his resolutions, attacks and intentions regardless of how immoral and harmful these intentions might be.[1]

Even when the creation of Johan Ludvig Heiberg's play is undoubtedly closely connected to the polemical writing published by his father the previous year, the son still draws totally different consequences from the preoccupation with the demonic will of the monarch. Again, in my opinion, the reference to Hegel's *Elements of the Philosophy of Right*, which allows the younger Heiberg to meet his father's argumentation, is, in a very subtle way, once again decisive here.

Hegel, namely, does not see any argument against the monarchy in the individualism of the king. Quite the contrary, he bases this type of state surprisingly explicitly on the unreasonable and absolute randomness of the person of the monarch. Accordingly, "[t]he concept of the monarch" was introduced by Hegel as "the most difficult for ratiocination—i.e., the reflective approach of the understanding."[2] The basis of the argumentation concerning this is once again formed by the idea that the sovereignty of the state cannot be expressed in an abstract concept but rather has to be

---

[1] Cited from Peter Andreas Heiberg, *Enevoldsmagtens Indførelse*, p. 54.
[2] Hegel, *Sämtliche Werke. Jubiläumsausgabe*, vol. 6, § 279, p. 382. (*Elements of the Philosophy of Right*, § 279, p. 318.)

embodied in a person: "The personality of the state has actuality only as a person, as the monarch.—Personality expresses the concept as such, whereas the person also embodies the actuality of the concept, and only when it is determined in this way is the concept Idea or truth."[1] This idea is central for Hegel since with *Elements of the Philosophy of Right* he tries to take the step from the philosophical abstraction up to a reality-based philosophy which also attempts to comprehend the state not abstractly but rather concretely. This is exactly why Hegel is interested in the will of the (corporeally constituted) monarch, who realizes the will of the people. Consequently, the sovereignty of the state is bound to one single person's expression of will. This will is not based on a set abstract idea or body of rules, but rather on the, as Hegel emphasized, "unfounded" self-determined decision of a subject:

> Sovereignty, which is initially only the *universal* thought of this ideality, can *exist* only as *subjectivity* which is certain of itself, and as the will's abstract— and to that extent ungrounded—*self-determination* in which the ultimate decision is vested. This is the individual aspect of the state as such, and it is in this respect alone that the state itself is *one*. But subjectivity attains its truth only as a subject, and personality only as a person….This absolutely decisive moment of the whole, therefore, is not individuality in general, but *one* individual, the *monarch*.[2]

Slavoj Žižek, who has analyzed this passage extensively, has tried to clarify Hegel's extremely daring conclusions. His political philosophy circles around an understanding of sovereignty that ultimately defines itself through an irrational moment of an "ungrounded self-determination of the will":

> The essential thing, here, is the irreducible abyss between the organically articulated rational Whole of the constitution of the State, and the

---

[1] Hegel, *Sämtliche Werke. Jubiläumsausgabe*, vol. 6, § 279, p. 382. (*Elements of the Philosophy of Right*, § 279, p. 317.)
[2] Hegel, *Sämtliche Werke. Jubiläumsausgabe*, vol. 6, § 279, p. 381. (*Elements of the Philosophy of Right*, § 279, pp. 316f.)

"irrationality" of the person, who incarnates supreme Power, by which the Power receives the form of subjectivity.[1]

Based on the politically privileged position that Hegel allocates the king, Žižek in turn surprisingly demonstrates the topicality of his philosophy. Hegel's speculation is not limited to pure fantasies of *sublation* (*Aufhebung*) but rather, by contrast, circle stubbornly around the incommensurability of the real:

> [T]he State as the rational organization of social life *is* the idiotic body of the Monarch....Herein lies the "last secret" of dialectical speculation: not in the dialectical mediation-sublimation of all contingent, empirical reality, not in the deduction of all reality from the mediating movement of absolute negativity, but in the fact that this very negativity, to attain its "being-for-itself," must embody itself again in some miserable, radically contingent corporeal leftover.[2]

Naturally, Hegel already addresses the question of which devastating consequences a government can produce that legitimizes itself only through the moment of an "ungrounded self-determination of the will." He thus already examines the problem of whether "it makes the affairs of the state subject to contingency—since the monarch may be ill-educated or unworthy of holding the highest office—and [whether] it is absurd for such a situation to be regarded as rational."[3] Hegel links the answer to this question with the plea for a constitutional monarchy with which the will of the monarchy is bridled by advisers:

> Representational thought can easily comprehend that the state is the self-determining and completely sovereign will, the ultimate source of decisions. But it is more difficult to grasp this "I will" as a person, for this formula does not imply that the monarch may act arbitrarily: on the contrary, he is bound by the concrete content of the advice he receives, and if the constitution is

---

[1] Slavoj Žižek, *Interrogating the Real*, New York: Continuum 2005, p. 127.
[2] Slavoj Žižek, *The Sublime Object of Ideology*, London: Verso 1989, p. 207.
[3] Hegel, *Sämtliche Werke. Jubiläumsausgabe*, vol. 6, § 280, Zusatz, p. 388. (*Elements of the Philosophy of Right*, § 280, Addition, p. 322.)

firmly established, he often has nothing more to do than to sign his name. But this *name* is important; it is the ultimate instance and *non plus ultra*.[1]

Hegel's argumentation circles around a paradox. On the one hand, the state should be linked to an unfounded free act of volition that ensures the sovereignty of the state without further appeal. On the other hand, this act of volition in particular has to be maintained within limits that prevent the excess of despotism.[2]

If one reads Heiberg's work *On Human Freedom*, that was published in Kiel in 1824, or his draft of a philosophy of contingency that originated in 1825, then one quickly notices how thoroughly he occupied himself with the described contradictions in Hegel's philosophy.[3] In both works, Heiberg examines a "dialectic of the will" that moves exactly between the insistence on the arbitrary contingency of an act of volition and the control of the will due to the necessity of reason:

> The first contradiction is this: if the will, as we have already seen, cannot determine itself (since then it would be at the mercy of chance), then it is determined by something external and is thus not free.

[1] Hegel, *Sämtliche Werke. Jubiläumsausgabe*, vol. 6, § 279, Zusatz, p. 386. (*Elements of the Philosophy of Right*, § 279, Addition, p. 321.)

[2] An article published in 1842 in Heiberg's *Intelligensblade* in which Rasmus Nielsen argues for a surprising synthesis of a structural constitution and the absolute claim of power of the monarch indicates just how much Danish Hegelianism influenced the dialectic outlined here. In his argument Nielsen lingers on Hegel's reflections on the free will of the monarch quoted above. It is this free will alone that can guarantee the sovereignty of the nation in the face of an external and unchanged body of law. See Rasmus Nielsen, "Konge og Constitution," *Intelligensblade*, no. 11, 1842, pp. 250-278.

[3] See Johan Ludvig Heiberg, *Om den menneskelige Frihed. I Anledning af de nyeste Stridigheder over denne Gjenstand* (in *Prosaiske Skrifter*, vol. 1, pp. 1-110) and *Der Zufall aus dem Gesichtspunkte der Logik betrachtet. Als Einleitung zu einer Theorie des Zufalls* (in *Prosaiske Skrifter*, vol. 11, pp. 325-362). This latter text is also available in English translation with helpful comments and notes. See *Heiberg's Contingency Regarded from the Point of View of Logic and Other Texts*, ed. and trans. by Jon Stewart, Copenhagen: Museum Tusculanum Press 2008 (*Texts from Golden Age Denmark*, vol. 4), pp. 53-75. Both texts are presented extensively and examined from the perspective of the history of philosophy in Jon Stewart, *A History of Hegelianism in Golden Age Denmark*, Tome I, *The Heiberg Period: 1824-1836*, Copenhagen: C.A. Reitzel 2007 (*Danish Golden Age Studies*, vol. 3), pp. 115-178 and pp. 191-198.

The second contradiction is this: the external motives that determine the will are freedom and necessity. Its determination is thus the necessary product of the relative strength of these motives; it thus concerns an arithmetical result for which one cannot be held responsible.

Both of these contradictions, as one can see, annul the concept of will.[1]

Heiberg too made it very clear that a free will can only be constituted through a borderline experience. The true free will cannot be determined through rational laws—even if it is the idea of freedom itself—but rather requires the contingency of an unfounded self-determination that even pushes it close to insanity.[2] He writes,

Only then does will express itself as will, when it wills; but if it wills, then it wills itself, is its own motive, or is free, indeed, even arbitrary, because it determines itself. But what determines it in every instant to either determine itself or to allow itself to be determined, either to want or not to want?— This is chance, as I want to say without much ado; chance, whose power it cannot, as I will explain in more detail, totally evade....If will did not hover on this border [between freedom and necessity, arbitrariness and chance], then it could also not sin, then it would also not be free in the empirical sense. Here it is, however, even if only in receding moments, arbitrariness, *libertas indifferentiae*, since arbitrariness is nothing other than a freedom that has not yet constituted itself through necessary laws; but only in the moment in which it hovers on the border can it express itself as such, since

---

[1] Heiberg, *Om den menneskelige Frihed. I Anledning af de nyeste Stridigheder over denne Gjenstand* (in *Prosaiske Skrifter*, vol. 1, p. 53).

[2] An extensive debate on determinism and free will, which arose from the question of the accountability of insane criminals, forms the starting point for Heiberg's treatise. Heiberg attempts nothing less than a dialectical unification of, on the one hand, the position of a psychological determinism, which his friend Franz Gothard Howitz developed in the essay "Om Afsindighed og Tilregnelse, et Bidrag til Psychologien og Retslæren" ("On Madness and Ascribing Responsibility: A Contribution to Psychology and Jurisprudence") published in 1824 in *Juridisk Tidsskrift*, and, on the other hand, the more traditional idealist position of a basic freedom of the will. In doing so he even involves himself in the risky attempt to outline the dialectical relationship between madness (uncontrolled desires) and the sovereignty of the free will. These considerations present without a doubt the basis for the preoccupation with the royal insanity in *King Valdemar Atterdag*. For a detailed examination of the Howitz debate, see Stewart, *A History of Hegelianism*, Tome I, pp. 134-152.

in the moment in which it does not constitute itself, it allows itself to be constituted and vice versa.[1]

The connection to Hegel is clear, even before the concluding passage of the citation in which the problem of the self-constituting will is completely determined dialectically through the synthesis of freedom (as a regulating necessity) and necessity (as free arbitrariness). It is thus no coincidence that Heiberg is also preoccupied with Hegel's peculiar legitimation of the king, which, in the end, draws the political consequences from this reflection about a constitution that is not constituted but rather constitutes itself. The most impressive evidence of his intensive study of Hegel's *Elements of the Philosophy of Right* and in particular for his extensive examination of its idea of the national will embodied in the subject of the monarchy is supplied by the "Letters to a Village Pastor," published by Heiberg in 1834 in *Kjøbenhavns flyvende Post. Interimsblade.*[2]

With this in mind let us return from the philosophical excursus to *King Valdemar Atterdag*. With the intention of examining the question of the monarchy's self-determination in the play, expressed in the quotation reproduced above, Heiberg reverts directly to the central subject of his own philosophical writings and at least indirectly to the political paradox described by Hegel. Nonetheless, he transfers the political conflict between the unfounded will of the king and the rationality of the state constitution as indicated by Hegel into the soul of his main figure, Valdemar Atterdag, who has to face the demonic arbitrariness of his own desire.

In doing so, the King's will is almost dialectically understood and divided into a rationally controlled part as well as a secretive, demonic, irrational moment of desire. The surprising point of the drama is that the King's sovereignty is oddly not only expressed in the rational actions with

---

[1] Heiberg, *Om den menneskelige Frihed. I Anledning af de nyeste Stridigheder over denne Gjenstand*, in *Prosaiske Skrifter*, vol. 1, pp. 57f.

[2] See Johan Ludvig Heiberg, "Breve til en Landsbypræst" in *Prosaiske Skrifter*, vol. 10, pp. 256-291. (English translation in *Heiberg's Contingency Regarded from the Point of View of Logic and Other Texts*, ed. and trans. by Jon Stewart, pp. 201-222.) There are numerous quotations in this article from Hegel's *Elements of the Philosophy of Right* which I also used in my argumentation. My thanks to Jon Stewart for pointing out this article.

which he speeds up the wedding of his daughter and thus the political alliance between the Nordic nations; rather, the King's actual sovereignty is first explained in the moment in which he produces a synthesis between the insanity of his dark and unreasonable desire and the rational actions supporting the state. This synthesis is established exactly at the point in which the King projects his desire onto an aesthetic sentiment for Danish nature.

This point is absolutely critical when we pursue the political implications of the play. Considering the fact that the King's advisor takes on an increasingly important role in the course of the story in order to control the King's impulsive actions, we can easily say that, based on Hegel, Heiberg here takes a position supporting a constitutional monarchy. This point, however, seems to be less exciting than the concrete way in which the King's desire in the play is finally tamed since when the monarch's desire is regulated at the end of the play through an aesthetic sentiment, the significance of the role that art could play in a monarchy in the early nineteenth century is at least hinted at. Art and in a special way the theater could contribute to aligning the subjective will of the monarch and his subjective aesthetic pleasure with the general welfare of the nation better than a team of advisors who, so to speak, externally regulate the will of the monarch. It is not cold reasons of state that form the basis of a constitution but rather an aesthetically based national sentiment that is built on the idea of the state as a self-determined individual. In this sense a political re-evaluation of the aesthetic is, in my opinion, hidden behind this play, if not a political re-evaluation of the royal stage itself on which *King Valdemar Atterdag* is to be performed. I do not have to emphasize the degree to which Heiberg, by basing the political on the aesthetic, moves away from Hegel's guidelines, which are shaped considerably by the interest of a philosophical impregnation of the real.

In the last section of my article, I would like to consider the draft of the play *King Valdemar Atterdag* once more since, as mentioned at the beginning, Heiberg once again turns to the Gurre material in the vaudeville *Day of the Seven Sleepers*, while at the same time he decisively modifies it as well. However, before I discuss *Day of the Seven Sleepers* I would like to briefly take a look at *Fata Morgana*, which can also be grouped among the series of Heiberg's royal dramas discussed here.

V. From Aesthetic Desire to a Philosophy of Love:
Fata Morgana *(1838)*

On January 28, 1838 Frederik VI celebrated his 70th birthday, and once again Heiberg provided a play for this occasion, which celebrated its premiere on January 29. *Fata Morgana* deeply disturbed the audience and was dropped from the program after only five performances. After being ignored for decades, the play has received a great deal of attention in recent research. Previously, the primary interest was directed at Heiberg's concept of a speculative drama, which, due to its far-reaching philosophical claims, anticipates modern aesthetic concepts.[1]

In this context, I nevertheless do not want to concern myself with the play's philosophical reflection,[2] but rather with its political content, which is once again closely linked with the question of royal desire. In contrast to the other royal plays by Heiberg that have been discussed here, this play takes place not in the north but rather in a fictional Sicily, that means the literary world of Ariosto's *Orlando Furioso*. Due to a political intrigue, the legal heir of Sicily's throne Clotaldo grows up as a foster-child of a poor fisherman. At the end of the play he will regain the throne. This potentially exciting political plot nonetheless stands in the shadow of the hero's personal development, which is described purely allegorically. Similar to Valdemar Atterdag, Clotaldo runs the risk of falling prey to the magic of an art object. The role of the ring is taken over by a pearl in this play, with which the goddess of illusion, Fata Morgana, attempts to influence the history of mankind. This pearl of illusion reflects exactly those images the observer desires the most. In this way it becomes literally an object of desire, for which everyone in the

---

[1] See Lasse Horne Kjældgaard, *Sjælen efter døden. Guldalderens moderne gennembrud*, Copenhagen: Gyldendal 2007, pp. 153-171; Jon Stewart, *A History of Hegelianism in Golden Age Denmark*, Tome II, *The Martensen Period: 1837-1842*, Copenhagen: C.A. Reitzel 2007, pp. 137-160; and Klaus Müller-Wille, " 'Blendværk'—Om en seendets kritik i C.J.L. Almqvists *Signora Luna* (1835) och J.L. Heibergs *Fata Morgana* (1838)," in *Ett möte. Svensk og dansk litterär romantik i ny dialog*, ed. by Gunilla Hermansson and Mads Nygaard Folkmann, Göteborg: Makadam 2008, pp. 53-72.

[2] At this point I refrain from a summary as well as an analysis of the philosophical structure of the play and instead refer readers to the contribution by Jon Stewart in this volume.

play yearns. Only after Clotaldo finds his true love and his love of truth does he gain the strength to free himself from the power of the pearl; that is, he gains the strength to free himself from the fantasy world with which the goddess of illusion befuddles his mind. Only as a result of this philosophical emancipation and the related change of direction towards "reality"[1] does he gain the power to join in the political debate. He reclaims the throne for the prince, whose daughter he marries.

Gunilla Hermansson, who thoroughly examines the subject of love in this play, demonstrates in a fine analysis to what extent Heiberg's concept of love differs from the contemporary romanticism: "the power of love in this play is completely copied from the romanticist rhetoric and is at the same time sexless and orphaned."[2] The specific form of Clotaldo's love is, in other words, equated with a completely asexual philosophical realization through which Clotaldo learns to emancipate himself from the illusionary power of art and to apply himself to the truth of reality.

If one reads the play as a response to the earlier draft of *King Valdemar Atterdag*, then it becomes clear how far Heiberg distanced himself from the supremacy of an aesthetic sentiment still connected to the dark driving forces outlined there. The role that national sentiment in the draft of *King Valdemar Atterdag* still plays as an instrument for cultivating the royal will is adopted in *Fata Morgana* from philosophy. While the aesthetic sentiment holds the hero captured in a world of imaginary desires and fantasies, true love, which in Heiberg's conception is only valid as philosophical love of truth, allows him to influence reality and to make a decision of will.

Still, these philosophical views are packaged in a drama with which Heiberg obviously hoped to influence the royal court. In this sense he

---

1 Once again we can here refer to Hegel's *Elements of the Philosophy of Right*, which describes the phase in his philosophy in which Hegel turns from speculation to a philosophical practice or in which he attempts to investigate the rational in the actual (in the "real").

2 Cited from Gunilla Hermansson, "Kärlek och katastrof. Tre romantiska dramer— Almqvist, Atterbom och Heiberg," in *Dramatikern Almqvist*, ed. by Anders Burman, Roland Lysell and Jon Viklund, Stockholm: Gidlunds 2010, pp. 61-83. Gunilla Hermansson also presents an extensive analysis of the subject of love in *Fata Morgana* in the chapter "Komedien. Heiberg" in her monograph *Lyksalighedens øer. Møder mellem poesi, religion og erotik i dansk og svensk romantik*, Gothenburg: Makadam förlag 2009 (*Centrum för Danmarksstudier*, vol. 23), pp. 194-234.

had not yet fully overcome the idea of an aesthetic education or even schooling of the royal will that embodied the nation. This is also expressed in the closing scene of the play in which the king with the aid of the allegory of poetry—of all things—goes into battle against the Queen of Illusion. To what extent Heiberg tried, despite this ending, to regulate the aesthetic sentiment through the philosophical speculation is evident in the entire conception of the for good reason unsuccessful play, whose brittle allegories could hardly have an aesthetic impact.

It may well have been a result of the catastrophic reception of *Fata Morgana* that Heiberg wrote a drama two years later in which he greatly distanced himself from his earlier royal dramas. Whereas all of these plays are influenced by the effort to substantiate the absolutist constitution aesthetically or philosophically, *Day of the Seven Sleepers* contributes to a radical deconstruction of such political fantasies.

VI. *Citizen, Poet and Phantom of the King:* Day of the Seven Sleepers *(1840)*

If one is to believe the autobiography of Johanne Luise Heiberg (1812-90), her husband had actually longed for the coronation of Christian VIII. Based on her description, however, it can be inferred that his relationship to the crown noticeably cooled after Christian VIII assumed office. Johanne Luise Heiberg even maintains that, due to his disappointment with a number of reforms that failed to happen, her husband downright refused to support the king against the attack of the liberal press and its desire for a new constitution:

> One day Christian VIII beckoned Heiberg and asked him to step in with his feather against the attacks to which he was exposed daily....Heiberg did not feel enough sympathy for the King to overcome his lack of desire for such a task. It seemed to him as if he had to sell out his convictions for it, and he excused himself on the grounds of his time being occupied by other tasks and that, moreover, he did not have the talent necessary for it—an excuse that was not so graciously accepted.[1]

---

[1] Cited from Johanne Luise Heiberg, *Et liv genoplevet i erindringen*, vols. 1-4, ed. by Niels Birger Wamberg, Copenhagen: Gyldendal 1973, vol. 1, p. 321.

This anecdote is from a late and surely not quite reliable source. I believe all the same that Heiberg's attitude towards the monarchy already manifested itself in the thoroughly peculiar play that he wrote on occasion of the new king's coronation and that celebrated its premiere on July 1, 1840.

Day of the Seven Sleepers is directly based on the earlier draft of *King Valdemar Atterdag.* Heiberg retains the Gurre material which he worked with in *King Valdemar Atterdag*, that is, the story of the king's sexual confusion triggered by the magical ring, with hardly any changes to it at all in *Day of the Seven Sleepers.* The historical portion of the original draft—that is, the story about the marriage of the princess and the related disputes with the diplomats of Norway and Holstein—nevertheless are completely eliminated. In return the play is supplied with a new plot that takes place in the present and which presents a number of citizens from Copenhagen who join in the festivities in Fredensborg around the coronation of Christian VIII. It is already clear early on that Heiberg supplements the material from the historical drama with a vaudeville plot, which—according to the conventions of this genre—circles around the relationship between love and economy.[1] It goes without saying that this peculiar form of mixed genres contributed to a radical modification of the historical drama.

The heroes of the vaudeville plot are the siblings Anna and Balthasar, who, as orphans, are in the custody of the stingy wholesaler Max. While Balthasar suffers because he is unable to afford clothes fitting of his position, Anna mourns for the forbidden love with an anonymous poet. Both of their sufferings are intensified during their stay in Fredensborg: Balthasar has to see how the smooth and fashionably clothed procurator Steier succeeds at snatching his beloved Constance away from him right from under his nose. Anna, on the other hand, receives a furious farewell letter from the hand of her poet. Both Anna and Balthasar decide to have a talk with the poet and to visit him in the ruins of the Gurre Castle where he supposedly is staying. There they fall asleep and awake in a dreamlike past as characters in the mentioned historical drama. At

---

[1] For a more extensive discussion on this see Leonardo F. Lisi, "Heiberg and the Drama of Modernity," in *Johan Ludvig Heiberg: Philosopher, Littérateur, Dramaturge, and Political Thinker*, ed. by Jon Stewart, Copenhagen: Museum Tusculanum Press 2008 (*Danish Golden Age Studies*, vol. 5), pp. 421-448.

the end of the play they leave the dream world as part of a trio, since by day the poet Thorstein, who married Anna in the historical dream, turns out to be the anonymous poet the two had sought. While Steier and Constance as well as Anna and the poet promise one another to marry at the end of the play, Balthasar is at least comforted with the prospect of new clothing: Steier reveals the secret that with the wedding the assets of the children, which up until then had been managed by the merchant Max, finally are passed on to them as legal heirs.

Already by designating the citizen's careers as "*renteskriver*," "*grosserer*" and "*procurator*," Heiberg draws attention to the prosaic law of a modern world, which stands in clear contrast to the examination of the royal power structures in the dream plot. The first scene of the play, in which a banquet table in one of the halls of Fredensborg Castle with a view of the gardens is shown, can also be read as an indication of the changed realities in the modern age. Those dining at the table are in no way aristocratic but rather the mentioned civil servants and bourgeois merchants.

The striking transformation of the original draft of the play, which is caused by this new contextual framing of the Gurre subject, is underlined by additional modifications of the material. Thus, the conclusion of the Gurre episode is significantly re-written. Whereas the ring in the original version from *King Valdemar Atterdag* remains sunk in Lake Gurre, in *Day of the Seven Sleepers* it is rescued from the lake by an allegorical embodiment of the power of imagination, Phantasus, and returned to the poet, who in turn passes it on to his beloved. This modified conclusion in the dream plot already indicates that the position of the poet, who manipulates the royal will, is even more clearly emphasized in *Day of the Seven Sleepers* than in the draft of *King Valdemar Atterdag*.

Nevertheless, this reading is also called into question in the text since in contrast to *Elves' Hill* and *King Valdemar Atterdag*, *Day of the Seven Sleepers* is concerned with a distinct meta-drama in which the function of theater is constantly referred to. This self-referential trait is expressed especially in the character of Phantasus, who, like Puck in Shakespeare's *A Midsummer Night's Dream* intervenes in the actions of the characters and comments on the events with poetological remarks. A further important meta-fictional trait of the play is the diverse inter-textual references. As Anna and Balthasar enter into the historical dream world of the Gurre Castle, they explicitly compare this incident

with corresponding literary experiences which they had while reading national romantic historical plays. In this sense, the Gurre episode in the text refers neither to a historical event nor to the relevant sources from folk literature, but rather to the processing and "re-functionalization" of historical material in Danish Romanticism.

Due to this fact, the image of the king that is developed in the play seems to be twice as eerie. On the one hand, the monarch is presented as a result of poetic delusions and bourgeois projections right from the start. In other words, the king appears throughout the entire play as a pure fantasy or dream product of the citizens' literarily schooled imagination. The synthesis between the king's two bodies that was targeted in *Elves' Hill* is fundamentally undermined because the king only appears within the frame of a dream event.

On the other hand, in the dream King Valdemar Atterdag himself is presented as a completely passive victim of the imagination, which is created by the ring. He is clearly staged as a powerless marionette, manipulated by various characters in the play. In contrast to the earlier draft of *King Valdemar Atterdag*, he does not at any point in time act as an autonomous subject. The synthesis between the subjective desire of the king and the state as a rationally constituted whole, which is a subject of *King Valdemar Atterdag*, is thus not realized in *Day of the Seven Sleepers*.

Since the play was to be performed for the coronation of the king, it does raise the suspicion that Heiberg did indeed continue the subversive political manner of his father. In any case, it is clear that in *Day of the Seven Sleepers* he no longer makes any effort to develop a subtle aesthetic legitimization of the monarchy based on Hegel's *Elements of the Philosophy of Right*. This interpretation is further emphasized through another important intertextual reference in the play. In a review of the play at the time, Peder Ludvig Møller (1814-65)[1] already drew attention to the fact that Heiberg adopted the crude mix of genres that characterized a play from Frederik Paludan-Müller (1809-1876). Paludan-Müller's play, *Adventure in the Forest* published in 1836, also lives from the tension

---

[1] Peder Ludvig Møller, "Syvsoverdag, romantisk Comoedie, skreven til Kroningen. Defensionsindlæg," in Peder Ludvig Møller, *Kritiske Skizzer fra Aarene 1840-47*, ed. by Hans Hertel, Copenhagen: Gyldendal 1971, pp. 68-94, here p. 70.

between a petty bourgeois farce and a romantic fairy tale play.[1] The connection to *Adventure in the Forest* also suggests itself in this context because this play is likewise characterized by a political subject. At the center of the comedy, which is in a number of ways reminiscent of Ludvig Holberg's *The Political Tinker* (1722), is the failed attempt to establish a republic. The presumptuous ambitions to power of the politically completely incompetent citizens and craftsman drive the community into total ruin. While Paludan-Müller uses the tension between the petty bourgeois farce and the fairy tale play in order to, so to speak, make fun of the presumptuous political ambitions of the citizens from the perspective of a timelessly valid (almost mythical) fairy world, Heiberg radically turns around the relationship between the bourgeois satire and the fantastical dream plot. In no way does the described dream world embody timelessly valid truths, but rather it is exposed as a historical product of bourgeois projections. With that, the political fantasies linked with the imaginary construction of historical kings and heroes are also resolutely undermined.[2]

The thesis outlined here is corroborated by a later essay published by Heiberg in 1842 in the *Intelligensblade*.[3] This treatise is dedicated to the phenomena of authority. Heiberg refers extensively to the crisis of the absolutist monarchy and establishes a connection between it and a general crisis of political and cultural authorities in his time. With this diagnosis he substantiates his fear that the liberal idea of a state founded on a social contract will ultimately lead to a complete atomization of society and to the disintegration of the nation. Even when this estimation of Heiberg gives evidence of conservative political views, the conclusions which he draws at the end of the article are astonishingly progressive. In doing so he refers to Hegel's concept of the "*List der Vernunft*" (the cunning of reason): "Reason makes a fool of the unreasonable individuals and makes them serve the idea while they think they are pursuing an entirely different purpose."[4] First, it is noticeable that kings no longer function as

---

[1] Frederik Paludan-Müller, "Eventyr i Skoven. Skuespil," in Frederik Paludan-Müller, *Poesier*, vols. 1-2, Copenhagen: C.A. Reitzel 1836, vol. 1, pp. 1-264.

[2] The court also seems to have noticed this tendency of the play since Henrik Hertz and not Heiberg was requested to write a play in 1841 for another wedding of crown prince Frederik, which Heiberg perceived as a conscious affront.

[3] Johan Ludvig Heiberg, "Autoritet," in *Prosaiske Skrifter*, vol. 10, pp. 328-349.

[4] Ibid., p. 345.

the highest political authority of the nation state, but rather the idea of historical world spirit itself. In this sense the political crisis of Heiberg's time is read as a necessary transitional phase of history. That means that the crisis of absolutism like the atomization of society that results from it is interpreted as a step in a dialectically progressive historical process. Apparently Heiberg hoped that this unpredictable process would prepare a new, organic constitution of the community.

The farewell to the political fantasies about the function of the monarch in a national state of the early nineteenth century suggested in this argumentation is in my opinion already anticipated in *Day of the Seven Sleepers*, in which Heiberg at least humorously shrugs off his earlier royal dramas. Furthermore, with the double wedding, which, during the play is situated in the shadow of the coronation ceremony, he indicates, in my opinion, the future of the collective imagination, which will replace the king in his function.

The union of Anna with the poet at least hints at the possibility that the poets will be the heirs of the kings. Poetry or more precisely the national theater takes over the symbolic function of the king to ensure the organic unity of the state. After all, a short time later in 1842 Heiberg published the important treatise "People and Public" in *Intelligensblade*, in which he carefully examined a corresponding function of the theater.[1] There he develops the idea that the amorphous mass of the public can only be formed into the organic totality of the people by the artistic experience.[2] The corresponding formulations are obviously reminiscent of the function which Hegel assigned to the king in a modern state.[3]

---

[1] See Johan Ludvig Heiberg, "Folk og Publikum," in *Prosaiske Skrifter*, vol. 6, pp. 263-283.
[2] With regards to this interpretation see George Pattison, "The Present Age: The Age of the City," *Kierkegaard Studies Yearbook*, 1999, pp. 1-20; and Klaus Müller-Wille, "Phantom Publikum. Theatrale Konzeptionen des corps politiques in der dänischen Ästhetik von Andersen bis Kierkegaard," in *Kollektive Gespenster. Die Masse, der Zeitgeist und andere unfaßbare Körper*, ed. by Michael Gamper and Peter Schnyder, Freiburg in Br.: Rombach 2006, pp. 105-128.
[3] Interestingly, the central political article in the *Intelligensblade*, in which the quite daring synthesis of a republican based absolutism is formulated, was not written by Heiberg, but by Rasmus Nielsen. See Rasmus Nielsen, "Konge og Constitution." Heiberg, however, occupied himself in this journal primarily with questions that affected the constitution of the theater.

The kings could, in other words, fulfill their function also as a dream-like phantom, who only flits around on the stage of the national theater. In this sense, the complex relationship between dream and reality that unfolds in *Day of the Seven Sleepers* and that no one less than the liberal critic Peder Ludvig Møller takes as his starting point for an enthusiastic review of the play[1] hints at Heiberg's attempt to be involved in a theater policy which at last renders the monarchy obsolete.

However, that Heiberg was not totally convinced of the national theater's regulating function as early as 1840 is indicated by the second wedding that was celebrated at the end of *Day of the Seven Sleepers*. The imaginary world, towards which the fashion-addicted Steier and the purely appearance-conscious Constance are oriented, has nothing to do with the idea of a holistic, organic and aesthetic national community. Rather, Steier and Constance orient themselves on a new ghost, the phantom of the *Zeitgeist* or the phantom of fashion, that leads not to a concentration, but rather, as Heiberg already commented on in the 1830 essay "On Our National Pleasures," to a pure distraction of a formless mass audience.[2]

At least the form of the play *Day of the Seven Sleepers* hints that Heiberg is also conscious of the aesthetic consequences of a drama directed at an audience addicted to distractions. In contrast to *Elves' Hill*, in which the different genres of vaudeville, historical drama and folk song still blend into a harmonic union, the appeal of *Day of the Seven Sleepers* is more in the crude mix of different text fragments and a very complex network of intertextual allusions, which do not join together in a harmonic work, but whose stylistic characteristics are irony and ruptures. Perhaps Heiberg was aware that the idea of an organic totality of state and art in 1840 was not entirely contemporary.

---

[1] See Møller, "Syvsoverdag, romantisk Comoedie, skreven til Kroningen. Defensionsindlæg."

[2] Johan Ludvig Heiberg, "Om vore nationale Forlystelser," in *Prosaiske Skrifter*, vol. 8, pp. 475-495.

The Danish Way to Fame and Power? Johan Ludvig Heiberg, Thorvaldsen, and the Popularity of Art

Wolfgang Behschnitt

On September 17th, 1838, after having spent more than four decades abroad, Bertel Thorvaldsen (1770-1844) returned as an international celebrity to his hometown Copenhagen. On the occasion of his homecoming, a whole series of celebrations was arranged. It began with a festive greeting of his ship in the roadstead of Copenhagen, and continued with a gala dinner at the Hotel d'Angleterre on October 7th, with a celebration at the students' union and a manifold of private invitations, and with the bestowal on him of the title of honorary citizen of the Danish capital on November 21st.

Many of these celebrations are well documented.[1] We have access to programs, honorary publications, poems and songs in tribute to the artist

---

[1] Important primary sources are the news coverage in *Kjøbenhavnsposten* (September 16 and 17, 1838) and *Dagen* (September 18, 1838) and, among others, eyewitness accounts in the following autobiographical works: H.C. Andersen, *Mit Livs Eventyr* (Copenhagen: C.A. Reitzel 1855, pp. 260-265), August Bournonville, *Mit Teaterliv. Erindringer og Tidsbilleder* (vols. 1-3, Copenhagen: C.A. Reitzel 1848-78, vol. 1, pp. 183-184), Hans Birch Dahlerup, *Mit Livs Begivenheder* (vols. 1-4, ed. by Joost Dahlerup, Copenhagen: Gyldendalske Boghandel, Nordisk Forlag 1908-12, vol. 2, pp. 198-218), Johanne Luise Heiberg, *Et liv genoplevet i erindringen* (5th rev. ed., vols. 1-4, ed. by Niels Birger Wamberg, Copenhagen: Gyldendal 1973-74, vol. 1, pp. 337-339), C.F. von Holten, *Erindringer* (Copenhagen: Gyldendalske Boghandels Forlag 1899, pp. 82-84), Alex Wilde, *Erindringer om Jerichau og Thorvaldsen ombord på Fregatten Rota 1838* (Copenhagen: Gyldendalske Boghandels Forlag 1884). On the centenary of Thorvaldsen's homecoming in 1938, an extensive historical description of the festivities was published: Sigurd Schultz, *Da Thorvaldsen kom*

composed by highly esteemed Danish authors like Adam Oehlenschläger (1779-1850), Hans Christian Andersen (1805-75), Nikolai Frederik Severin Grundtvig (1783-1872), Henrik Hertz (1798-1870), Johan Ludvig Heiberg (1791-1860) and others. In addition, we have at our disposal newspaper articles, illustrations, letters, and many eyewitness accounts found in biographies and memoirs. An important source is the first extensive biography of Thorvaldsen, written by Just Mathias Thiele (1795-1874), who, as a leading member of the celebration committee, was one of the driving forces behind the homecoming festivities. Additionally, we can rely on the autobiographical writings of many of Thorvaldsen's contemporaries: Johanne Luise Heiberg (1812-90), August Bournonville (1805-79), Hans Birch Dahlerup (1790-1872), who was the captain of the frigate *Rota* which brought the artist and his work safely from Italy to Denmark, Alexander Wilde (one of Thorvaldsen's travel companions on the ship) and, probably best known, the account given by H.C. Andersen in his autobiographical *The Fairy Tale of My Life*.

The relevance of these celebrations in the collective memory of Thorvaldsen's contemporaries becomes all the more apparent in light of the fact that the solemn opening of the Thorvaldsen Museum ten years later was scheduled exactly on the anniversary of the homecoming, September 17th, 1848. The place of this homecoming in Danish national history was then definitively secured by the murals on the outside walls of the Thorvaldsen Museum. Jørgen Sonne's (1801-90) famous frieze depicts several scenes of Thorvaldsen's homecoming: the boat parade and the artist's reception by the citizens of Copenhagen, the unloading of the *Rota* and the, somewhat unhistorical, transport of the artworks to the museum.[1]

The particular circumstances of the celebrations and the way in which Thorvaldsen's art and personality were incorporated as essential assets into the national heritage—by way of the museum, its location,

hjem. Billeder fra hans sidste aar i København og paa Nysø, 1838–1844, Copenhagen: Foreningen Fremtiden & Thorvaldsens Museum 1938.

[1] The depiction of the unloading of the *Rota* and the transport to the museum is fiction. The construction of the museum had not even begun when the *Rota* arrived in Copenhagen. Also, many of Thorvaldsen's sculptures were transported to Denmark by other ships.

Detail from Jørgen Sonne's frieze on the Wall of Thorvaldsen's Museum
(Painting on colored plaster, 1846-50,
Courtesy of Thorvaldsen's Museum, Copenhagen.)

architecture, decoration, etc.—make quite clear that we are dealing with something more than just a tribute to an eminent artist. The tributes to Thorvaldsen were also a national event. They were planned, as *Kjøbenhavnsposten* writes the day before the artist's arrival, as "a truly national celebration";[1] they were staged as such and were stamped into the collective memory as a both glamorous and popular representation of the Danish nation.

The 1830s were a crucial period in Danish nation-building, although the foundations for a Danish identity were laid earlier, in the second half of the eighteenth century in an increasing effort to assert Danish autonomy vis-à-vis the preponderance of German culture and language in the United Monarchy. But in the aftermath of the French July Revolution of 1830 and parallel to the foundation of the Assembly of Estates in 1831 as the first political representations in the absolutist

---

[1] [anonymous], "Nyheds-Post," *Kjøbenhavnsposten*, September 16, 1838.

Danish state, we see the emergence of a political movement that took
up the cause of constitutionalism and liberalism. Liberal leaders like
Tage Algreen-Ussing (1797-1872) and Orla Lehmann (1810-70)
were no revolutionaries, but they propagated constitutional reforms
of the Danish state and the idea of the nation as the basis of political
representation. It must be observed, though, that at this time, around
1838, many intellectuals and artists had not yet started to share the
liberal enthusiasm for political reforms and national ideas. Memories
of the French Revolution's terror still being fresh, they mistrusted
democratic ideals and feared the uncontrollable powers of the unleashed
mob. Instead, they firmly supported the traditional monarchic system.[1]
An illustrative example of the artists' loyalty towards the absolute ruler
can be found in Poul Martin Møller's (1794-1838) poem "The Artist
Among the Rebels" from 1837.[2] It tells the dramatic tale of the great
artist who, in spite of being threatened with death, refuses to join a
rioting crowd and defeats the insurgence with an oak club taken from a
Hercules statue. The poem fits our context especially well, since the artist
in Møller's poem is a sculptor—the description of his work and studio
showing several similarities with Thorvaldsen's.

   With this historical background, it is interesting to note that the
Thorvaldsen celebrations of 1838 can be described as a variation of
Møller's "The Artist Among the Rebels." As a national event, according
to the intentions of the respectable citizens in the organizing committee,
the artist and his symbolic capital were appropriated for the national
community and its heritage. As a mass event, according to the actual
development of the festivities, the artist was appropriated by the crowd—
quite materially, as will be shown later. The monarch and the institutions
of the absolute state, however, were remarkably absent.

   In this article I want to take the Thorvaldsen celebrations as a
point of departure for an investigation into the complex and dynamic
interrelations between an emerging national self-perception, the pursuit
of constitutional and democratic reforms, and aesthetic concepts which

---

[1] Obviously, there were exceptions like Steen Steensen Blicher and Nikolai Frederik
    Severin Grundtvig, writers who were eager to advance the national cause already
    during the 1830s.

[2] Poul Martin Møller, "Kunstneren mellem Oprørerne," in *Nytaarsgave fra danske
    Digtere*, vols. 1-4, ed. by H.P. Holst and Christian Winther, vol. 4, 1838, pp. 82-94.

show a new interest both in the national and in the popular. In order to discuss these subjects I will first analyze the celebration itself and then focus on Johan Ludvig Heiberg, one of the leading intellectuals and at the same time a foreground figure in the arrangement of the celebrations. He composed the verses to the tribute song which not only was sung to greet Thorvaldsen but also was published in the newspapers and mentioned in many eyewitness accounts. But he is also interesting in the context of the rising national awareness. Like many of his literary colleagues, Heiberg was a monarchist rather than a partisan of the national liberals, and he certainly did not cherish democratic ideas. It was not until the 1840s that he in essays such as "On the National and the Provincial" (1842) and "Danish and German" (1843)[1] resorts to the political notion of "the nation."[2] But on the aesthetic level, notions of "the national" and "the popular" started playing a role in Heiberg's thinking already around the time of Thorvaldsen's homecoming (namely, in his critique of Henrik Hertz's *Svend Dyring's House* in 1837).[3]

An analysis of the Thorvaldsen celebrations with special focus on Heiberg's welcome poem seems therefore apt to unfold some problems connected to the intricate relation between art, popularity and nationality in the Danish Golden Age.

I. Thorvaldsen's Homecoming: The Celebration

The celebration of Thorvaldsen's homecoming was prepared meticulously. A committee, led by Just Mathias Thiele, planned and coordinated the welcoming, the result being a virtual choreography. The program starts with a parade of boats receiving the royal frigate with Thorvaldsen on

---

[1] Heiberg, "Det Nationale og det Provindsielle," in *Prosaiske Skrifter*, vols. 1-11, Copenhagen: C.A. Reitzel 1861-62, vol. 10, pp. 350-373; "Dansk og Tydsk," ibid., vol. 10, pp. 374-394.

[2] See my discussion of Heiberg's conception of the national in *Wanderungen mit der Wünschelrute. Landesbeschreibende Literatur und vorgestellte Geographie Deutschland und Dänemarks im 19. Jahrhundert*, Würzburg: Ergon 2006, pp. 301-308.

[3] Johan Ludvig Heiberg, "Om den romantiske Tragedie af Hertz: *Svend Dyrings Huus*. I Forbindelse med en æsthetisk Betragtning af de danske Kæmpeviser," *Perseus. Journal for den speculative Idee*, no. 1, 1837, pp. 165-264.

Program.

1. Baadene passere ud igjennem Bommen under Nationalflag, uden Musik, og roe faa langsomt, at alle kunne følge med.
2. Stabsflagene heises og Musikken stemmer i, saasnart Baadene ere ordnede udenfor Bommen.
3. Under Fregatten gives 3 Gange Hurra. Derefter standser Musikken og almindelig Stilhed iagttages.
4. Baadene ordne sig i en Halvkreds ved Styrbord, saaledes, at de decorerede Baade ligge foran og Musikbaadene samlede bagved.
5. Musikken istemmer Melodien: „Vi Søemænd gjør ei mange Ord." Ved første Repetition begynder Sangen.
6. Efter Sangen følger: Thorvaldsen leve! med 3 Gange Hurra.
7. Skeer der et Ophold, inden Thorvaldsen forlader Fregatten, musiceres i Mellemtiden.
8. Naar han stiger fra Borde og har taget Sæde i Chaluppen bringes Fregatten Rota et Hurra.
9. Derefter bringes Fregattens Chef et: Længe leve!
10. Endelig et Hurra for Fregattens Besætning.
11. Under Tilbagetoget musiceres.
12. Under Tilbagetoget iagttages saameget som muligt, at den Chaluppe, hvori Thorvaldsen befinder sig, paa begge Sider og bagved i behørig Afstand fra hinanden omgives af de decorerede Baade.
13. Naar Thorvaldsen stiger iland paa Toldboden bringes ham tre Gange Hurra.

Program of the Festivities on September 17th, 1838
(*From Sigurd Schultz,* Da Thorvaldsen kom hjem, *p. 9*)

board; each boat carries the representatives of a particular group (artists, poets, actors, doctors, students, etc.) and is decorated with their respective symbols. Flags are flown, music plays, and after a threefold "Hurrah!" Thorvaldsen is greeted with Heiberg's welcome poem, sung to the popular melody of "Vi Sømænd gjør ej mange Ord." Still on board, Thorvaldsen is presented the royal promotion to the title "Konferensraad." After some more cheers, Thorvaldsen is rowed ashore in the captain's shallop.

Contemporary witnesses tell us that an overwhelming crowd greeted Thorvaldsen ashore. The director of the Art Academy, Christian Frederik Hansen (1756-1845), awaited him in a carriage to take him to Charlottenborg where a studio and residential rooms had been prepared for him. From Charlottenborg's balcony, Thorvaldsen greeted the excited crowd on Kongens Nytorv. Thorvaldsen's biographer Thiele recounts:

A storm of loud rejoicing of the exalted crowd swept around him and it was like wind blowing in his silver hair. The whole square seemed like a carpet, braided of faces looking upwards and arms waving hats, from the center of which arose the equestrian statue and the lampposts, richly decorated with young admirers.[1]

With the fall of night, young artists paraded with torches while a band provided the music. Sigurd Schultz concludes, "No Danish artist was ever received in such a way, either before or since. All contemporary reports agree that it exceeded all description."[2]

The outstanding importance of Thorvaldsen's homecoming in the consciousness of his contemporaries also becomes evident in the way in which the reports endowed the event with a sacral aura. Higher powers seemed to have contributed to its glory. When Thorvaldsen reached Danish waters, northern lights were seen in the sky—in the same way as they had illuminated his former visit to his home country in 1819. Even his arrival in the roads of Copenhagen was blessed by a celestial phenomenon: at the very same moment when the ship arrived and the celebration was about to begin, the rain stopped, the clouds gave way to sunshine and a rainbow arched the scene. Hans Christian Andersen comments enthusiastically: "The sun was shining, and there stood a beautiful rainbow stretched over the sound: 'An arch of honor for Alexander!'"[3] The scene is depicted in several illustrations, but is best known in Christoffer Wilhelm Eckersberg's (1783-1853) brilliant painting. Another visual depiction has played an even more decisive role for the inscription of Thorvaldsen's homecoming into the cultural memory of the Danish nation, namely, Jørgen Sonne's frieze on the murals of the Thorvaldsen Museum, where the event is immortalized on the side oriented towards the canal and the city.

---

[1] Just Mathias Thiele, *Thorvaldsens Leben*, vols. 1-3, Leipzig: L. Wiedemann 1852-56, vol. 3, p. 12.

[2] Schultz, *Da Thorvaldsen kom hjem*, p. 17.

[3] Hans Christian Andersen, *Mit Livs Eventyr*, in *Samlede værker*, vols. 1-18, ed. by Klaus P. Mortensen et al., Copenhagen: Det Danske Sprog- og Litteraturselskab and Gyldendal 2003-2007, vol. 17, *Selvbiografier II*, p. 237.

Thorvaldsen's Arrival in the Copenhagen Roadstead on September 17ᵗʰ, 1838
(Painting by C.W. Eckersberg, 1839,
Courtesy of Thorvaldsen's Museum, Copenhagen.)

Central themes of the festivities are, on the one hand, the tribute to Thorvaldsen as an outstanding artist, and, on the other, the celebration of his return to the bosom of the Danish nation. Clearly, the 1838 Thorvaldsen celebrations were to a large extent national festivities. Johan Ludvig Heiberg's welcome poem may serve as an example. The first stanza says:

On Danes' way to fame and power
We greet You, whose honor
Has brought the fatherland's honor
To the world's far-away towns.
When the heart under the Pole of the North
Did send you sighs of longing,
Then you moved from your warm sun
Hither to your cold cradle.

Paa Danskes Vei til Ros og Magt
Vi hilse Dig, hvis Hæder
Har Fædrelandets Hæder bragt
Til Verdens fjerne Stæder.
Da Hjertet under Nordens Pol
Dig sendte Længsels-Sukke.
Da drog du fra din varme Sol
Hid til din kolde Vugge.[1]

Heiberg makes use of a repertory of national stereotypes to contrast north and south, home and foreign places, to heighten the honor of Denmark and to express the longing, the emotional link between the nation and its famous son. Not surprisingly, we find the same metaphors and motifs in other poems written for the same occasion. N.F.S. Grundtvig apotheosizes the homecoming with the words: "Fatherland! / Brighter twinkles your star, / the son comes home from afar" [*"Fædreneland! / Lysere tindrer din Stjerne, / Sønnen kom hjem fra det Fjerne"*].[2] And Henrik Hertz evokes similar nostalgic feelings when contrasting far away and home: "Fatherland! In far-away, beautiful countries, / whose air is so mild, whose sky is always blue, / my want draws me to those coasts, / where I as a child carefree looked up to the sky" [*"Fædreneland! i fjerne, skjønne Lande, / Hvis Luft er saa mild, hvis Himmel stadig blaa / Drager mig Savn hen til de Strande, / Hvor jeg som Barn til Himlen sorgløs saae"*].[3] More interesting than this well-known national repertory, however, was the struggle to incorporate the famous artist into the national community, as is manifested in the subsequent stanzas of Heiberg's poem. It is a problematic enterprise because neither the artist nor his work really seems to fit the national canon. Thorvaldsen was an international artist *par excellence*—he spent most of his life abroad, worked and won his reputation outside of Denmark—and his artistic work was entirely international in both theme and style. Certainly, his Danish admirers could relate to an established picture of Thorvaldsen as the heroic "Nordic" counterpart to the more graceful Italian Antonio

---

[1] Heiberg, "Thorvaldsens Ankomst paa Fregatten Rota," in *Poetiske Skrifter*, vols. 1-11, Copenhagen: C.A. Reitzel 1862, vol. 8, p. 351.
[2] Cited in Schultz, *Da Thorvaldsen kom hjem*, p. 67.
[3] Ibid., p. 68.

Canova (1757-1822). But even in the frame of this aesthetic debate it would be difficult to nationalize Thorvaldsen's neoclassicism, which at the time of his return to Denmark had long since been surpassed by more "national" romantic art movements.

The problem is mirrored in Heiberg's welcome poem. Since Thorvaldsen's work refuses its appropriation as truly Danish or Nordic, the patriotic sound of the poem remains abstract and generalizing. The artwork appears in many of the tribute poems, and likewise in Heiberg's, as a symbolic capital (cf. "honor," "fame") which is brought home from "the world's far-away towns." The last stanza evokes the idea that "Denmark's name" now shines in the sky of art—a realm which is basically imagined in concepts and metaphors borrowed from classical antiquity. But there is another level in Heiberg's poem in which the reference to Denmark becomes more substantial; it is the level of economic instead of symbolic capital. The first line of the poem, which is repeated in the last stanza, refers with astonishing explicitness to this context. The "Danes' way to fame and power," of course, is the sea, a central motif of the poem. This becomes still more obvious in the melody, the popular tune "Vi Sømænd gjør ej mange ord," which was established in the popular Danish song tradition when Johan Clemens Tode used it in the final choir of his play *Søofficererne* (1782) and would immediately lead thoughts to the field of naval enterprises and the times of Denmark as a major naval power.[1] Sung in the roads of Copenhagen on the occasion of the arrival of a ship loaded with precious goods, the poem clearly refers to Denmark as a seafaring nation. The "Danes' way to fame and power" has not only symbolic and political connotations but implies the Danish way to commercial success as well. Thorvaldsen's homecoming and its festive celebration, thus, can be described as an analogy to the preferred economic strategy of a seafaring and trading nation in the nineteenth century. The fortunate arrival of the ship brings back home, multiplied, the capital invested abroad. In his formidable study of Jørgen Sonne's mural frieze, John Henderson points to the minuteness and authenticity that characterize the representation of the unloading of the frigate *Rota*. One of the scenes, says Henderson,

---

[1] Hans Kuhn, *Defining a Nation in Song: Danish Patriotic Songs in Songbooks of the Period 1832-1870*, Copenhagen: C.A. Reitzel 1990, pp. 252f.

"shows us precision, know-how, teamwork" and at the same time "highly dangerous, heavy-duty, effort."[1] He continues,

> The "adventus" of Thorvaldsen is in this sense an ideal occasion…for the celebration of nothing less than a nineteenth-century European "cargo-cult." Pouring out of the ship's hold comes a bonanza of "symbolical capital" that carries international credit wherever boats dock, shipments are loaded, and merchandise is ferried.[2]

II. The People

Apart from the question if the artist Thorvaldsen and his work can be appropriated for the national heritage as characteristically "Danish," there is another aspect to the national intentions of the Danish intellectual bourgeoisie which was responsible for the organization of the celebrations. Thorvaldsen's art as well as his personality were thought to exert an educative influence, to contribute to the cultivation and formation of the nation. Johanne Luise Heiberg writes in her memoirs: "It is a great fortune for a nation to have such a personality in its midst, whose sole presence tunes all around him in a higher key and forces even the raw crowd to a feeling of piety which it is in such great need of."[3] The project of the Thorvaldsen Museum was imbued by the same ideas, as again is expressed by Johanne Luise: "And when finally the Thorvaldsen Museum was opened for everybody, one often saw people there from the lower classes, who with great interest contemplated the immortal works. It can truly be said that these works have exerted considerable influence on the nation's sense of beauty."[4]

---

[1] John Henderson, *The Triumph of Art at Thorvaldsens Museum*, Copenhagen: Museum Tusculanum Press 2005, pp. 86f.

[2] Ibid., pp. 87f.

[3] Johanne Luise Heiberg, *Et liv genoplevet i erindringen*, vols. 1-4, ed. by Niels Birger Wamberg, 5th rev. ed., Copenhagen: Gyldendal 1973-74, vol. 1, p. 339: "*Det er en stor lykke for en nation at have en sådan personlighed i sin midte, hvis blotte nærværelse stemmer alt omkring sig i en højere toneart og tvinger selv den rå mængde til en pietetsfølelse, som den har så godt af at besidde.*"

[4] Ibid., pp. 339f.

Johan Ludvig Heiberg phrases the educative intention in a similar way in his poem "Thorvaldsens Museum," originally published in the illustrated album *Denmark: A Painter's Atlas* in 1842.[1] His conclusion, though, is clearly more skeptical. His skepticism is first of all expressed in the distance Heiberg sees between classic art and his contemporaries. The lamentable lack of aesthetic sense of his times makes great works of art utterly necessary indeed, but, Heiberg asks, will the public be capable of grasping them, too? Can his contemporaries subordinate their conceit, their limited judgment, to the universal truth of art? "Whoever is used to / thunder judgments, / Should learn here to subordinate / His meaningless critique." [*Hver, som Dommerord at tordne, / Raad at give har for Skik, / Lære her at underordne / Sin unyttige Critik.*"][2] Certainly, the skepticism of Heiberg the critic is informed by the difficult relationship of Heiberg the artist to his public. Later on, I will elaborate on his fundamental criticism of the contemporary "*Publicum*" in his essay "People and Public" from 1842. Here, it may suffice to state that the possibilities of the artist to exert some educative influence on the formation of the nation and his contemporaries seemed rather limited. The people were not educated as easily as proponents of some idealistic notions about the power of art would have liked to assume.

Actually, Johanne Luise in her report about the Thorvaldsen home-coming also refers to the shortcomings of the citizens of Copenhagen to do justice to the aesthetic value of the artistic work. Most of the people, she writes, lacked a thorough knowledge of Thorvaldsen and his work, and she indicates a general ignorance about the art of sculpture in Denmark:

But they heard that he was famous abroad—something people here have a certain respect for, and they heard that he had become a rich man due to his works—a circumstance which contributed a lot to their interest becoming more lively and relevant. Later, when the time of his arrival drew closer, so much was written and talked about him that the crowd was agitated and set into motion, although it did not quite know what it was enthusiastic

---

[1] Johan Ludvig Heiberg, "Thorvaldsens Museum," in *Poetiske Skrifter*, vol. 8, pp. 166-169.
[2] Ibid., p. 169.

about....If you know the Copenhageners' curiosity and their desire to be where others are, you will understand that one did not need a third of these preparations to get the whole population going.[1]

Obviously, there was a gap between the solemn tributes to the power of art and the confidence that it would serve as an effective tool in the pedagogical efforts of the bourgeois elite to mould the Danes into a nation, on the one hand, and the real needs and desires of the Copenhagen population, on the other.

The descriptions of the Thorvaldsen celebrations give the impression that the enthusiasm of the public, but most of all its mere size—an unprecedented quantity of spectators—caused the program, which was planned so meticulously, to get out of control. While the program prescribed: "During the return to shore one should pay the greatest possible attention that the shallop with Thorvaldsen onboard, be surrounded on both sides and in the back by the decorated boats which hold proper distance from each other,"[2] already on the water there was such a jostle of boats that Thorvaldsen's shallop had trouble making its way. Still worse was the situation on land. In order to make it possible for the honored artist to go ashore, several sailors had to go and make a path through the crowd by force in advance. Sigurd Schultz tells about the situation:

[A]nd they succeeded in their endeavor to guide Thorvaldsen through the crowd to the carriage only thanks to the support of a dozen strong masons and carpenters in yellow leather trousers. They set their backs against the crowd at the same time as they yelled "Hurrah" as powerfully as possible and filled the air around them with the stench of brandy.[3]

The final appropriation of the great artist by the crowd, then, was enacted symbolically, when the masses unhitched the horses and drew Thorvaldsen's carriage through Copenhagen—a fact which Thorvaldsen, as is reported, did not even notice at the moment but grew very angry

---

[1] Johanne Luise Heiberg, *Et liv genoplevet i erindringen*, vol. 1, p. 338.
[2] Schultz, *Da Thorvaldsen kom hjem*, p. 9.
[3] Ibid., p. 14.

about when he was informed about it later on.[1] Later, on its way to
Charlottenborg, the crowd crossed the royal court at Amalienborg,
something which was prohibited. A turmoil arose, in which a student
was hurt by a bayonet, "but the sentry who wanted to stop the carriage
was swept aside without further ado."[2] The absolute disregard for royal
authority, which is manifested in the incident, corresponds to the complete
absence of royals and clergy from the celebration. That the Thorvaldsen
homecoming was considered a celebration of and for the people is also
observed by John Henderson with respect to Jørgen Sonne's frieze: "This
is to show us how Copenhagen would like to see itself....No, they saw
no need for the presence of royalty, guard of honour with guns, robed
and bemedalled nobility, or mitred church fathers: for here is an Art 'of
the people,' stepping ashore."[3]

III. The Art

But how is this "Art" and how are "the people" to be conceived in the
particular case of Thorvaldsen and the Danish public? Johanne Luise
Heiberg's retrospective reflections on the educative influence of the
great artist on the "raw crowd," respectively "the lower classes," obviously
betray an idealistic vision of the social and pedagogical force of art on
the people. Poul Martin Møller's sculptor who is forced to exert his
pedagogical mission on the people with the raw force of Hercules' club
appears as a grotesque double of these idealistic notions. Anyway, both
hint at a central area of aesthetic and political debate: the question of
representation and of the political imagination in times of transition to
modern mass society. Are the people—as sovereign and political body—to
be imagined as contemplating visitors in the temple of art or as a rioting
crowd of insurgents? The celebrations of Thorvaldsen's homecoming
were undoubtedly a primary occasion for a staging of the nation as an
aesthetic and political body. And we see very clearly the contradictory
traits of the performance: from the pre-modern, corporative structure

---

[1] Ibid., pp. 14f.
[2] Ibid., p. 15.
[3] Henderson, *The Triumph of Art at Thorvaldsens Museum*, pp. 87-89.

manifested in the boat parade to the unleashing of the crowd in modern mass society.

These contradictions and dynamics in the actual development of the celebrations, the meticulously prepared choreography getting out of control, lead our thoughts to Heiberg's reflections about *"Folk"* and *"Publicum"* as published four years later in *Intelligensblade*. It is the lack of discipline of the theater audience which inspired Heiberg to his ideas (first in his criticism of Carsten Hauch's *Svend Grathe*,[1] then in "People and Public,"[2] both published in 1842). He considers *"Publicum"* an unorganized atomistic mass, while *"Folk"* is an organic whole, a corporeal body in which each single part functions and receives its value in relation to the entirety. For the concept of *"Folk,"* differentiation and organization mean hierarchy: the claim for leadership through the people's "conscious organs," the intellectual elite. They express and represent the unconscious impulses of the people and its national genius: "You can say that the people [*Folket*] themselves compose verse and write, i.e., unconsciously, with the help of their conscious organs—those people, who are called poets and writers in the proper sense of the word."[3] And by means of literature, the other way round, the intellectual elite educates the people. Literature then appears as "an institution of education, from which they [the people] shall receive their formation; they must therefore respect literature's *authority* and *superiority*, and they can do this all the better since these have originated from themselves."[4]

Almost the same thought is coined by Heiberg in his poem on Thorvaldsen's Museum (also from 1842). I have to make the reservation "almost the same," because he mentions the authority and superiority of art but has nothing to say about the organic relationship between artist and people which here appears as "crowd" (*Mængden*). Thus, he highlights their distance: "The mass stares upon the great / Guests from a foreign country, / Asks: Can this amuse me? / Can this educate my mind?" [*"Mængden stirrer paa de store / Gjæster fra et fremmed Land, / Spørger:*

---

[1] Heiberg, "C. Hauchs: Svend Grathe," in *Prosaiske Skrifter*, vol. 4, pp. 378-402.
[2] Heiberg, "Folk og Publicum," in *Prosaiske Skrifter*, vol. 6, pp. 263-283.
[3] Ibid., p. 273.
[4] Ibid.

Kan mig dette more? / Kan det danne min Forstand?"][1] This distance
and lack of intimacy may be caused by the international character of
Thorvaldsen's art, which appears "foreign" to the people ("guests from
a foreign country"). But certainly, it is caused by the incapacity of the
actual public (the crowd, *Mængden*) to respect and esteem the genuine
work of art.

In an illuminating article, Klaus Müller-Wille describes the crisis
of aesthetic and political self-representation in the Danish 1840s, in
particular as it is reflected in Heiberg's essays. He raises the question
of how the traditional concept of the king's body as representation of
the state can be transformed and adapted to the concept of the nation
state, to the idea of the people's body.[2] The idealistic notion of the great
artist, "whose sole presence tunes all around him in a higher key and
forces even the raw crowd to a feeling of piety,"[3] as expressed by Johanne
Luise Heiberg, seems to advance the romantic idea that the artist's
personality could function as a substitute for the king, a center of gravity
around which the people's body would be formed. Indeed, Thorvaldsen's
homecoming festivities appear in many ways as the staging of a royal
event. And does not Johan Ludvig Heiberg in his "People and Public"
in a similar way present us with a notion of the organic formation of the
people (*Folket*)? But against the background of his Hegelian schooling,
Heiberg very clearly discerns that the historical progress necessarily
will lead the present state of fermentation to new forms of organization
in which the dialectic of *Folk* and *Publicum* might reach a synthesis.[4]
His concept of *Folket*, then, serves as a tool to analyze a social and
aesthetic crisis (which in the first place is a crisis of an integral aesthetic
representation of the nation), but it cannot be used as a forward-looking
political imagery for the body of the nation.

---

[1] Heiberg, "Thorvaldsens Museum," in *Poetiske Skrifter*, vol. 8, p. 168.
[2] Klaus Müller-Wille, "Phantom Publikum. Theatrale Konzeptionen des corps
politiques in der dänischen Ästhetik von Andersen bis Kierkegaard," in *Kollektive
Gespenster. Die Masse, der Zeitgeist und andere unfaßbare Körper*, ed. by Michael
Gamper and Peter Schnyder, Freiburg i. Br.: Rombach 2006, pp. 106ff. From
Heiberg's essays, Müller-Wille proceeds to an analysis of Thomasine Gyllembourg's
Two Ages (1845) and Søren Kierkegaard's *A Literary Review* (1846).
[3] Johanne Luise Heiberg, *Et liv genoplevet i Erindringen*, vol. 1, p. 339.
[4] Müller-Wille, "Phantom Publikum," pp. 112f.

But is there no concept of art that would correspond to the ideal claim to form and represent the nation to be found in Heiberg's aesthetics? In fact, we can find such a concept, but it was developed some years before the skeptical essay in *Intelligensblade*: in his article on Henrik Hertz's romantic tragedy *Svend Dyring's House* from 1837. Heiberg here discerns the national character of Hertz's work, and at the same time praises it for being popular:

> There is something in this poetry which must captivate every Dane; it is the National in it, which at the same time has become popular, so that it captures the whole public. It is not written for one or another class, not only for the educated people, not only for "the dignified part," but for everybody without exception.[1]

Before it can exert an influence on the people, the truly national work of art must become popular. In contrast to Thorvaldsen's work, there is no contradiction between great art and the public. On the contrary, the popularity of the play is praised as one of the tragedy's finest qualities. But what does "popular" mean to Heiberg? It does not mean that it appeals to sensuality, to the lower instincts of the audience. Popularity, that is, in Heiberg's sense the power "with which every true work of art captivates a whole people, both educated and uneducated,"[2] is based on a special kind of beauty. In *Svend Dyring's House* it is the tone of the old Danish folk poetry, the *Kæmpeviser*. This tone captures the audience immediately and irresistibly, as "a magic power," which appears "at the same time so old and so new, so familiar and so strange."[3]

This concept of true art as national art obviously does not apply to Thorvaldsen. Of course, beauty is the main motif even in Heiberg's

---

[1] Heiberg, "Om den romantiske Tragedie Svend Dyrings Huus," in *Prosaiske Skrifter*, vol. 4, p. 169.

[2] Ibid., p. 171.

[3] Ibid., pp. 171f. A couple pages later, the author adds: "*Forunderlig er den Trolddom, som ligger i Folkepoesien og i Folkemusiken....I vore danske Kæmpeviser have vi Danske en levende Fornemmelse af vor fædrelandske Natur, af Havet, Bøgeskoven og de duftende Enge; vi føle, at disse Sange ere vore, og ingen Andens i Verden; i dem gjenkjende vi danske Følelser og dansk Tænkemaade; og at Dette ikke er en Illusion fremkaldt ved Vanen eller ved indpodede Forestillinger, viste den Enthusiasme, hvormed de gamle Folkemelodier i Elverhøi bleve optagne....*" (ibid., p. 173).

tribute poem to Thorvaldsen: the birth of beauty in the metaphor of Aphrodite rising from the foam of the sea. The overlap of the national and the classic, however, leads to a realistic-mythological catachresis. The national welcome scene, the loaded ship in the roadstead of Copenhagen, is superimposed with pictures from classical mythology: Nereus' daughters peek from out of the water in order to catch sight of Thorvaldsen; they remember "How Beauty rose from the bottom of the sea / And was born as a goddess,"[1] which serves as a point of departure for the idea of beauty reborn in Thorvaldsen's art, "Whose thought has room for beauty, / and makes it be reborn."[2] The last stanza returns to the present scenery without, however, refraining from the mythological picture: "And the wave is rejoicing once again / And storming towards the ship, / And around its concha sounds a song / For him, who forms Gods." [*"Og Bølgen jubler anden Gang / Og høit mod Skibet stormer, / Og om dets Concha toner Sang / For Ham, den Gudeformer."*][3] The concha refers to works of visual arts (representations of Venus in the shell) as conveyed since antiquity, but it is hard to see how this picture convincingly can be conferred to the ship in the roadsteads of Copenhagen.

The poem does not succeed in integrating organically classical beauty and Danish nationality; so much can be said without engaging in a more profound critique. It just superimposes them by way of a quite artificial metaphor. Besides, its train of thought is often cumbersome. It is hard to imagine that its meaning could easily be grasped when performed by a choir located on boats on the open water. We may not forget, however, that the tribute song was an old and well-established genre. Its successful performance depended on much more than the qualities of the text: on the staging, for instance, but just as much on the music. The tune "Vi Sømænd gjør ej mange Ord" was, as Hans Kuhn shows,[4] a very popular one, and it was used in many different contexts in the patriotic song tradition of the time. It was closely connected to naval themes and to the idea of Denmark's glorious past as a seafaring nation. Its "cheerful

---

[1] Heiberg, "Thorvaldsens Ankomst paa Fregatten Rota," in *Poetiske Skrifter*, vol. 8, p. 352.
[2] Ibid.
[3] Ibid.
[4] Kuhn, *Defining a Nation in Song*, p. 171.

marching rhythm"[1] and its inherent patriotic message secured, we may suppose, the success of the performance as a patriotic tribute song independently of the intricate textual figuration of the poem.

IV. Conclusion

The relationship of the Danish intellectual elite (and more specifically of Johan Ludvig Heiberg) to Thorvaldsen as it is manifested in the celebrations around his homecoming in 1838 directs our attention to areas of special interest within Danish society and aesthetics of the Golden Age.

With respect to aesthetics, attention is focused on the function of art (both literature and visual arts) in the nation-building process. Heiberg's aesthetic reflections touch on the question of how art in times of social change, more specifically in a process of transition to democracy and mass society, can represent and at the same time mould the people, the sovereign of the nation. For Heiberg, in his essay on Hertz's *Svend Dyring's House*, "popularity" is a key word in this context. True national art must be popular in order to be able to fulfill its function of uniting and educating the people. But being truly popular implies, at the same time, being rooted in the national, in one's own heritage. This must be appropriated anew in order to appear "at the same time so old and so new, so familiar and so strange."[2] As highly estimated as Thorvaldsen's classic sculpture may have been, it certainly does not fit such a concept of popular national art. This, on the one hand, makes us discern the narrow limits of the concept, whereas it, on the other hand, explains Heiberg's skepticism with respect to Thorvaldsen's educative influence on the public (as "*Publicum*").

With respect to society, an analysis of the Thorvaldsen discourse and practices in the context of the homecoming celebrations directs the focus towards political and economic change, in which the value and function of art have to be situated. Heiberg's tribute poem, as well as the

---

[1] Ibid.

[2] Heiberg, "Om den romantiske Tragedie Svend Dyrings Huus," in *Prosaiske Skrifter*, vol. 4, p. 172.

choreography of the welcoming in the roads of Copenhagen, connects seafaring and commerce, symbolic and economic capital, directly to the material and pecuniary qualities of art as a commodity. This signals the growing social importance of the bourgeoisie compared to the traditional elites (royalty, nobles, clergy). At the same time, however, the collapse of the bourgeois staging under the pressure of the lower classes or simply the mass of spectators announces the advent of mass society.

II. Theater and Philosophy

The Opera Hater? Johan Ludvig Heiberg and the Musical Theater

Joachim Grage

I. Introduction

In his *History of Opera in Denmark*, Gerhard Schepelern deems Johan Ludvig Heiberg unsuccessful as the director of the Royal Theater in Copenhagen. Schepelern describes the years under Heiberg's leadership (1849-56) as the decline of opera, marked by a dramatic slump in the performance numbers of operas and *singspiele*.[1] Even one so sympathetic to Heiberg as Morten Borup confirmed that it was not a "golden time"[2] for opera in Denmark during the mid-nineteenth century. In the seven years under Heiberg's auspices only three new works were performed in the musical theater genre. According to Borup, during this time Copenhagen was devoid of opera in the true sense, with "*Syngestykker*" (meaning here "*singspiele*") being performed almost exclusively.[3] Whereas Borup traces this back not only to Heiberg's lack of support but also to the public's lack of interest, Schepelern makes Heiberg alone responsible since he was of the opinion "that opera should actually be abolished."[4]

---

[1] See Gerhard Schepelern, *Operaens historie i Danmark*, Copenhagen: Munksgaard Rosinante 1995, pp. 72f.

[2] Morten Borup, *Johan Ludvig Heiberg*, vols. 1-3, Copenhagen: Gyldendal 1947-49, vol. 3, p. 104: "*ingen Glansperiode.*"

[3] Ibid.

[4] Schepelern, *Operaens historie i Danmark*, p. 73.

Thus, playing on a variation of a title from a famous novel written by
Klaus Rifbjerg,[1] Schepelern simply called him the "opera hater."[2]

The question mark in the title of this article already indicates that
I would like to re-examine this assessment. In 1855, in an article in the
Berlingske Tidende, Heiberg defended himself against the accusation
that he was not at all interested in opera. According to his appraisal, he
actually saved it from extinction after having found it in absolute decay.[3]
A verdict on Heiberg's role as a theater and opera director can only be
made after a thorough examination of the history of theater, based on
archival materials. However, the question of whether or not he disputed
opera's right to exist as a genre can also be critically investigated based
on his aesthetic writings. In the following I will attempt to reconstruct
Heiberg's systematic considerations regarding the relationship
between opera and drama. Moreover, I will try to indicate *aporiae* and
contradictions in his aesthetic thought and demonstrate that he clearly
had a vision for musical theater, which he obviously did not see fulfilled
in the opera productions of his time. I will also occasionally address
similarities and differences between Heiberg's aesthetics of the musical
theater (when one can speak of them) and Hegel's aesthetics. This will
serve to determine Heiberg's position more precisely and to place him
within the context of the debates about musical aesthetics in the mid-
nineteenth century.

Borup's distinction between "opera" and "*singspiele*" already indicates
that there were various forms or genres of productions within musical
theater and that they were valued differently. Heiberg undertakes such
classifications as well. I use the term "musical theater" as a generic
term for the genres which Heiberg speaks of in the aesthetic writings
discussed here, that is, for musical dramas with or without singing.
Included among these are operas, operettas, *singspiele* and vaudeville, on
the one hand, and, on the other hand, those pieces performed with stage

---

[1] Klaus Rifbjerg, *Operaelskeren*, Copenhagen: Gyldendal 1966. (Although this book
has not been translated into English, the title could be translated as "The Opera
Lover.")

[2] Schepelern, *Operaens historie i Danmark*, p. 72 and p. 82: "*operahaderen.*"

[3] See Borup, *Johan Ludvig Heiberg*, vol. 3, p. 104.

music usually composed specifically for them and which often contain melodramatic passages.[1]

II. Heiberg's Musical Theater Aesthetics and his Aesthetic System

Heiberg developed his systematic thoughts on musical theater primarily in three essays, including *Vaudeville as a Dramatic Genre and its Significance for the Danish Stage* (1826)[2] and two shorter essays "A Few Comments Regarding Opera and *Singspiel* (On Occasion of Robert the Devil)" from 1836[3] and "Italian Opera" from 1842.[4] Although a systematic approach is clearly recognizable in his comments, they are always related to specific incidents, events or constellations in Copenhagen's theater scene.[5] The context alone in which he explores questions of the musical theater illustrates that it is not the center of his interests: he deals with it in relation to vaudeville (which Heiberg considered to be more drama than *singspiel*) or in celebration of particular performances or the Italian opera company's stay in Copenhagen.

Heiberg thinks about musical theater from the perspective of someone working in the theater and not from a musician's standpoint. Moreover, when it comes to music he is obviously a layman without any practical musical education. Yet his biographer, Borup, declares

---

[1] The term "melodramatic" is used here in the sense common to music theory, that is, as a connection between spoken text and music—not as an identification of a sentimental play.

[2] Johan Ludvig Heiberg, *Om Vaudevillen som dramatisk Digtart og om dens Betydning paa den danske Skueplads. En dramatisk Undersøgelse*, in *Prosaiske Skrifter*, vols. 1-11, Copenhagen: C. A. Reitzel 1861-62, vol. 6, pp. 1-111.

[3] Johan Ludvig Heiberg, "Et Par Bemærkninger om Operaen og Syngespillet. (I Anledning af Robert af Normandiet)," in *Prosaiske Skrifter*, vol. 6, pp. 141-146. Giacomo Meyerbeer's opera *Robert le Diable* was performed under the title *Robert af Normandiet* in Copenhagen.

[4] Johan Ludvig Heiberg, "Den italienske Opera," in *Prosaiske Skrifter*, vol. 6, pp. 147-170.

[5] See also Vilhelm Andersen's characterization of Heiberg's vaudeville essay: Heiberg's system is based on a historically dependent and restricted situation; it is a "Copenhagen aesthetic from and for 1825," Carl S. Petersen and Vilhelm Andersen, *Illustreret dansk Litteraturhistorie*, vols. 1-4, Copenhagen: Gyldendal 1919-25, vol. 3, Vilhelm Andersen, *Det nittende Aarhundredes første Halvdel*, p. 423.

him "thoroughly musical,"[1] and Niels Schiørring found "his very strong musical sense,"[2] with which he selected suitable melodies for the vocal numbers of his vaudevilles, the key to the great success and popularity of his pieces. In his vaudeville essay, Heiberg complains a number of times about dilettantes daring to have an opinion about questions of art. He also goes on to protest that the vaudevilles in Copenhagen are judged by censors who are not musically inclined,[3] a remark, which, according to Borup, is aimed at Knud Lyne Rahbek (1760-1830).[4] Heiberg himself rarely expresses an opinion about music, but rather comments first and foremost about the dramatic quality of musical theater when he refers to specific pieces. Some of the passages within his text indicate that his basic understanding of music is bound to a romantic musical aesthetic— for example when he writes that "the mere tones are already prophets of a greater and ideal world."[5] Nonetheless such general comments about the essence of music are rare, and especially because they are so isolated they tend to sound stereotypical and not reflected.

That statements such as this are not theoretically supported is a result of Heiberg not having published any cohesive, systematic work on aesthetics. However, he had already written one quite early on: *Grundlinien zum System der Aesthetik als speculativer Wissenschaft*, written in German in 1824, is available as a 153-page manuscript in the Rigsarkiv in Copenhagen. Jon Stewart has shown that the basic concepts of this work are based in many ways on Hegel's lectures on aesthetics, which Heiberg knew well from a student's written record of them.[6] In Chapter

---

[1] Borup, *Johan Ludvig Heiberg*, vol. 3, p. 104.
[2] Niels Schiørring, *Musikkens historie i Danmark*, vols. 1-3, Copenhagen: Politikens Forlag 1977-78, vol. 2, p. 207.
[3] See Heiberg, *Om Vaudevillen som dramatisk Digtart og om dens Betydning paa den danske Skueplads*, in *Prosaiske Skrifter*, vol. 6, p. 56.
[4] See Borup, *Johan Ludvig Heiberg*, vol. 2, p. 57.
[5] Heiberg, *Om Vaudevillen som dramatisk Digtart og om dens Betydning paa den danske Skueplads*, in *Prosaiske Skrifter*, vol. 6, p. 20.
[6] See Jon Stewart, *A History of Hegelianism in Golden Age Denmark*, Tome I, *The Heiberg Period: 1824-1836*, Copenhagen: C.A. Reitzel 2007 (*Danish Golden Ages Studies*, vol. 3), pp. 178-185. Heiberg's biographer Morten Borup also mentions a systematic aesthetic that was supposedly developed in a manuscript in 1832; it is unclear whether the piece from 1824 is meant here. Cf. Borup, *Johan Ludvig Heiberg*, vol. 3, p. 180.

VI of the essay ("Von den Natur-Categorien der Schönheit") music is also discussed (§§ 122-129 "Hörbare Natur-Categorien der Schönheit, oder Töne").[1] A Heibergian aesthetic can perhaps not be reconstructed alone from the few general comments about music sprinkled throughout his published writings, however, Heiberg's published comments on musical theater indicate that his thoughts originated in an aesthetic system that had also existed for several decades. Already in his vaudeville essay, he develops an outline of a systematic theory of dramatic art which he implicitly refers to in later writings.

III. Reconstruction of the Systematic Musical Theater Aesthetic

Heiberg's aesthetic theory is clearly bound to a dialectical Hegelian reasoning and gives the appearance of being able to specifically locate every artwork in the system.[2] The basic idea is that art unfolds within a field of tension between two main principles reflected to varying degrees in the individual types of art and genres. In the vaudeville essay he apodictically states: "All art is either plastic or musical because it acquires objectivity either within space or in time."[3] The either/or, however, is qualified in that each of the two arts in which these basic principles come into existence (or as Hegel wrote, "[are] presented to contemplation and feeling"[4]) also contains the other element in the sense of an "as well as." Thus, the same opposition that determines art on the whole is found in each art object, whereby poetry is the one art which unites these oppositions (and one cannot resist using the Hegelian term "mediation" here). This comes down to a basic three-way division: there

---

[1] Stewart, *A History of Hegelianism in Golden Age Denmark*, p. 179.

[2] With regard to the dialectical derivation of vaudeville in Heiberg's poetological writings, compare also Jens Kr. Andersen, "Efterord," in *Johan Ludvig Heiberg, Dramatik i udvalg*, ed. by Jens Kr. Andersen, Copenhagen: Det Danske Sprog- og Litteraturselskab and Borgen 2000 (*Danske Klassikere*), pp. 539-543.

[3] Heiberg, *Om Vaudevillen som dramatisk Digtart og om dens Betydning paa den danske Skueplads*, in *Prosaiske Skrifter*, vol. 6, p. 45.

[4] G.W.F. Hegel, *Sämtliche Werke. Jubiläumsausgabe*, vols. 1-20, ed. by Hermann Glockner, Stuttgart: Friedrich Frommann Verlag 1928-41, vol. 12, p. 148 (English translation: G.W.F. Hegel, *Aesthetics: Lectures on Fine Art*, trans. by T.M. Knox, vols. 1-2, Oxford: Clarendon Press 1998, vol. 1, p. 101.)

are two extremes and (at least) one middle course. This triadic structure continues in the filiations of the system.

First, the three main genres of art can be arranged within this field of tension. The plastic (as a substitute for the visual arts in general) is the nearest to the plastic principle and music is the closest to the musical principle. In between—merging plastic and musical elements—is poetry, which according to Heiberg is the art "in which the general concept of art is realized the most."[1] One can already note: the golden mean is always the middle course for Heiberg. The three main genres of poetry can in turn be arranged within this field of tension. Epic poetry is closest to the plastic, lyric to the musical, and dramatic poetry represents the middle course. The contrast between epic and lyric manifests itself within dramatic poetry as the synthesis of the situation (epic) and the characters (lyric), while the plot represents the merger of character and situation. In his paper on Italian opera published fifteen years later, Heiberg locates the difference between tragic (= plastic) and comic (= lyric, = musical) in the strong contrast between the plastic and the musical.[2]

Within this system syntheses between types of art, independent of the levels in which they surface within the system, are also now possible. One of these syntheses is musical theater, which arises from the connection between dramatic poetry and music. It thus surfaces in the field of tension between the dramatic and the musical within which the different forms of musical theater can then be located. Thus the opera without any spoken text is the most musical, and melodrama (i.e., spoken theater with music added) the most dramatic. In between these stand the two forms which combine music and spoken text: the *singspiel* and vaudeville. The musical dramatic forms are thus systematically derived.

IV. The Borders between Genres

In this universe of art everything therefore seems to have its place. Nonetheless, in other passages it becomes clear that Heiberg does not

---

[1] Heiberg, *Om Vaudevillen som dramatisk Digtart og om dens Betydning paa den danske Skueplads*, in *Prosaiske Skrifter*, vol. 6, p. 46.
[2] See Heiberg, "Den italienske Opera," in *Prosaiske Skrifter*, vol. 6, p. 161.

want to allow a place for everything and that he is very critical of a few hybrids. While praising the connection between drama and music as an element created from two types of art, he rails quite vehemently against the fusion of two types of poetry, which he finds more and more rampant and which he depicts as a serious threat to art. Heiberg believes that dilettantism is responsible for this and finds that German literature is especially infected by this, although he also has fears regarding Danish literature. In particular he focuses on the play *Preciosa*, a Cervantes adaptation by the actor and playwright Pius Alexander Wolff (1782-1828) to which Carl Maria von Weber (1786-1826) had written stage music:[1]

> ...the famous actor [is] a master in his field, but quite a mediocre dilettante in writing, for which he demonstrated his incompetence by failing to even understand the subtleness in Cervantes' superb novella from which he threw together his *Preciosa*, a play which, due to Weber's music and scenic coquettishness, but first and foremost due to the audience not knowing the Spanish material, could have what one calls success.[2]

The fact alone that an epic text (a novella) is adapted into a play arouses suspicion of failure. Heiberg views poetry as responsible for the transgression, for poetry is more prone to dilettantism than music because "due to its initial challenges, it [music] scares the mobs away from its sanctum."[3] Letters are easier to write than notes; thus, there are more appalling poets than appalling composers.

Above all, *Preciosa* irritates Heiberg because it blurs the borders between the individual dramatic genres. He finds this problematic, because in his opinion each genre only has its specific character and thus its significance within its borders. *Preciosa*, however, belongs to the plays

---

[1] See Helmut Wirth, "Bühnenmusik," in *Die Musik in Geschichte und Gegenwart*, ed. by Friedrich Blume, vols. 1-17, Kassel: Bärenreiter 1951-86, vol. 2, p. 444. Wirth is also of the opinion that "the quality of the composition clearly exceeds that of the poetry."

[2] Heiberg, *Om Vaudevillen som dramatisk Digtart og om dens Betydning paa den danske Skueplads*, in *Prosaiske Skrifter*, vol. 6, p. 15.

[3] Ibid., p. 7.

that blend all of the dramatic genres together "in the same way that medical charlatans mix an entire pharmacy into one prescription accor-ding to the principle 'if the one does not help, the other one will.'"[1] It is one of those "so-called lyrical dramas with songs, chorus, dance and pageantry, or in other words: a hotchpotch of tragedy, comedy, drama, melodrama, opera and ballet apart from a number of other ingredients that do not belong in art and are to some degree unworthy of it."[2] He illustrates what irritates him the most about these mixed genres using Christoph Ernst Friedrich Weyse's (1774-1842) stage music for Shakespeare's *Macbeth*. Here, the tragedy is not rewritten into a complete opera, but rather only individual parts are operatically adapted. In no way is he protesting against musical dramatic adaptations of spoken plays, quite the opposite. He even found it "interesting to see the Shakespearian questions unraveled by means of music and then especially by that kind of music [sc. Weyse's]."[3] Nonetheless, it is not allowed to cross over the borders between the genres. Whereas he dismisses the songs sprinkled throughout the play's plot as misplaced, he believes that it could be completely set to music because this follows other rules. In an opera, songs do not need to have a motivation; they are a natural part of it, "because here music is the only language and is the basis upon which all rests."[4] However, in the tragedy, songs represent a break in the fiction as long as they are not dramaturgically motivated (for example, in the form of diegetic music) and thus represent a foreign element. In the same way, Heiberg criticizes adding elements of dialogue into an opera afterwards, for example, in the case of Wolfgang Amadeus Mozart's *Le Nozze di Figaro* or Gioacchino Rossini's *Il barbiere di Siviglia*, which in contemporary adaptations were performed with spoken dialogues originally from Pierre-Augustin Caron de Beaumarchais' plays.[5] Either/ or, and no experiments, that is what Heiberg's aesthetic dogmas seem to dictate here.

Keeping the genres pure is a question of taste for Heiberg, that is, taste is the category which is the basis of any judgment about art. Taste

---

[1] Ibid., p. 19.
[2] Ibid.
[3] Ibid., p. 20.
[4] Ibid., p. 21.
[5] See ibid., p. 29.

is not evident in the details like appropriate manners or following social rules, but rather "in general, in recognizing the objective in art and in one's subordination to the scepter of this power."[1] What these objectives are remains unclear. Heiberg uses this term in his essays in very different contexts. It is not clear if, as Carl Henrik Koch suggests, the outline of a formal aesthetic arises here,[2] since there is some doubt as to whether this objective means the same thing that Heiberg calls in other places "the beautiful form…through which every subject first becomes an art object."[3] Perhaps, one has to think here from the perspective of Hegel and start with the concept of an objectivization of ideals in art similar to Hegel's characterization of beauty as the "pure appearance of the Idea to sense."[4] However, that is just speculation because Heiberg does not elaborate on this thought. For him, taste means the respect for already existing genres as well as the aim to maintain these in their purity and not to fall behind the artistic development the great masters have given us. The conservative thrust of this concept is still corroborated with the observation that taste in art is the same as the *pietas* in the family and belief in religion,[5] a foundation, which may not be shaken without the order being threatened.

Moreover, the rigorism with which Heiberg polemicizes against the softening of the genres' borders is also disconcerting. He thus expressively welcomed the fact that each of the Parisian theaters committed themselves to just one section of the spectrum of theatrical genres and that this arrangement was supported "by governmental regulations and police

---

[1] Ibid., p. 40.

[2] See Carl Henrik Koch, *Den danske idealisme 1800–1880*, Copenhagen: Gyldendal 2004 (*Den danske filosofis historie*, vol. 4), p. 234.

[3] Heiberg, *Om Vaudevillen som dramatisk Digtart og om dens Betydning paa den danske Skueplads*, in *Prosaiske Skrifter*, vol. 6, p. 30.

[4] Hegel, *Sämtliche Werke. Jubiläumsausgabe*, vol. 12, p. 160. (*Aesthetics*, vol. 1, p. 111.)

[5] See Heiberg, *Om Vaudevillen som dramatisk Digtart og om dens Betydning paa den danske Skueplads*, in *Prosaiske Skrifter*, vol. 6, p. 40. The word *pietas* became a key term in the nineteenth century for a conservative patriarchal familial ideology; cf. Helmut Scheuer, " 'Autorität' und 'Pietät'. Wilhelm Heinrich Riehl und der Patriarchalismus in der Literatur des 19. Jahrhunderts," in *Familienmuster—Musterfamilien. Zur Konstruktion von Familie in der Literatur*, ed. by Claudia Brinker-von der Heyde and Helmut Scheuer, Frankfurt am Main: Lang 2004, pp. 135-160.

surveillance."[1] In the *Académie Royale de Musique* only French operas were performed, and in the Italian theater only Italian, just as institutions for musical theater and spoken theater were strictly separated. It is exactly this spatial separation and restriction that prevents the mixing of genres harmful to the taste of the general public. Furthermore, the government's organizational actions demonstrate how highly they regard the theater. The law enforcement agency is transfigured here into the executor of the rules of art—yet this is only referred to as a pleasant side-effect of the rather questionable state control of the theater:

> Whether it is really about caring for art or for other subordinate reasons that France's government exercises such strict control over the theater is none of our concern....The government's activities could also very well have a negative impact on the freedom of the theater, especially when the censorship is too strict or entrusted to those who follow their own subjective tastes instead of orienting themselves according to the valid objectives.[2]

The role of the state with regard to art is thus just as ambivalent as the necessity of borders between the genres. The state threatens artistic freedom, on the one hand, and, on the other hand, ensures the stability of the art system that Heiberg designs and wants to see emulated in public institutions: each genre should have its own theater. Apparently, the rules of art are not enough to arrange the literary market, or there is a lack of instruments other than the state authority for asserting these rules. The desire for such a public control, however, has to be considered in light of the fact that Heiberg had endeavored in vain to establish a private theater for vaudeville. This theater was to appeal to a different audience than that of the Royal Theater, where, according to Heiberg, operas and ballets should be performed. The spoken theater was to have its home on a third, private stage. However, this three-house model was thwarted by political resistance as well as economic necessity; ultimately, it was just too large for Copenhagen at the time.[3] As a result, vaudeville

[1] Heiberg, *Om Vaudevillen som dramatisk Digtart og om dens Betydning paa den danske Skueplads*, in *Prosaiske Skrifter*, vol. 6, p. 25.
[2] Ibid., pp. 25f.
[3] See *Dansk teaterhistorie*, ed. by Kela Kvam, Janne Risum and Jytte Wiingaard, vols. 1-2, Copenhagen: Gyldendal 1992, vol. 1, pp. 210-212.

had to hold its own on the royal stage next to opera and the spoken theater and against other mixed genres.

V. Aporiae *and Contradictions in Heiberg's Systematic Aesthetics*

The decision about when a hybrid form is permissible (such as vaudeville) and when not (such as the work of dilettantes) seems to be arbitrary. However, it cannot be overlooked that the passionate plea for good taste and the observance of literary rules inherent within the traditional and established genres are part of a polemic against the poor quality in contemporary drama productions. Heiberg, therefore, uses the authority of tradition as an argument when he tears apart the dilettante work he sees flooding the Royal Theater. He is everything but conservative, though, when he hails vaudeville as an innovative genre and a way out of the theater's crisis. The decisive criteria for when a hybrid has to be classified as an illegitimate or legitimate form is taste,[1] which nonetheless cannot be systematically explained. Heiberg describes it as a consequence of a literary education process, in which the theater itself as an institution plays a fundamental role:

> By whom else should the audience that judges the play preferably be instructed than by the playwright himself?...It is no contradiction that the audience that judges should be schooled by the poet since no one is able to make a judgment about something—regardless of whether it be in aesthetic or legal things—without first learning how to judge.[2]

Especially because the theater develops the taste of its audience and because it should raise the audience to be critical and discerning viewers,

---

[1] With regard to Heiberg's rhetorical strategy of the legitimization of vaudeville, see Kirsten Wechsel, "Herkunftstheater. Zur Regulierung von Legitimität im Streit um die Gattung Vaudeville," in *Faszination des Illegitimen. Alterität in Konstruktionen von Genealogie, Herkunft und Ursprünglichkeit in den skandinavischen Literaturen seit 1800*, ed. by Constanze Gestrich and Thomas Mohnike, Würzburg: Ergon Verlag 2007 (*Identitäten und Alteritäten*, vol. 25), pp. 39-59.

[2] Heiberg, *Om Vaudevillen som dramatisk Digtart og om dens Betydning paa den danske Skueplads*, in *Prosaiske Skrifter*, vol. 6, pp. 5f.

the work of dilettantes poses a danger for the institution. The *aporia* of Heiberg's argument exists in that he, on the one hand, preaches a separation between the genres while he, on the other hand, but at the same time, proclaims a previously unestablished, and in contemporary Copenhagen highly debated, mixed genre as the savior for the theater's crisis. It was not without good reason that he already emphasized in the title of his essay that it was concerned with the significance of vaudeville for the Danish stage. The systematic derivation of vaudeville serves to retrospectively legitimize the not yet solidly established genre which stands apart from the traditional order and which Heiberg himself had implemented on a trial basis.

Nevertheless, Heiberg's argument leaves a number of questions unanswered. How can it be that a new "type of poetry" is supposed to establish itself in the venerable system of traditional forms? And why is this new genre a hybrid of spoken and musical theater? Heiberg strived to differentiate vaudeville from other hybrids in that he also spoke of a "mixture";[1] however, in the vaudeville case it is with the sense of a merging of two arts resulting in the creation of a new "unity of art."[2] Accordingly, the divergence between the original genres, opera and spoken drama, is resolved in vaudeville. This line of thought may be referred to as Hegelian dialectic; nonetheless it is not explained. Moreover, with the implementation of vaudeville Heiberg has to accept an inconsistency in his triadic system of genres, because vaudeville is not the only mediating genre but rather shares the position with *opéra comique* or *singspiele* (which Heiberg considered the same). The novelty of the form compared to the other mixed genres lies in its different proximities to each of the two original genres. Whereas the writer of the *singspiel* is closer to opera and is governed by the rules of music, where the dialogue just represents a transition between musical situations, vaudeville leans towards drama, in that it is subject to the primacy of the dramatic dialogue, and the music is only introduced at its climaxes, more or less like icing on the cake. With that, however, the resolution of the oppositions in the mediating genres once again has to be called into question. If the proportions of

---

[1] Ibid., p. 42.
[2] Ibid., "*Kunst-Eenhed.*"

drama and opera continue to be so easily extracted from the two hybrid genres, then the "unity of art," be it in vaudeville or in *singspiel*, is a little shaky.

In fact, Heiberg discusses vaudeville almost exclusively from a literary perspective in that he presents it as a contemporary successor to the Holbergian comedy. When Heiberg locates vaudeville as a form of musical theater which is closer to pure drama than opera, one can also recognize a distancing from the musical whose essence remains strangely undetermined in the vaudeville essay.

VI. Heiberg's Use of Music in Vaudevilles

As already indicated, Heiberg also expresses himself about the question of introducing music in vaudeville and again in differentiation to *singspiele*. While *singspiele* are centered on music, and dialogues are only transitions between individual musical scenes, spoken dialogues are the focus in vaudevilles, and the music replaces the dialogue at the point it climaxes. Thus, in vaudeville the dialogue culminates in the music:

> In the *singspiel* the dialogue replaces the music; in vaudevilles the music replaces the dialogues, which is why one uses to a large extent known and light melodies in it. The listener's attention should not be bound to the musical elements here but rather peacefully oriented on the dialogue currently supported and clarified through known melodies, whose memories put the listener in the mood that the writer calls for at each and every point.[1]

In vaudevilles the old debate in the history of music about the dominance of speech or music in musical theater is vehemently decided in favor of speech, whereas music is made to serve it. The music is not allowed to draw the attention of the audience to itself since this would then distract attention from the dramatic events; rather, it serves more subliminally to create the mood. Heiberg is concerned first and foremost with the sung "melodies." That this melody should be "light" serves in turn the function

---

[1] Ibid., p. 43.

that the listener focuses not on the musical production, but rather on the text. At the same time, this also has practical reasons: it allows actors without trained singing voices to be able to manage the parts. This was particularly applicable with regard to the French vaudeville that Heiberg became familiar with during his stay in Paris; he himself had to pay little attention to the competence of the ensemble since the personnel at the Royal Theater in Copenhagen were also trained to appear in operas and musicals.[1]

The second key requirement for the melodies was that they should be "known." This too stemmed from the tradition of French vaudeville, which almost exclusively used contemporary songs and arias from popular musicals and operas. It was not the originality of the music that made it appealing, rather the originality of its use. The listener should recognize it and establish references to its original use or to the lyrics that were initially added to it. Such multiple uses of melodies are referred to as parodies in music theory; however, Heiberg also used them in his vaudevilles as parodies in the sense used in literary theory, in that he built on the recognition effect and played with the tension between the original (con)text and the current usage. With that the music also maintains what the texts alledge: Heiberg's vaudevilles often refer to current events and unfold their significance by tightly weaving together innuendos and inter-textual references.

The dramaturgical function of the music can be illustrated by taking a look at Heiberg's vaudeville *The Reviewer and the Animal* (1826). The twelve pieces of music are frequently found at the end of a scene and consequently maintain the postulate of being at the point of the dialogue's culmination. Most of the melodies used have been forgotten today; however, the songs and arias used were firmly rooted in the cultural memory of the 1820s. In fact, they were already to some degree previously employed in other *singspiele* and vaudevilles. Among these were popular songs of the time such as the Tyrolean song "Steh' mal auf, steh' mal auf, junger Schweitzerlbub"[2] or melodies from *singspiele* that

---

[1] With regard to the role of music in Heiberg's vaudevilles, see Torben Krogh, *Heibergs Vaudeviller. Studier over Motiver og Melodier*, Copenhagen: Branner 1942 (*Studier fra Sprog- og Oldtidsforskning*, vol. 189), p. 35.

[2] See Heiberg, *Dramatik i udvalg*, pp. 274f.

had already made the rounds as popular songs,[1] and opera numbers such as the chorus "Das klinget so herrlich" from Mozart's *Zauberflöte*, which, as an exception was sung here in Heiberg's vaudeville with the original text.[2] Only two numbers are original: six variations and one coda about the bridal song "Wir winden dir den Jungfernkranz" from Weber's *Der Freischütz*[3] stem from Giuseppe Siboni (1780-1839), and one melody was written by Heiberg himself. This becomes part of the vaudeville's showpiece, the quintet in the 16th scene, in which five persons at the end sing five different texts in four languages to five different melodies simultaneously, and to top it all off, one of the singers stutters. With this, Heiberg satirically parodies the operatic ensemble songs in which the text completely recedes behind the musical arrangement.

The dominance of the dialogue over the music also means that the text sung is understandable, which, as we all know, is not always the case in operas. This in turn is achieved due to the melodic simplicity, the comfortable range and the clear diction of the singers (who employ their speaking voices rather than their singing voices). The orchestral accompaniment frequently arranged by Ludvig Zinck (1776-1851), the principal singing master, also played an important role in the piece.[4] Heiberg praised Zinck in one of the footnotes in his paper "Contemporary Vaudeville and its Influence on Literature": "In our case, the principal singing master L. Zinck tastefully tries to combine a proper and pleasing accompaniment with the songs and to make it as elaborate as the clarity of performing the text allows."[5] Under no circumstances is the music allowed to displace the text, whether with regard to its complexity or with regard to the loudness of the accompanying orchestra. The essay on vaudeville explains that this genre represents the ideal form of a musical drama for Heiberg. The dramatic text takes on the dominant

---

[1] See the melody "Hør Skjønne, hvis I prøve vil" from the *singspiel Lønkammeret* by the French composer J.P. Solié (1753-1812), which already circulated as "*klubvise.*" Ibid., pp. 283f. and pp. 611f. (notes).

[2] See ibid., p. 356.

[3] Heiberg thus also used melodies from operas of whose dramaturgical quality he was not convinced: with regard to *Der Freischütz* see below.

[4] See Krogh, *Heibergs Vaudeviller*, pp. 36-40.

[5] Johan Ludvig Heiberg, "Om den nuværende Vaudeville og dens Indflydelse paa Litteraturen," in *Prosaiske Skrifter*, vol. 6, pp. 112-138; here pp. 117f.

part and the skillfully selected music supports the text. Moreover, as quotations, the melodies produce references to other texts and manners of use. The music has a function, and its compositional quality must serve that function: it has to be popular and meet the tastes of a wide audience. Originality tends to be counterproductive, even though Heiberg can imagine vaudevilles that use music created exclusively for them: this music then should be composed "in a light song or dance style."[1]

VII. Music and Text in Opera

A decade later, in his short essay "On Opera and *Singspiel*" Heiberg once again dedicates himself to the relationship between music and text. The essay is written on the occasion of a performance of Meyerbeer's opera *Robert le Diable* (in Danish as *Robert af Normandiet*), whose text and treatment met with Heiberg's disapproval. He puts forward the question: does a bad play become more bearable through the music or is the music devaluated by a bad play? This problem surfaced already in the vaudeville essay in which Heiberg reprimanded the librettist of Weber's *Freischütz* for his extensive use of supernatural appearances and poor dramaturgical adaptation of truly epic fairy tale material. This piece could not even be saved by the music since "the beauty of the music is in no way allowed to be an excuse for the author."[2] Hegel comes to a similar conclusion in his consideration of texts suitable for being set to music. Their content must be distinguished by "true solidity": "Nothing musically excellent and profound can be conjured out of what is inherently flat, trivial, trumpery, and absurd; the composer can add what seasoning and spices he likes, but a roasted cat will never make a hare-pie."[3] However, the differences between Hegel and Heiberg are clear. Hegel demands that the libretto be of average quality, which allows a space for the music to unfold: "what the words convey must not be all too difficult thoughts

---

[1] Heiberg, *Om Vaudevillen som dramatisk Digtart og om dens Betydning paa den danske Skueplads*, in *Prosaiske Skrifter*, vol. 6, p. 44.
[2] Ibid., p. 37.
[3] Hegel, *Sämtliche Werke. Jubiläumsausgabe*, vol. 14, pp. 201f. (*Aesthetics*, vol. 2, p. 945.)

or profound philosophy."[1] That said, the libretto must also not have the "precious, artificial, and screwed up naïveté" that Hegel recognized in "the so-called 'romantic' poetry."[2] Instead he calls for

> a certain intermediate kind of poetry which we Germans scarcely allow to be poetry at all, whereas the French and Italians have had a real sense for it and skill in it: a poetry which in lyrics is true, extremely simple, indicating the situation and the feeling in few words, and in drama without all too ramified complications, clear and lively, not working out details but concerned as a rule to provide sketches rather than to produce works completely elaborated poetically.[3]

Certainly, Heiberg also considered Italian and French operatic and musical texts acceptable, but one could not expect him to relativize the quality of the text as Hegel did. Heiberg, instead, thinks in absolute categories: a text either has dramatic qualities or it does not. In his essay "On Opera and *Singspiel*" he once again addresses this problem and undertakes an explicit ranking of the arts, in which he claims that music, despite all of its merits, falls below poetry.[4] He therefore sees the composer as serving the text and thus, the playwright: "The composer should express what the playwright has assigned him to; if he does not, he is a poor composer. But when the playwright has not assigned him anything dramatic, either regarding the character or the situation, the music cannot express what is not there."[5] It is also the composer's responsibility to evaluate if a text is suitable for a "musical dramatic treatment."[6] If someone writes good music or a poor play, the result remains the same. Heiberg regards undramatic texts as poor particularly in the Italian genre *opera seria*, which his attention returns to in his essay "Italian Opera."

---

[1] Hegel, *Sämtliche Werke. Jubiläumsausgabe*, vol. 14, p. 202. (*Aesthetics*, vol. 2, p. 945.)
[2] Ibid.
[3] Hegel, *Sämtliche Werke. Jubiläumsausgabe*, vol. 14, p. 203. (*Aesthetics*, vol. 2, p. 946.)
[4] Heiberg, "Et Par Bemærkninger om Operaen og Syngespillet. (I Anledning af Robert af Normandiet)," in *Prosaiske Skrifter*, vol. 6, p. 143.
[5] Ibid., p. 144.
[6] Ibid., p. 149.

VIII. *The Cultural War about Opera and the Vision of a "Universal, Cosmopolitan Opera"*

In 1842, Heiberg launched his article on Italian opera in the journal, *Intelligensblade*, while an Italian opera company was visiting the city and was being met with approval from the people. Since the post as director of music at the Royal Theater was vacant at the time and since Heiberg saw that selecting a candidate meant making a decision about the direction of the theater, he railed against establishing Italian opera at the theater, that is, against the company being given a permanent appointment. He pleas for a strict institutional division, considering a separate Italian theater plausible and even prestigious, since Paris also had that; however, under no circumstances should Italian opera arrive in the temple of Danish national culture. Heiberg supports this with a pattern of argumentation that is characteristic of *cultural warfare*. The Italian opera is a national institution—but only in its own homeland; everywhere else it is "unnational."[1] He unceremoniously declares Italy to be "outside of the current cultivated world,"[2] to which he counts only the Nordic and that means Protestant countries: Denmark, Germany and France (the latter of which is Catholic but demonstrates for him sufficient Protestant influences). Heiberg remarks that Southern Catholics suggest "stiffened forms" and "fossilized immobility,"[3] while he bluntly snubs the character of Italian art as "generally plastic."[4] Here, Heiberg falls back once again on the aesthetic system he outlines in the vaudeville essay. Even in the least plastic of arts, music, the quintessentially plastic of the Italians is evident. Because although Italian singing has a body, it has no soul—by which at the same time its essence is missed, since, Heiberg then apodictically adds, "song is the art of the soul."[5] The performers of Italian opera can only serve a Nordic audience as an example because of their extraordinary singing technique.

Heiberg's polemic against Italian opera reaches its highpoint as he takes on the libretti. These consist of nothing but exclamations such as

---

[1] Heiberg, "Den italienske Opera," in *Prosaiske Skrifter*, vol. 6, p. 155.
[2] Ibid., p. 156.
[3] Ibid.
[4] Ibid., p. 157.
[5] Ibid., p. 156.

"Oh heavens!," "Oh no!," "Oh horrors!" and interjections such as "Oh" and "Oh woe." Heiberg adds, "but as everyone knows the interjection is the one part of speech, in which human concept and articulation disappears and which therefore approaches the language of animals."[1] In view of such passages the term "opera hater" is in fact plausible. Nevertheless, the malice remains restricted to the Italian opera, since Heiberg continually resorts to examples from German, French and Danish *singspiele* in order to belittle the Italian. The homogeneity of Mozart's *Don Giovanni* is set against Donizetti's operas, which Heiberg considers to be pieced together from individual numbers without any guiding thread; in the buffa genre, he deems Weyse's *singspiel Sovedrikken* (*The Sleeping Draught*) to be as far above Donizetti's pieces as the sky is above the earth.[2]

However, in the same essay in which Heiberg polemicizes against Italian opera, when he reflects about the musical presentation and the singers' performance he seems to concede that opera generally has its own dramatic aesthetic that differs from the spoken theater. Here, the first signs that he considers musical theater from more than just the perspective of drama are evident. The singers' dramatic art, says Heiberg, inevitably has to differ from that of theater actors, since its dramatic arrangement is articulated in the presentation of music, being minimally supported "by a merely skilled plastic art [sc. gestures and bodily expression] that does not let us feel an absolute emptiness in its positions and movements."[3] Only so much could be asked of a singer since a singer is not capable of presenting a character as in a spoken play. This insight, however, represents a contradiction to Heiberg's neat aesthetic system, where character is ascribed to the lyrical and therefore more musical principle, whereas here it explicitly means that the music suppresses the portrayal of the character.

In the same essay Heiberg reveals his vision of a "universal, cosmopolitan opera,"[4] which naturally can only be realized in the Protestant north. Whether or not this transnational genre already exists is not truly clear. It almost seems as if Heiberg avoids relating

---

[1] Ibid., p. 158.
[2] See ibid., pp. 160f.
[3] Ibid., p. 164.
[4] Ibid., p. 165.

this concept, which he uses a number of times, to concrete examples of German, French, or Danish opera productions. In the singing of this new universal opera "imagination as feeling, and poetic passion—in a word the romantic spirit—first comes into its own."[1] One becomes alert when at other points Heiberg writes of the "new opera…in which the instrumentation plays such a dominant role and, like an invisible choir, expresses the reflections of the world spirit about the individual characters and occurrences."[2] This coincides in conspicuous ways with Richard Wagner's (1813-83) opera aesthetic and the way he deals with the orchestra. In 1849 Wagner wrote in *The Art Work of the Future*: "The orchestra is…the loam of endless, universal feeling, from which the individual feeling of the separate actor draws power to shoot aloft to fullest height of growth."[3] However, Heiberg had great difficulty with Wagner's concrete implementation of this vision. When Heiberg wrote his essay on opera, Wagner was just working on *The Flying Dutchman*. In 1856, Heiberg had the opportunity to attend a performance of this "romantic opera," which he wrote about extensively in a "travelogue."[4] He had already heard of Wagner's project to renew opera and had learnt of the quasi-religious worship of the composer. He ironically called him "the preacher of the one true gospel of opera."[5] Heiberg sees Wagner as the antagonist of the "empty and meaningless so-called wealth of melodies from the newest Italian composers"[6] and considers himself on the same side. Nonetheless, it was his opinion that the task had been accomplished a long time ago

> by Gluck, Cimarosa, Mozart, Mehul, Boieldieu and many others, who all created the most pleasant and at the same time characteristic melodies while supporting these with an orchestral accompaniment that gave the

---

[1] Ibid., p. 157.
[2] Ibid., p. 164.
[3] Richard Wagner, *The Art Work of the Future*, in *Richard Wagner's Prose Works*, trans. by William Ashton Ellis, vols. 1-8, London: Kegan Paul, Trench, Trübner & Co. 1892-99, vol. 1 (2nd ed. 1895), p. 190.
[4] Johan Ludvig Heiberg, "En Rejse-Erindring," in *Prosaiske Skrifter*, vol. 7, pp. 441-451.
[5] Ibid., p. 443.
[6] Ibid., p. 444.

deeper explanation of the importance of singing voices, and who, so to speak, initiated the listeners into the secrets of composition.[1]

This sounds as if Heiberg's ideal of an opera had long been realized, that is, in the eighteenth-century and pre-romantic nineteenth-century musical theater. Thus, what remained for Wagner to do? Curiosity drove Heiberg to the Prague opera house, and here he was forced to realize that the central element of his music aesthetic, the melody, was finished off by Wagner: "An effective remedy for avoiding dull melodies is to avoid every single melody. This is so obvious that I have to be ashamed that I did not think of this method myself, this method which is so clear and simple."[2] The musical-scenic impression irritates him so much that he, who often enjoyed absurd situations in his vaudevilles, felt like he was sitting in a madhouse:

> The longer I looked at these mad boats, and listened to the passionate, wild, crazy howling on the stage, in which even the orchestra joined—thus blocking the last possible way to escape—the more I had to ask myself: are you sitting in a real audience, that…paid for its seats, and are you seeing a performance in the real Royal Bohemian Theater, or are you in a madhouse, where madmen are performing a play for madmen?[3]

Heiberg's expectations were generated by the broad discussion about Wagner's music, his writings and Wagner himself. Both these expectations and Heiberg's disappointed reactions in the opera house are typical of the Wagner reception in the nineteenth century. When the new cannot be integrated into one's own aesthetic horizon—it is considered "crazy." This goes to show that even though people share an opposition to a cultural practice, it does not follow that they have the same views on aesthetics.

The question of whether Heiberg was an opera hater or not, therefore, has to be specified in a number of respects. If opera is used as a synonym for musical theater, the answer is no. Heiberg himself was

---

[1] Ibid.
[2] Ibid., p. 445.
[3] Ibid., pp. 450f.

a musical dramatist who drew from the full breadth of contemporary operas and musical productions for his own work. In that he referred in a parodic way to other musical-dramatic works, he strengthened their position in the cultural memory. If one understands opera as a form within the spectrum of the musical-dramatic genres, then Heiberg was anxious to demarcate it. He sets an elite form against a popular one, which he conceptualizes as a mediation between opera and drama. That does not mean that opera became superfluous as a result, since vaudeville can only take the place assigned to it alongside the other genres, and therefore Heiberg could hardly be of the opinion that opera deserved to be abolished. On the other hand, if one means contemporary opera, then it must be said that Heiberg's ideal of an opera was already realized around 1800 and that he considered both Weber's romantic German operas and Wagner's musical dramas as well as the Italian operas of the mid-nineteenth century by Bellini, Donizetti and Verdi to be inferior in comparison to the classical masters; consequently, he fought against them in his critical writings. Nonetheless, even his attacks against the Italian opera served the function of helping him to demarcate and derive his own opera aesthetic. Heiberg thought too dialectically to be able to hate.

Heiberg's Conception of Speculative Drama and the Crisis of the Age: Martensen's Analysis of *Fata Morgana*

Jon Stewart

Johan Ludvig Heiberg was one of the leading figures in theater life in Golden Age Denmark. He was also a Hegelian. According to his own autobiographical statements, these two aspects of his intellectual activity were in perfect harmony with one another.[1] Hegel's philosophy provided the abstract and theoretical background for his concrete and practical works on aesthetics and theater. However, later commentators have often found it difficult to grasp exactly how these two things fit together in a harmonious manner and have been keen to point out contradictions in his general program. Indeed, there was substantial confusion about this in Heiberg's own time since he was criticized by both sides, that is, by philosophers and by theater critics, being rebuked for both bad philosophy and bad theater.

Perhaps his most overt attempt to combine these two interests was his ambitious work, *Fata Morgana* (which premiered on January 29, 1838), an allegorical piece in which he attempts to bring Hegel to the

---

[1] Heiberg, "Autobiographiske Fragmenter," in Heiberg's *Prosaiske Skrifter*, vols. 1-11, Copenhagen: C.A. Reitzel 1861-62, vol. 11, p. 501. (English translation: "Autobiographical Fragments," in *Heiberg's On the Significance of Philosophy for the Present Age and Other Texts*, ed. and trans. by Jon Stewart, Copenhagen: C.A. Reitzel 2005 (*Texts from Golden Age Denmark*, vol. 1), p. 66.)

stage.[1] He regarded this as a new genre which he designated "speculative drama." This claim to novelty or innovation was a contentious one at the time. In this article I wish to explore what Heiberg meant by this designation. I wish ultimately to try to come to an assessment of his claim to have created a new dramatic form with this work.

The piece was badly received at the time and was thus in need of some explanation. Before the play was ever produced, Heiberg's wife, the actress Johanne Luise Heiberg (1812-90), had a negative premonition about how things would go. In her memoirs she explains this as follows:

> In the season 1837-38 Heiberg wrote his play *Fata Morgana*, at the request of the board of directors of the theater, for the celebratory performance on occasion of Frederik the VI's birthday. His mother [sc. Thomasine Gyllembourg] and I had often urged him to write something for the theater again, saying that we now longed to receive this work. Over the past few years, Heiberg had occupied himself almost exclusively with philosophical studies, and his *Fata Morgana* is strongly influenced by this, indeed probably all too strongly. With excitement and anticipation we sat one evening around our living room table in order to hear him read his new piece aloud. I was excited beyond words to hear once again something from his pen, but while he was reading I became more and more uneasy and distressed—not because I did not find this work worthy of a poet—but because I knew the audience and knew that this kind of allegorical poem would be impossible for them to comprehend, and, moreover, the actors at the theater's disposal would be unable to understand or present what was placed in their hands.[2]

Johanne Luise Heiberg, who played the role of Fata Morgana herself in the piece, correctly foresaw that the work would not be comprehensible to those who were not already initiated into the intricacies of Hegel's philosophy.

[1] Johan Ludvig Heiberg, *Fata Morgana, Eventyr-Comedie*, Copenhagen: J.H. Schubothes Boghandling 1838. (Reprinted in *Poetiske Skrifter*, vols. 1-11, Copenhagen: C.A. Reitzel 1862, vol. 2, pp. 93-226.)
[2] Johanne Luise Heiberg, *Et liv genoplevet i erindringen*, vols. 1-4, Copenhagen: Gyldendal 1973, 5th revised edition, vol. 1, p. 296.

Fata Morgana.

Eventyr=Comedie

af

Johan Ludvig Heiberg.

Kjøbenhavn.
Schubothes Boghandling.
Thieles Bogtrykkeri.
1838.

Title Page of Fata Morgana
(Private Collection)

As it turned out her fears were confirmed. The play only saw a total of five performances and was removed from the billboard after February 21, 1838.[1] There were many dramatic works at the time that had a short lifespan—indeed, works quickly came and went—but this one was particularly troublesome due to its special role as a ceremonial work for

[1] The five performances were on January 29 and 30; February 3, 15 and 21, 1838. See Thomas Overskou, *Den danske Skueplads i dens Historie, fra de første Spor af danske Skuespil indtil vor Tid*, vols. 1-7, Copenhagen: Samfundet til den danske Literaturs Fremme 1854-76, vol. 5, pp. 311-312. Arthur Aumont and Edgar Collin, *Det danske Nationalteater 1748-1889*, vols. 1-5, Copenhagen: J. Jørgensen 1896-1900, vol. 5.1, p. 224.

the king. The premiere was attended not just by the king and the court but also by a host of Danish and foreign diplomats, ambassadors and high-ranking officials. The theater critic and historian Thomas Overskou (1798-1873) gives a detailed account of the event. According to his description, the audience was so perplexed that no one applauded after the show was over.[1] There was a numbed silence, as people scratched their heads and looked at one another in the hope that their neighbor had understood it and could explain it.

Problems at the box office meant financial losses for the ticket scalpers, who would buy tickets for an entire loge and then sell their own tickets at a reduced rate to as many people as could fit into it. However, if the piece was unpopular, this practice was a tricky matter since it was uncertain if they could make enough money even to cover their own costs for the price of the original tickets if there were not enough people who wanted to see the piece. Overskou reports that a painfully embarrassing scene took place at the second performance, when one of the loge hucksters aggressively booed and hissed the work and encouraged the rest of the audience to do the same, in the hope that the theater's board of directors would be moved to discontinue the piece as soon as possible.

In his review of this second performance Overskou, who was a traditional ally of Heiberg, rebukes this uncultivated practice and tries to give as positive an assessment of the piece as he can.[2] He seems to support Heiberg's view that the work represents a new genre in drama since, in his defense of the piece, he argues, "it is the first work of this kind which has been brought to our stage." *Fata Morgana* was also the subject of a satirical rhymed letter that appeared in the journal *Den Frisindede*.[3] The letter, which is addressed "To a Friend in the Countryside," refers to Overskou's review as the lone supporter of Heiberg's piece: "It [sc. *Fata Morgana*] is likewise praised by no one except / the editor of the journal, *Dagen*, / who is especially pleased to find in it / a particularly brilliant presentation / of Heibergian-Hegelian philosophy / and Calderón's

---

[1] Thomas Overskou, *Den danske Skueplads*, vol. 5, p. 320.
[2] This review appears under the heading, "Kjøbenhavn, 31. Januar," *Dagen*, no. 27, January 31, 1838 (no page numbers). The review covers most of the first page.
[3] xx., "Til en Ven paa Landet," *Den Frisindede*, vol. 4, no. 13, February 13, 1838, pp. 49-50.

poetry."[1] Heiberg could not let this stand and wrote a response, also in the newspaper, *Dagen*, in which he claims that trying to please such a base and uncultivated member of the audience was like casting pearls before swine, thus alluding to the pearl, which is a central motif in the dramatic work.[2]

The important role of Heiberg's friend Hans Lassen Martensen (1808-84) in relation to all of this has in general remained unrecognized. I wish to argue that it was Martensen who provided Heiberg with the original inspiration for the piece. Moreover, while Heiberg was still licking his wounds from the poor reviews and catcalls, Martensen attempted to repair the damage by writing a defense of the work. His goal was to explain its allegorical meaning to those critics who were quick to dismiss it. What is particularly interesting about this review is that Martensen attempts to defend Heiberg's claim to have invented a new literary genre. This was a particularly controversial point, as I will try to sketch in what follows.

I. Møller's Criticism

At the beginning of the 1830s Heiberg had a good relation to the poet and philologist Poul Martin Møller (1794-1838). At this time they were both associated with the new trend of Hegelianism that they jointly defended in any number of works.[3] However, by the time of the

[1] Ibid., p. 49: "*Den roses ei heller af Nogen, undtagen / Af Redacteuren for Bladet: Dagen, / Der frydes især, ved at finde deri / Af heibergsk-hegelsk Philosophie / Og Calderonisk Poesie / En særdeles genialsk Fremstillelse.*"
[2] J.L. Heiberg, "Til Riimbrev-Skriveren i *Den Frisindede* Nr. 13," *Dagen*, no. 39, February 14, 1838 (no page numbers): "*At* Fata Morgana *Dig ei behager, / Og at i det Hele Du Perler vrager, / Er troligt, men Skylden er ikke min, / Thi skjøndt jeg en Perle har foræret, / Saa har det dog aldrig min Hensigt været, / At ville kaste Perler for Sviin.*" See also P.R., "En lille Vise for *Den Frisindede*," *Søndagen. Et Tillægsblad til Dagen*, no. 6, February 11, 1838.
[3] See Frederik Ludvig Bang Zeuthen, *Et Par Aar af mit Liv*, Copenhagen: G.E.C. Gad 1869, p. 44, where he refers as follows to his dissertation *De notione modestiae, inprimis philosophicae* (Copenhagen: J.D. Qvist 1833): "The content of the work was essentially directed against the philosophical immodesty which appeared or seemed to me to appear in Hegelianism, which in particular Heiberg and Poul Møller at that time represented in Copenhagen."

performance of *Fata Morgana* the two had had a falling out, in part due to Møller's distancing himself from Hegel's philosophy in his well-known treatise on the German debates about immortality, a work that appeared the previous year.[1] Heiberg responded to this in the first volume of his philosophical journal *Perseus* by referring to Møller as a "deserter" with regard to the cause of Hegelianism.[2]

In a letter shortly before his death, Møller gives an extended account of his view of *Fata Morgana* and its claim to originality. The letter is addressed to the poet Carsten Hauch (1790-1872) and represents a follow-up to a discussion that they had in person, perhaps on occasion of one of the performances of the piece. Møller begins in a fairly generous manner, acknowledging that the work does contain some positive poetic elements:

> I recently said some things to you on occasion of Heiberg's *Fata Morgana*, which I have hastily run through, and I now want to write down a few words about it. No one can deny that there are beautiful, well-conceived things in this poem, and it is certainly a rarity that a theater piece which was made to order, indeed, ordered with a very short deadline, was so successful.[3]

This positive tone, however, quickly changes. Møller focuses on what he regards as a misunderstanding about the nature of the work that he believes Heiberg himself is responsible for promulgating: "But I believe that the author and his friends have mistaken ideas about it. They regard it as a wholly new genre in art, to which they give the name a 'philosophical drama.'...I cannot make any sense of this."[4] Møller is

[1] Poul Martin Møller, "Tanker over Muligheden af Beviser for Menneskets Udødelighed, med Hensyn til den nyeste derhen hørende Literatur," *Maanedsskrift for Litteratur*, vol. 17, 1837, pp. 1-72, pp. 422-453.
[2] Johan Ludvig Heiberg, "Recension over Hr. Dr. Rothes *Treenigheds- og Forsoningslære,*" *Perseus, Journal for den speculative Idee*, no. 1, 1837, p. 33. (Reprinted in Heiberg's *Prosaiske Skrifter*, vol. 2, pp. 41-42. (English translation in *Heiberg's Perseus and Other Texts*, ed. and trans. by Jon Stewart, Copenhagen: Museum Tusculanum Press 2011 (*Texts from Golden Age Denmark*, vol. 6), p. 107.)
[3] *Poul Møller og hans Familie i Breve*, vols. 1-3, ed. by Morten Borup, Copenhagen: C.A. Reitzels Boghandel 1976, vol. 2, letter 168, p. 109.
[4] Ibid., vol. 2, letter 168, pp. 109f.

perplexed primarily by the claim that *Fata Morgana* represents a new genre of poetry.

He goes on to recount what he takes to be Heiberg's argument for this. What does it mean to designate a work a "philosophical drama"? Møller continues,

> It is a philosophical drama—so it is argued—for in it the "*Idea*" is expressed that there are illusions which have meaning and completely empty illusions. But it is my conviction that, taken in this manner, every true work of poetry, or almost every one, contains a "philosophical idea."...One would particularly expect a philosophical formalist such as Heiberg to recognize this. However, H.[eiberg] with his oral statements about this has put his opinion about his work into circulation, and every schoolboy who keeps step with the city's aesthetic tradition says that *Fata Morgana* is a philosophical comedy.[1]

Møller is skeptical about this claim since he fails to see anything new with respect to genre. There are many poetical works that contain various philosophical ideas. Just to make use of certain philosophical questions or doctrines in verse form is not enough to justify designating the work a new genre of poetry. The only thing new is the designation that Heiberg has given it: "philosophical drama" or "philosophical comedy." Møller seems to be correct in his assessment that this view was widely held as a result of Heiberg's influence. Many years later Hans Friedrich Helweg (1816-1901) still refers to *Fata Morgana* as a "speculative drama" in his article on Hegelianism in Denmark.[2]

As Møller notes, these terms are an echo of Heiberg's earlier designation of "speculative poetry." This was a term that Heiberg used in *On the Significance of Philosophy for the Present Age* in 1833 in order to designate the highest form of poetry at the time.[3] This was the apex

---

[1] Ibid., vol. 2, letter 168, p. 110.
[2] Hans Friedrich Helweg, "Hegelianismen i Danmark," *Dansk Kirketidende*, vol. 10, no. 51, December 16, 1855, p. 826.
[3] E.g., Johan Ludvig Heiberg, *Om Philosophiens Betydning for den nuværende Tid. Et Indbydelses-Skrift til en Række af philosophiske Forelæsninger*, Copenhagen: C.A. Reitzel 1833, pp. 36ff. (Reprinted in *Prosaiske Skrifter*, vol. 1, pp. 417ff.) (English translation in *On the Significance of Philosophy for the Present Age and Other Texts*, pp. 107ff.)

of the genres of poetry. Moreover, it was the artistic equivalent of what Hegel called "absolute knowing" in the sphere of philosophy. According to the account given there, Heiberg seems to take speculative poetry to be the ability to create a large systematic overview in the way that, for example, Dante does in the *Divine Comedy*. Then with this grand system, the author has the ability to shift perspectives from the very large to the very small, from the most abstract and sublime, to the most empirical and base. With this shift of perspective the author demonstrates his mastery of the whole and conveys the organic unity to the reader. In that work Heiberg goes through a long list of well-known poets who are either praised as "speculative" poets or criticized as reactionary, empirical poets. While the English poets bear the brunt of the hardest criticism, Goethe, Dante and Calderón come out best on his account. Given this earlier analysis, the implication seems to be that with *Fata Morgana* Heiberg is following in the footsteps of these great poets by creating a speculative drama.[1]

In his letter Møller expresses his frustration with the fact that Heiberg seems too fixated on the specific term and is not able to discuss its actual meaning. He writes in confidence to Hauch:

> What I here tell you I would never dream of saying to Heiberg himself; we have long since ceased to get along. He seems to me to have sometimes one favorite word and sometimes another with which he connects a half-mystic, wholly subjective meaning, for example, the way he once used "speculative" poetry....But when one presses him for a more precise explanation about what he actually means, then he withdraws into the snail shell of his subjectivity. He seems to me to lack either the ability or the good will for a really lively conversation in which the participants can exchange their views without reservations.[2]

Here Møller rightly associates the earlier designation "speculative poetry" with the new one "philosophical drama." Møller calls into question the meaningfulness of these designations and ultimately the originality of

---

[1] For another account of speculative poetry see Heiberg's "Til Læserne" in *Perseus, Journal for den speculative Idee*, no. 1, 1837, p. viii. (English translation: "To the Readers," in *Heiberg's Perseus and Other Texts*, p. 76)

[2] *Poul Møller og hans Familie i Breve*, vol. 2, letter 168, p. 110.

Heiberg's contribution. Although his remarks appear in a private letter, it can probably be assumed that his criticisms were shared by others at the time.

II. Martensen's Anticipation of Fata Morgana

Fata Morgana met with such misunderstanding and lack of appreciation that it seemed clear that some explanation was required. Martensen was uniquely placed to mount this defense due to his intimate knowledge of Hegel's philosophy and his friendship and private conversations with Heiberg. Thus although Martensen was known for his theology or philosophy of religion and not for his aesthetics, this review demonstrates beyond any doubt that he had a profound understanding of this field as well.

Before we turn to the review itself, Martensen's inspiration for the work should be made clear. This inspiration has not been recognized in the secondary literature, presumably because Heiberg does not mention Martensen in his introductory comments to the piece. Instead, there he names Ariosto's *Orlando Furioso* as his principal source for the work.[1] The term "fata morgana" refers to an actual meteorological phenomenon common to the Sicilian coast. It is a kind of fog that produces mirages. In Ariosto's work this is, following Sicilian tradition, represented by the fairy Morgana, who is thought to cause illusions. Heiberg then develops this figure of folklore into a major character in his piece. While Heiberg does not mention Martensen in this account, there is very good evidence that in fact it was Martensen who was, if not the original source, then the proximate source for this work.

In the first issue of Heiberg's Hegelian journal *Perseus* from 1837, Martensen published an article on a version of Faust, by the Austro-Hungarian poet Niembsch von Strehlenau (1802-50), whose pseudonym was Nicolaus Lenau.[2] This article, entitled "Observations on the Idea of

---

[1] See "Forerindring" in Johan Ludvig Heiberg, *Fata Morgana, Eventyr-Comedie*, Copenhagen: Schubothes Boghandling 1838 (on unnumbered pages). (Reprinted in Heiberg's *Poetiske Skrifter*, vol. 2, p. 95.)

[2] Nicolaus Lenau, *Faust. Ein Gedicht*, Stuttgart: Verlag der J.G. Cotta'schen Buchhandlung 1836.

Faust with Reference to Lenau's *Faust*,"[1] was a modified Danish version
of a short monograph that Martensen published upon his return from
his journey abroad,[2] during which he met Lenau in person.[3] In this work
Martensen interprets Lenau's efforts as speculative in Heiberg's sense.
He thus makes use of Heiberg's designation of speculative poetry in
order to understand Lenau's contribution and to distinguish its merits
from Goethe's famous version of the Faust legend.

In his Faust article, Martensen draws on the thesis of his dissertation,
*On the Autonomy of Human Self-Consciousness in Modern Dogmatic
Theology*.[4] This work, which appeared in the same year, argues that the
shortcoming of the modern systems of theology—primarily those of
Kant, Schleiermacher and Hegel—is that they are based on a misguided
conception of autonomy, which is the general principle of modern
thinking. The principle of autonomy undermines the true religious view
of theonomy. By claiming to know the truth by means of, for example,
pure reason or speculative dialectics, these modern thinkers deny the
need for God. By contrast, Martensen argues that we must return to a
principle of theonomy and accept our dependence on God for our lives
and truth.

Martensen then applies this theological principle from his dissertation
to the interpretation of Lenau's *Faust*. According to this view, the figure
of Faust is a paradigm case for autonomous thinking. Faust is a scholar
who has a deep-seated belief in the achievements of secular knowing. He
is proud of what the human mind can achieve on its own and not least of
all of his own learning. Martensen writes, he embodies "the deep feeling
of the corruption of the human will, its desire to transgress the divine law,
its arrogant striving to seek its center in itself instead of in God."[5] Given
this, Faust's fate is unsurprising. He has no use for God or religion. He
rejects the principle of theonomy and fails to recognize his dependence

[1] Hans Lassen Martensen, "Betragtninger over Ideen af Faust. Med Hensyn paa
Lenaus *Faust*," *Perseus, Journal for den speculative Idee*, no. 1, 1837, pp. 91-164.
[2] Johannes M.......n, *Ueber Lenau's Faust*, Stuttgart: Verlag der J.G. Cotta'schen
Buchhandlung 1836.
[3] Martensen, *Af mit Levnet. Meddelelser*, vols. 1-3, Copenhagen: Gyldendalske
Boghandels Forlag (F. Hegel & Søn) 1882-83, vol. 1, p. 167, p. 170.
[4] Johannes Martensen, *De autonomia conscientiae sui humanae in theologiam dogma-
ticam nostri temporis introducta*, Copenhagen: I.D. Quist 1837.
[5] Martensen, "Betragtninger over Ideen af Faust," p. 94.

on the divine. In his arrogance and hubris he spurns the divine. The character of Lenau's Faust thus provides Martensen with a vivid literary example of the dangers of modern thinking that he attempted to sketch in the context of theology in his dissertation.

What is of particular interest for our purposes is that Martensen draws on Heiberg's aesthetics in his analysis. Specifically, he designates Lenau's work as an example of speculative poetry. In this context he seems to mean by that via a specific character a universal type is represented. Martensen explains, speculative poetry's "essence does not lie in the poetic presentation of the external event or the development of the *single* individual, but since its creations are individuals, they are also universal and symbolic, i.e., they are absolutely penetrated by the speculative Idea, which has, so to speak, been incarnated in them."[1] Seen in this light, Faust represents symbolically the principle of modern autonomy that Martensen is so keen to sketch. Faust "represents the human race's striving to ground a realm of *intelligence* without God."[2] This is not just an individual shortcoming but, according to Martensen, it represents a general tendency of the modern age. Thus, Faust functions as a useful symbol for this.

Like Heiberg, Martensen cannot resist the temptation to give a general outline of the development of poetry through the ages. His goal is to place the Faust story in this scheme in order to understand its significance more clearly. According to this pseudoHegelian triad, there are three historical stages of poetry, each with its own paradigmatic work. The first stage is the poetry of the ancient world, and instead of choosing a well-known Greek or Roman classic, such as Homer, or Virgil or Hegel's favorite Sophocles, Martensen claims that its characteristic work is the biblical Book of Revelation.[3] Martensen's argument is that this work represents the stage of immediacy, the point in early Christianity, where the new religion definitively broke away from Judaism and the pagan religions. Martensen's second stage of poetry is the Middle Ages, and its paradigmatic work is Dante's *Divine Comedy*.[4] Heiberg had already hailed this work as a great speculative poem in *On the Significance of Philosophy*

---

[1] Ibid., p. 96.
[2] Ibid., p. 97.
[3] Ibid., pp. 99f.
[4] Ibid., pp. 100-102.

for the Present Age.[1] There Heiberg portrays Dante's masterpiece as a speculative poem because its three parts, hell, purgatory and paradise, represent the Hegelian triad of immediacy, mediation and mediated immediacy. Martensen, however, emphasizes the religious dimension, arguing that this second historical stage is that of Catholicism. The third stage is the modern world, which is associated with Protestantism.[2] This is the proper context for understanding Faust since it is, according to Martensen, the representative work of the modern world. The world of the Middle Ages was caught up in visual images and representations, and for this reason painting and the visual arts flourished. By contrast, the modern world is no longer satisfied with this sensible element and demands to know not in terms of an image or picture but in terms of a concept. Martensen is clearly influenced by Heiberg's preference for Dante and Goethe, whose Faust is obviously the important forerunner for Lenau. He thus understandably draws on Heiberg's literary heroes to illustrate the notion of speculative poetry.

In this text Martensen also takes up in two different passages the key motif of Heiberg's *Fata Morgana*, which was written only a few short months after the Faust article had appeared.[3] In the first passage in question Martensen discusses the development of human knowledge and science. He argues as follows: "In its striving for the knowledge of the speculative truth, it [sc. spirit] loses heart, and the truth of the idea seems to be a mere appearance, a *fata morgana*, when compared with the immediate, palpable reality of experience."[4] The idea here is that at the initial stage of empiricism, the human mind is captivated by the richness of the senses. Empirical experience seems to be more real and more substantive than a mere idea. Martensen employs the *fata morgana* motif in an inversion of its usual usage. It is natural to think of a *fata morgana* as representing a deception of the senses due to the fact that it

[1] Johan Ludvig Heiberg, *Om Philosophiens Betydning for den nuværende Tid*, pp. 41f. *On the Significance of Philosophy for the Present Age*, p. 110.
[2] Martensen, "Betragtninger over Ideen af Faust," pp. 102ff.
[3] In a letter dated November 25, 1837, Heiberg was requested by the Board of Directors of the Royal Theater to write a special work that could be used to celebrate the birthday of the Danish King Frederik VI. He thus had precious little time to compose the work, when one considers that it premiered on January 29, 1838. *Breve og Aktstykker vedrørende Johan Ludvig Heiberg*, vols. 1-5, ed. by Morten Borup, Copenhagen: Gyldendal 1946-50, vol. 2, Letter 377, p. 289.
[4] Martensen, "Betragtninger over Ideen af Faust," p. 114.

is a deception of the eye, the empirical faculty of vision. The eye thinks its sees something, but it turns out to be a mere mirage. Here, by contrast, Martensen turns the image on its head and refers not to the realm of the senses but to the realm of thought as a *fata morgana*. By this he wishes to underscore the ephemeral nature of ideas, which from the perspective of empiricism, seem to be insubstantial. For the empiricist, they represent an illusion with nothing behind them, whereas the world of the sense is the domicile of truth.

The second passage comes from Martensen's specific analysis of the story of Lenau's Faust. He explains how Faust disdains all of existence and attempts to eliminate it from his thinking. However, he is unable to do so since he cannot escape his own history. He is unable to create himself, as it were, *ex nihilo*, or as Martensen says, *a priori*. Martensen writes, "Thus even at the beginning of his [sc. Faust's] trip, the earth and his life's better spirits, which he had cast out, were already showing themselves in the dream's *fata morgana*, and he had to struggle with melancholy's final feeling."[1] This time the *fata morgana* does not create an illusion or hide a falsehood but rather veils something true, Faust's past. This is in accordance with Heiberg's use of the motif. Heiberg wishes to point out that there is no essence behind the appearance, no thing in itself behind the representation; in short, there is nothing that we can grasp absolutely. We are always dependent on the appearances and our ways of perceiving. Thus the truth lies not in a correspondence of the appearance with some hidden truth or reality but rather in the appearances themselves without reference to some other term. In Heiberg's play the goddess of illusion Fata Morgana says,

> I show him [sc. man] the golden phenomenon,
> His eyes are blinded, his thought captivated by it,
> And he does well to be satisfied with this;
> For if he wants to penetrate the phenomenon,
> Wants to seek the truth on the other side of it,

---

[1] Ibid., p. 154. This appears as follows in Martensen's earlier monograph in German: "*So zeigten sich ihm schon im Anfange seiner Reise die Erde und jene besseren Gestalten seines Lebens, die er von sich gestoßen hat, noch in der Fata morgana des Traumes, und er mußte mit dem letzten Gefühl der Wehmuth kämpfen.*" Johannes M........n, *Ueber Lenau's Faust*, p. 48.

Then he creates for himself the worst illusion.
For him no other truth exists,
Except that from which my mirage borrows its outline:
The magic castle which I show him in the sky,
He can find as real on earth.
But if he thinks that there is behind the heavenly image
A truth, which is not borrowed from the earth,
But comes from above to the phenomenon;
And he forces his way to see it,
Then he will meet only me, and I will destroy him.[1]

Fata Morgana attempts to cultivate the illusion of a transcendent truth beyond the appearances. But the moral to the story is, as one learns from the later school of phenomenology, that the truth is in the appearances.

Martensen clearly was aware that Heiberg was working on *Fata Morgana* intensively after he had been commissioned to produce the work at the end of November 1837. Indeed, given the references in his Faust article, it is quite possible that he discussed this motif with Heiberg during this time. In any case, he refers to it once again in a private correspondence with Heiberg on January 4, 1838, only three weeks before the premiere of the piece. In the letter Martensen announces to Heiberg that he is engaged to be married:

I have followed your own guidelines and struggled against it [sc. marriage] as long as I could. The opinion cannot, however, be that such a conflict should continue in a bad infinity, or when it is once sublated, that it should end with a merely negative result. On the contrary—if love is more than a *fata morgana*—and mine certainly is, then the result must be the knowledge that it is not some illusion, regardless of the finite view it could easily seem

---

[1] Heiberg, *Fata Morgana*, p. 26. (*Poetiske Skrifter*, vol. 2, pp. 121f.) *"Jeg viser ham det gyldne Phænomen, / Hans Øie blendes, Tanken fanges i det, / Og klogt han gjør at slaae sig der til Ro; / Thi vil han Phænomenet gjennemtrænge, / Vil søge Sandhed paa dets anden Side, / Da skaber han sig selv det værste Blendværk. / For ham er ingen anden Sandhed til, / End den, hvoraf mit Luftsyn laaner Omrids: / Det Trylleslot, jeg viser ham paa Himlen, / Det kan han finde virkeligt paa Jorden. / Men troer han, at der bag et himmelsk Billed / En Sandhed er, som laantes ei fra Jorden, / Men kommer ovenfra til Phænomenet; / Og trænger han igjennem for at see den, / Da møder han kun mig, og jeg ham knuser."*

to be; it must be recognized as an absolute reality, an ideal power, which can be reconciled but not reasoned away.[1]

Clearly, there is a playful tone in this letter. Martensen refers to a number of philosophical motifs that both he and Heiberg had discussed and written about, especially in connection with Hegel's philosophy: the bad infinity, the sublation of the negative, the finite and the infinite, etc. The allusion to the illusion of love as a *fata morgana* can hardly be coincidental. By declaring his love to be more than a *fata morgana*, Martensen makes explicit appeal to a motif that Heiberg was working on at the time. This might be taken as evidence that he had perhaps already seen part of Heiberg's work in progress. In any case, given all this, there can be little doubt that Martensen was a cardinal source of inspiration for the piece.

III. Martensen's Review of Fata Morgana

Martensen's defense of Heiberg came in the form of a review that appeared in the *Maanedsskrift for Litteratur* for April of 1838.[2] As he was writing the review, he shared it with Heiberg both orally and in writing. This is clear from what Heiberg writes in a letter to Martensen, dated March 5, 1838:

> Perhaps we could soon have the pleasure of hearing your review from start to finish. We are all longing very much for this, and I, for my part, cannot omit repeating my thanks for the great pleasure which you gave me the day before yesterday by communicating to me a large part of it. Not only was I glad to see so many points of my own aesthetic view set forth with such talent that I must hope that they in this way will find entry among the reading public, but also your presentation of my own poetic activity has, so to speak, raised me in my own eyes and is for me almost the dearest reward that I have yet received for it.[3]

---

[1] *Breve og Aktstykker vedrørende Johan Ludvig Heiberg*, vol. 2, Letter 381, p. 293.

[2] Martensen, "*Fata Morgana, Eventyr-Comedie* af Johan Ludvig Heiberg. 1838. 125 S. 8°. Kjøbenhavn. Schubothes Boghandling," *Maanedsskrift for Litteratur*, vol. 19, 1838, pp. 361-397.

[3] *Breve og Aktstykker vedrørende Johan Ludvig Heiberg*, vol. 2, Letter 389, p. 298.

Here one can see confirmation that Martensen's review is wholly in line with Heiberg's intentions and the Heibergian aesthetics in general. Heiberg seems particularly impressed with Martensen's gift for communicating some of these difficult ideas in a didactically effective manner. Just as Heiberg was enthusiastic about the draft that he saw, so also was he profoundly moved by the published version of the review when it appeared a few weeks later. In a letter dated April 1, he writes the following words of unrestrained praise to Martensen: "I have now also read your review slowly and carefully so that I could give myself the chance to examine every word in it. It is without doubt the best treatise on aesthetics which has been yet produced in this country."[1]

Martensen organizes his review of *Fata Morgana* in the same way that he did his article on Lenau's *Faust*. He uses the first part to give a general assessment about the current status of poetry and dramatic poetry in particular, and then the second part is dedicated to a more detailed examination of the work under review.

Martensen takes some of his inspiration from the first two volumes of Hegel's *Lectures on Aesthetics* that had recently appeared.[2] Hegel traces how different forms of art come and go with specific historical time periods. As the human spirit develops, so also do the different artistic genres. Certain forms of art appeal to the human mind at a rudimentary stage, but then seem hollow and lifeless once that stage has been surpassed. Each historical epoch thus has its own preferred form of art, which matches its own level of development. Heiberg had also defended this view in *On the Significance of Philosophy for the Present Age.* Now Martensen takes it up again. His claim is that with the development of the human spirit, poetry and specifically dramatic poetry has been displaced from its once central role in culture. He regrets that it is no longer taken seriously as it once was. The reason for this, he argues, is that the human mind has progressed to a higher level, and dramatic writers

---

[1] Ibid., vol. 2, Letter 394, p. 304.
[2] *Vorlesungen über die Aesthetik*, vols. I-III, ed. by Heinrich Gustav Hotho, vols. 10.1-3 [1835-38], in *Georg Wilhelm Friedrich Hegel's Werke. Vollständige Ausgabe*, vols. 1-18, ed. by Ludwig Boumann, Friedrich Förster, Eduard Gans, Karl Hegel, Leopold von Henning, Heinrich Gustav Hotho, Philipp Marheineke, Karl Ludwig Michelet, Karl Rosenkranz, and Johannes Schulze, Berlin: Verlag von Duncker und Humblot 1832-45.

have not kept pace. Thus, they continue to produce works that are no longer appealing to the intellect of the modern age. As a result, theater in general looks lifeless and uninteresting as a genre. The challenge that confronts the modern age is then to develop drama further so that it better suits the needs of the modern audience. The present age is thus in a crisis—to use Heiberg's expression—since it wallows in an indeterminacy and uncertainty as it taps in the dark, searching for a new form of poetry in step with the time.

In this context Martensen launches into a polemic against Romantic poetry, which he regards as characteristic of the artistic crisis of the age. Romanticism presents truth and beauty as something abstract or unattainable.[1] Truth is something out of reach for human beings, a mere idea that we hope for or long after. The present age is thus lost in a relativism or agnosticism that is unsatisfying for those who take art seriously and regard it as a vessel of truth. The Romantics enjoy pointing out to their readers the transitoriness of human existence and empirical things. All truth claims and beliefs are hollow since the real truth cannot be obtained. In this crisis human beings simply wallow in a confused jumble of appearances with no truth or validity. Since, for the Romantics, we are only left with mutable and transitory appearances, there is in effect no truth. Martensen argues that the key to the solution to this crisis is to realize that there is a truth in the appearances themselves and that there is no need to posit some transcendent sphere in order to validate them.[2] Specifically, the speculative Idea can be found in the perceived phenomena and not outside them. Here one can start to see the point of Heiberg's *Fata Morgana*. It demonstrates this philosophical insight by means of dramatic poetry.

In this context Martensen makes his central claim that Heiberg has in fact managed to create the new poetic genre that is needed, and that *Fata Morgana* is the first example of this. Thus Martensen not only attempts to defend or explain the misunderstood work, but his claim is far more ambitious: *Fata Morgana* represents the solution to the current crisis of art. Here it is clear that there is much more riding on the question posed at the outset, namely, whether or not this work represents a new poetic

---

[1] Martensen, "*Fata Morgana, Eventyr-Comedie af* Johan Ludvig Heiberg," pp. 370f.
[2] Ibid., p. 373.

genre. Now what is at stake is no less than the salvation of art as such in a confused age. For Martensen to make this plausible, he must persuade his readers that in fact Heiberg has developed a new genre; for indeed if he is simply repeating an old genre, then he too would be stuck in the same reactionary situation as the other dramatic authors who fail to realize that human spirit has moved on, while they continue to produce the same old works. Instead, Martensen's case must be that Heiberg has rightly diagnosed the artistic crisis of the day and has offered the age a concrete solution to it by means of an entirely new poetic genre that is consonant with the current historical level of spiritual and intellectual development.

Martensen tries to make his case by arguing that the human mind has reached the level of speculative thinking. It is no longer satisfied with grandiose displays for the sense, but rather now the mind wants to understand by means of the speculative Idea. For this reason speculative poetry is a perfectly understandable solution since it attempts to do just this: to demonstrate the truth of the speculative Idea by means of poetic expression or in the case of *Fata Morgana* by means of dramatic-poetic expression.[1]

According to Martensen's interpretation, Heiberg's piece points the way towards human freedom. The message of the work is that we can break out of the current crisis of relativism and nihilism if we have the will for action. But in order to do so, we must follow the lead of Clotaldo, who destroys the illusions of the goddess Fata Morgana by destroying the magic pearl, which is responsible for creating the illusions.[2] Once this is done, then we will be able to grasp the truth of the appearances. Again the sphere of truth and beauty will be available to humanity.[3] This is a defiant act that each individual must undertake for him- or herself. After he sees the beauty of his beloved Margarita, Clotaldo says in delight, "I feel my mind liberated, / When I sacrifice the image of the illusion / for the true appearance."[4] At first, he was enchanted and infatuated by the

---

[1] Ibid., p. 367.
[2] Ibid., p. 391.
[3] Ibid., p. 389.
[4] Heiberg, *Fata Morgana*, p. 45. (*Poetiske Skrifter*, vol. 2, p. 141.) *"Frigjort føler jeg mit Sind, / Naar jeg offrer Illusionens / Blendværk for det sande Skin."*

Johanne Luise Heiberg and N.P. Nielsen in Fata Morgana *(1838)*
(Colored copper engrawing by Christian Wolmar Bruun in his
Danske Theater-Costumer, Copenhagen: n.p. 1826.)

imaginary picture of the princess in his mind, but this is discarded when he perceives her true beauty in person, that is, the empirical beauty that corresponds to the speculative Concept. At the end Clotaldo enjoins the audience to a similar act of rebellion. When he receives the Duke's sword for his heroic services, he declares, "With this sword I will be reminded of / The fight which is made for the actual; / And the poet in his world of images / Shall not himself be held in illusions / But struggle for the real truth."[1] Finally, in his triumphant speech to Fata Morgana, Clotaldo defiantly exclaims in their decisive violent encounter, "Poetry is truth, although it / Consists of images."[2]

---

[1] Heiberg, *Fata Morgana,* p. 62. (*Poetiske Skrifter,* vol. 2, p. 160.) *"Ved dette Sværd skal jeg erindres om / Den Kamp, der for det Virkelige føres; / Og Digteren skal i sin Billedverden / Ei være selv i Illusioner hildet, / Men kæmpe for den virkelige Sandhed."*

[2] Heiberg, *Fata Morgana,* p. 112. (*Poetiske Skrifter,* vol. 2, p. 212.) *"Poesie er Sandhed, om den / End i Billeder bestaaer."*

Martensen points out Heiberg's critical portrayal of Pierrot, the president of the Academy of Sciences, and Arlechino, the Superintendent of the Academy of Arts.[1] These figures are keen to maintain the status quo and to cultivate the world of illusions, and thus they guard the pearl as something precious. But by doing so, they prevent humanity from rising above the current crisis and seeing its correct solution. This is clearly a critical reference to Heiberg's contemporaries, who are, in his view, overly fixated on the empirical and who fail to see the truth of the speculative Idea. These are the same people that Heiberg's speculative journal *Perseus* is intended to do battle with.

Martensen attempts to understand *Fata Morgana* in the context of the general overview of the development of poetry as it appears in Hegel. According to Hegel's hierarchy, comedy is a higher dramatic form than tragedy.[2] While tragedy still takes seriously the reality of established customs, institutions and the external world generally, comedy calls all of this into question. In so doing, it shifts the locus of truth to the individual. Thus the principle of subjective freedom is introduced. Martensen explains, "Comedy rests on the doctrine that the mundane does not exist; its principle can be designated, to use a word which Hegel has introduced in a different context, as *acosmism* or the denial of the reality of the mundane, while tragedy, by contrast, rests on the conviction of the absolute reality of mundane endeavors and interests."[3] Given that comedy is the highest dramatic form, it is natural for Heiberg to make use of it in his attempt to create something even higher. Thus, while *Fata Morgana* may look on the face of it to be simply a traditional form of comedy, in fact with its use of Hegelian speculative thinking, it presents something new that goes beyond the standard forms of comedy.

IV. Critical Evaluation

Given this analysis, it is clear that the goal of Martensen's review is far more ambitious than a simple *apologia* for a box office fiasco. In fact, he addresses a major issue about the current status of art in society in general.

---

[1] Martensen, "*Fata Morgana, Eventyr-Comedie* af Johan Ludvig Heiberg," pp. 396f.
[2] Ibid., p. 376.
[3] Ibid., p. 378.

Given his agreement with Heiberg about the current artistic crisis of the age, his attempt to see Heiberg's *Fata Morgana* as a solution to it makes perfect sense. Since the age now demands speculative knowing, it is only appropriate that art meet this demand by creating works that produce this speculative knowing in different artistic forms. Given that Hegel had in his lectures traced the development of art to its end in drama, which then had its end in comedy, it was natural for Heiberg to use comedy as his point of departure since that was, up until that point, the highest form of art. He then simply needed to modify this by adding a speculative dimension to it. Thus Heiberg attempts to put a new gem in the Hegelian crown by taking the next step. Just as the present age needs Hegelian speculative philosophy to emerge from its crisis of knowing, so also it needs speculative drama in order to emerge from its crisis of art.

Heiberg, Martensen and Overskou all attempt to play down the fact that the work was a disaster with the audience; they appeal to the argument that this was understandable given that Heiberg's piece was something pioneering and entirely new. However, the reaction of the audience can be interpreted in a different manner. It might well be taken as evidence that in fact there was no grand crisis of the age as Heiberg claims. Perhaps the theater-going public was not, after all, yearning for something new. Perhaps the demands of the age were met perfectly well by other more traditional works. The fact that the audience did not understand the piece can be taken as evidence that the age was perhaps not yet ready for speculative knowing. In *On the Significance of Philosophy for the Present Age*, Heiberg talks about how specific gifted individuals such as Goethe or Hegel in effect run ahead of the common mass of humanity and lay the groundwork for their epoch. They thus play an ambiguous dual role as being, on the one hand, representatives of their age and, on the other, misunderstood anticipators of a new age, who will only be truly understood by a future generation.[1] Heiberg acknowledges that the work of Goethe has been at least in some respects appropriated by his contemporaries; however, Hegel's work remains poorly understood and is still waiting to be embraced by the wider masses.[2] With the

---

[1] Heiberg, *Om Philosophiens Betydning for den nuværende Tid*, pp. 36f. *On the Significance of Philosophy for the Present Age*, pp. 107f.

[2] Heiberg, *Om Philosophiens Betydning for den nuværende Tid*, pp. 50f. *On the Significance of Philosophy for the Present Age*, pp. 116f.

disappointing reception of the piece, Heiberg could perhaps congratulate himself as being one of the harbingers of the new age, but it could be that he simply got his diagnosis of his contemporary historical period all wrong.

With regard to the question of the novelty of *Fata Morgana* as a new genre, one can also claim that this remains an open and ambiguous issue. While Møller's objection that many poetic works contain philosophical motifs seems immediately intuitive, it cannot be denied that drama has developed enormously since Heiberg's time and perhaps his dramatic works played some role in these developments. In order to make good on the argument that Martensen wants to make on Heiberg's behalf, one would have to claim that these later developments have more and more invested drama with elements of Hegel's philosophy. This would of course be a difficult case to make since Hegel's philosophy is today no more generally accepted or intuitive than it was in Heiberg's time. However, one might nonetheless still try to argue that with the subsequent developments in, for example, the visual arts that art has become more about the cognitive dimension than about the sensible one. Indeed, today some special training in modern aesthetics or art theory is virtually a requirement for an appreciation of contemporary art works. With regard to theater specifically, the so-called theater of the absurd, made famous by Beckett and Ionesco in the 1950s and '60s, clearly rests on an abstract theoretical foundation that is not necessarily immediately obvious from the absurd dramas themselves. Thus in order to make any sense of these pieces, one must be familiar with the theory that informs them. This is something cognitive and not something empirical. On this point the Hegelian aestheticians seem to be correct: modern art appeals more to the intellect than to the senses. But Heiberg's influence and role in this wider development of art remains an open question.

Kierkegaard's Hidden Satire on Heiberg's Poetics of the Vaudeville in *Either/Or* and *Repetition*

Mads Sohl Jessen

I. *The Thesis of the Article*

Danish Golden Age writers were generally much more aware of polemics and satire as rich literary traditions dating back to Greek and Roman antiquity than Danish writers today. Søren Kierkegaard at one time before settling on the theme of Socrates and the concept of irony thought of writing his master's thesis on the Roman satirists.[1] Kierkegaard also refers in a journal entry from 1847 to polemics as one of his own definite character traits. Poul Martin Møller had called him "the most thoroughly polemical human being,"[2] a phrase which Kierkegaard did not seem to have had any objections to. Likewise Johan Ludvig Heiberg in the foreword to the publication of his three tomes of

---

[1] *SKS* 17, 241, DD:58 / *KJN* 1, 232. (*SKS* = *Søren Kierkegaards Skrifter*, vols. 1-28, K1-K28, ed. by Niels Jørgen Cappelørn, et al., Copenhagen: Gads Forlag 1997-2013. *KJN* = *Kierkegaard's Journals and Notebooks*, vols. 1–11, ed. by Niels Jørgen Cappelørn, Alastair Hannay, David Kangas, Bruce H. Kirmmse, George Pattison, Vanessa Rumble, and K. Brian Söderquist, Princeton and Oxford: Princeton University Press 2007ff.) For an introduction to Kierkegaard's reading of the Roman satirists see *Kierkegaard and the Roman World*, ed. by Jon Stewart, Aldershot: Ashgate 2009 (*Kierkegaard Research: Sources, Reception and Resources*, vol. 3).

[2] *SKS* 20, 83, NB:107. For an article on Kierkegaard's relations with Møller, see Finn Gredal Jensen, "Poul Martin Møller: Kierkegaard and the Confidant of Socrates" in *Kierkegaard and His Danish Contemporaries*, Tome I, *Philosophy, Politics and Social Theory*, ed. by Jon Stewart, Aldershot: Ashgate 2009 (*Kierkegaard Research: Sources, Reception and Resources*, vol. 7), pp. 101-168.

prose writings, published in 1841-43, underlines the fact that "a lot of my shorter writings are polemical; indeed those which do not contain traces of polemics constitute a very minor part of the shorter writings."[1] It could be argued that Heiberg and Kierkegaard, as literary writers, do not distinguish between high literature and low polemics and satire as we tend to do now.

Reading Heiberg's genre manifesto *On Vaudeville* from 1826 one can easily detect his polemical drive. Heiberg is especially frustrated by one objection against his first vaudevilles from 1825-26 which he wants to contest: "What is the main reason our reviewers fault them? First and foremost that they are farces and buffoonery and marketplace pieces."[2] On the next page Heiberg calls these reviewers "critical cockerels," and taunts them by calling them mere dilettantes.[3] Heiberg is preoccupied with differentiating his own vaudevilles from the concept of farce in *On Vaudeville*. It is clear that Heiberg found highly objectionable the claim that there was no real difference between ordinary farce and his own vaudevilles.

In this article a specific thesis on Kierkegaard's highly complex relations to Heiberg will be put forward. It will be argued that Kierkegaard, when writing the sixth text in the first part of *Either/Or*, "The First Love. A Comedy in One Act by Scribe. Translated by J.L. Heiberg," undertakes a hidden satire on Heiberg as a vaudeville translator and canonizer of the contemporary French vaudeville writer Augustin Eugène Scribe (1791-1861). Furthermore, it will be maintained that Heiberg was so infuriated by this satire that he sought to retaliate by secretly polemicizing

[1] Johan Ludvig Heiberg, "Fortale," in *Prosaiske Skrifter* vols. 1-3, Copenhagen: J.H. Schubothes Boghandling 1841-43, vol. 1, p. vii.
[2] Heiberg, *Om Vaudevillen, som dramatisk Digtart, og om dens Betydning paa den danske Skueplads*, Copenhagen: Jens Hofstrup Schulz 1826, p. 64 (in *Prosaiske Skrifter*, vol, 1, p. 204).
[3] For a reprint of some of these reviews see Morten Borup, *Johan Ludvig Heiberg* vols. 1-3, Copenhagen: Gyldendal 1947-49, vol. 2, pp. 199-209. For an introduction to the emergence of Heiberg's vaudevilles in Copenhagen theater life, see Julius Clausen, *Kulturhistoriske Studier over Heibergs Vaudeviller*, Copenhagen: Fr. G. Knudtzons Bogtrykkeri 1909, pp. 5-29. See also Kirsten Wechsel's article: "Herkunftstheater. Zur Regulierung von Legitimität im Streit um die Gattung Vaudeville," in *Faszination des Illegitimen. Alterität in Konstruktionen von Genealogie, Herkunft und Ursprünglichkeit in den skandinavischen Literaturen seit 1800*, ed. by Constanze Gestrich and Thomas Mohnike, Würzburg: Ergon Verlag 2007, pp. 39-60.

against the author of *Either/Or* in four different articles in his journal *Intelligensblade* in 1843. Kierkegaard was well aware of these attacks and was set for a covert literary fight with Heiberg; he therefore takes his own sort of highly original revenge by writing *Repetition*. Thus it is part of the thesis of the article that Constantin Constantius' sarcastic deliberations on the writer of *"posse"* are to be read as an analogous hidden satire of Heiberg's career as a vaudeville writer. To sum up the thesis, it could be said that Kierkegaard in issuing these satires in *Either/Or* and *Repetition* is actually aligning himself with Heiberg's early reviewers. However, whereas the early reviewers try to mock Heiberg's vaudevilles in a direct and straightforward way for being farces, Kierkegaard in his indirect and subtle manner especially targets Heiberg's poetics of the vaudeville as it is set forth in *On Vaudeville*.

II. *An Elaboration*

In my dissertation I tried to present a new thesis on Kierkegaard's highly complex relations to Heiberg by contending that Kierkegaard already began to secretly polemicize against Heiberg in 1838 in the foreword to his first independent publication, *From the Papers of One Still Living*.[1] Though most Kierkegaard scholars have so far been negatively disposed to this thesis, there is some degree of consensus that I may be right in arguing that Kierkegaard is not in any way praising Heiberg in the last chapter of his master's thesis *On the Concept of Irony* from 1841, which the discovery of some highly negative allusions to Heiberg's writings shows.[2] The Danish word *"tyvesproget"* (literally, thief language) from the title of my dissertation cannot be translated directly into English. Generally in Danish a *"tyvesprog"* is defined as a "language which is only understandable to a certain group of initiated people."[3] In this definition

---

[1] The thesis and readings of this article are based on the ones to be found in my *Tyvesprogets mester. Kierkegaards skjulte satire over Heiberg i* Gjentagelsen, Copenhagen: Unpublished Ph.D. dissertation 2010.

[2] See Mads Sohl Jessen, "Kierkegaard's Hidden Polemics against Heiberg and Martensen in the Last Chapter of *On the Concept of Irony*," *Danske Studier*, 2010, pp. 95-106.

[3] *Ordbog over det danske Sprog* 1-28, founded by V. Dahlerup, Det Danske Sprog- og Litteraturselskab, Copenhagen: Gyldendal 1918-56, vol. 24, column 1369.

it is taken for granted that the users of a *"tyvesprog"* are in positive
agreement as to the rules of the language. In my use of the concept I try
to highlight an opposite and very difficult aspect of Kierkegaard's literary
rhetoric. The thesis can be formulated in this way: Kierkegaard's allusions
are extremely difficult to grasp because he only wanted his polemical
enemies to understand them; among Kierkegaard's contemporaries the
initiated people of his *"tyvesprog"* were potentially his opponents.

Morten Borup, Heiberg's great biographer, stated "it is evident that
the polemical Kierkegaard has been a pupil in J.L. Heiberg's school."[1]
I think Borup is right. Heiberg was Kierkegaard's important precursor
on this very point. Heiberg did himself conduct very complicated
pseudonymous polemics in his first journal *Kjøbenhavns flyvende Post*
(1827-28, 1830, 1834-37), and Kierkegaard surely studied these with
a very deft ear and mind. In terms of pseudonymous writing, Heiberg
and Kierkegaard agreed on these two laws: "Do not reveal an allusion!"
and "If you do, you are an amateur in the art of polemics and satire!"
Neither of these two writers were amateurs in literary warfare, though
only Kierkegaard knew how to turn it into great literature. Kierkegaard
was a very fierce upstart crow in the art of hidden satire in Golden Age
Denmark in the early 1840s, and he was set on making Heiberg, the man
of cultural power, his chosen secret target.

III. An Example of Analysis

In a journal entry from 1848 Kierkegaard, well aware that posterity would
study his journals, confirms that he has "an inborn talent for intrigues,"[2]
and as late as 1854 Kierkegaard even affirms that "I have far more
intelligence, far more intrigue than the most intelligent and scheming
man among my contemporaries."[3] The concepts of intrigue and scheme
are not used in a negative sense in this article, but on the contrary as
objective terms. For Kierkegaard, literary intrigues were to some degree
simply the way to write excellent literature. This may seem farfetched to

---

[1] Borup, *Johan Ludvig Heiberg*, vol. 2, p. 104.
[2] *SKS* 21, 176, NB6:55.
[3] *SKS* 25, 462, NB30:94.

some readers, but one example of the way of reading Kierkegaard that I am in favor of might be useful here.

Henning Fenger wrote, "large parts of *Either/Or* are aesthetic analyses from the 1830s in the spirit of Heiberg."[1] I would argue that Kierkegaard, on the contrary, is parodying and scheming against Heiberg's aesthetic analyses in the first part of his debut as a pseudonymous writer. For example, the aesthete in "The Immediate Erotic States" might seem to offer Heiberg a great acknowledgement when he compares him to Molière and states that Heiberg's version of "Don Juan" has the virtue of being "more correct"[2] than Molière's. Kierkegaard apparently seems to imply that Heiberg's achievement is even greater than Molière's, but one needs to bear in mind that to be "more correct" is in aesthetic terms a rather ambivalent sort of praise. Kierkegaard is actually alluding to a striking phrase on the last page of Heiberg's *On Vaudeville*, where Heiberg in a humoristic way is trying to be modest (and perhaps turns out to be the opposite according to Kierkegaard): "I dare to say, that if my genius were as great as my taste is correct, I would venture to compare myself with any of our poets."[3] Heiberg's version of *Don Juan* is to be found in *Marionette Theater* from 1814, which, besides *Don Juan*, consists of another work called *Walter the Potter*. Heiberg writes in the foreword in regard to the latter piece: "The second piece is less fearfully presented to the audience than the first, since there is no famous example, with which it can be compared; it is wholly, both in regard to invention and execution, a free play of the writer's own fantasy."[4] Writing a play entitled "Don Juan," Heiberg was aware that he might be faced with critical comparisons to Molière. Kierkegaard's aesthete can be said to make a parodying inversion of Heiberg's use of the concept of correctness. For Heiberg, the concept refers to matters of taste, but the aesthete uses it to denote the internal aesthetic quality of a specific work. Where Heiberg in fact had been expressing "fearful" modesty in regard to the possible comparison to Molière's masterpiece, the aesthete ludicrously

---

[1] Henning Fenger, *Familjen Heiberg*, Copenhagen: Museum Tusculanum Press, p. 8.
[2] *SKS* 2, 113 / *EO2*, 110.
[3] Heiberg, *Om Vaudevillen*, p. 98 (in *Prosaiske Skrifter*, vol. 1, pp. 246f.).
[4] Heiberg, *Marionettheater*, Copenhagen: Fr. Brummer 1814, the foreword is not paginated.

lauds his play for being more correct than Molière's. Kierkegaard, in his *"tyvesprog,"* is actually teasing Heiberg by alluding to this very sentence from *On Vaudeville*, and I think one would be mistaken if one were to believe that Heiberg was not capable of understanding Kierkegaard's ironic allusions.

Kierkegaard's literary intrigue in this text is more complicated than this example reveals, but suffice it to say that it may be fruitful to investigate *Either/Or* from a completely new perspective. Instead of seeing this work as a "Heibergian apprentice work,"[1] as has been customary in the reception history of Kierkegaard's pseudonymous debut, it should be examined as an anti-Heibergian apprentice work.

IV. Scribe as a Didactic Poet

Kierkegaard traveled to Berlin on the 25th of October 1841 for his first and longest trip to the capital of Prussia. He returned to Copenhagen on the 6th of March 1842. In a letter to his friend Emil Boesen from the 14th of December 1841, Kierkegaard writes: "NB send me as soon as you can: *The First Love*, translated by Heiberg; you can find it in the Theater Repertoire and buy it at Schubothe, but don't let anyone know it is for me."[2] Schubothe was a bookshop in Copenhagen. Boesen most likely complied and sent Heiberg's translation of the French dramatist's work to Kierkegaard's address in Berlin. It is thus possible to conclude that Kierkegaard already at the end of 1841 had a specific text in mind that would end up having an ambiguous title: "The First Love: A Comedy in One Act by Scribe, translated by J.L. Heiberg." What seems to be Kierkegaard's irony in his choice of title? One must notice that the title has not been formulated by Kierkegaard himself. Kierkegaard has simply quoted the title of Heiberg's translation exactly as it appears in the Theater Repertoire. Kierkegaard could thus be said to insinuate that to invent an original title for a review of this piece of drama is not even worth the effort. Who was Scribe?

---

[1] Henning Fenger, *Kierkegaard-Myter og Kierkegaard-Kilder*, Odense: Odense Universitetsforlag 1976, p. 193.

[2] *Breve & Aktstykker vedrørende Søren Kierkegaard*, vols. 1-2, ed. by Niels Thulstrup, Copenhagen: Munksgaard 1953, vol. 1, p. 82.

The French dramatist Augustin Eugène Scribe (1791-1861) governed Parisian theater life for 40 years, producing around 350 vaudevilles, comedies, and operettas; most of them were collaborative efforts. Between 1824 and 1874 Scribe was the most played dramatist at the Royal Theater, where he with the mediation by J.L. Heiberg had around 100 pieces performed.[1]

In the 1830s Heiberg must have spent quite a lot of time translating Scribean drama to be used at the Royal Theater in Copenhagen. *The First Love* was one of Scribe's greatest successes in Denmark. The Heiberg bibliographer C.J. Ballhausen mentions, "it was played 139 times, from June 10, 1831 to 1887."[2] Though Scribe is not well-known today, many among Kierkegaard's contemporaries knew who he was, and in Denmark his name was inevitably linked to that of Heiberg.

The ethical narrator of the second part of *Either/Or*, Judge William, mentions Scribe in both his letters to the young aesthete. The first time makes it clear that William has read the nameless aesthete's review of *The First Love*: "I recall that you once sent me a little review of Scribe's *The First Love* that was written with almost desperate enthusiasm. In it, you claimed that it was the best Scribe had ever written and that this piece alone, properly understood, was sufficient to make him immortal."[3] Reading this paragraph from the second letter, it is obvious that William's hero is by no means impressed by Scribe's comedy:

> Our hero has seen your favorite play, *The First Love*. He does not credit himself with enough culture to be able to evaluate the play esthetically, but he finds it unfair of the author to have Charles sink so low in the eight years. He readily admits that such a thing can happen in life, but he does not believe that this is what we ought to learn from a writer.[4]

By using the verb "learn" Kierkegaard is alluding to Heiberg's canonization of Scribe in *On the Significance of Philosophy for the Present Age* from 1833:

---

[1] Quoted from *SKS* K2-3, p. 175.
[2] C.J. Ballhausen, *Peter Andreas & Johan Ludvig Heiberg. En annoteret bibliografi*, Copenhagen: C.A. Reitzels Forlag 2000, p. 125.
[3] *SKS* 3, 27-28 / *EO2*, 19.
[4] *SKS* 3, 283-284 / *EO2*, 300.

Scribe, who with hundreds of works, clothed in the most popular form, i.e., theatrical works, won the constant praise and thundering applause of both the cultured and the uncultured masses, while he, like the speculative philosopher, set down in these works—which are admired by the cultured public and the riffraff alike—his age's highest perception and deepest comprehension of nature, the state, religion, philosophy—in short, of all life's interests. He was also a didactic poet.[1]

According to Heiberg's genre system, the "didactic poet" represents the summit of literary greatness. Heiberg's Danish word for "didactic poet" is *"læredigter."* By writing, "He was also a didactic poet," Heiberg in fact is arguing that Scribe is on the same level as Dante, Calderón and Goethe. Kierkegaard ridicules this paragraph by jokingly insinuating that what one can learn from the great *"læredigter"* Augustin Eugène Scribe is to become a sort of immoral scoundrel like Charles. Kierkegaard, again in his "thief language," is directing sentences like this one directly at Heiberg, when William in the same letter rhetorically asks: "I wonder if Scribe is so modest as to assume that one learns nothing at all from his plays."[2] Kierkegaard is thus using William as narrator to secretly point the finger at Heiberg's earlier idolization of Scribe as a *"læredigter."* This may be one of the reasons why Heiberg chose to attack Kierkegaard in his review of *Either/Or,* an attack which will be analyzed in section VII below.

V. Heiberg's Two Notes on Scribe in Prose Writings

Between 1841 and 1843 Heiberg published his three volumes of prose writings. In the first volume the reader can find his manifesto on vaudeville. Heiberg wrote a number of notes for this republication, including two on Scribe: "In terms of the direction Scribe in his later years has given his *singspiel* and vaudeville, he has too clearly demonstrated what one

---

[1] Johan Ludvig Heiberg, *Om Philosophiens Betydning for den nuværende Tid,* Copenhagen: C.A. Reitzel 1833, pp. 41-42. (English translation: *On the Significance of Philosophy for the Present Age and Other Texts,* ed. and trans. by Jon Stewart, Copenhagen: C.A. Reitzel 2005, p. 111.)

[2] *SKS* 3, 307 / *EO2,* 325.

would reluctantly believe: he is, despite his great talent, not even a poet."[1] Heiberg's note clearly has a defensive character, since some readers would be capable of remembering that it was Heiberg himself who had canonized Scribe in 1833 as a "didactic poet" worthy of comparison with Dante, Calderón and Goethe. Heiberg's second note has a more moralistic form. Heiberg writes that the accusation against Scribe that "he really does not know good company and brings the culture of his compatriots in neglect"[2] becomes more and more founded. Heiberg certainly no longer wishes to suggest that Scribe belongs to the great company of didactic poets whom everybody has something to learn from. On the contrary, Scribe is now to be seen as a morally corrupt poet with no great merits to his name. Kierkegaard was most likely aware of these two notes, and it is not impossible that the notes were Kierkegaard's starting point for inventing his text. When Judge William argues that nothing is to be learnt from Scribe, Kierkegaard on a deeper ironic level can be said, not only to remind Heiberg of his former infatuation with the French dramatist but also to accuse him of being an aesthetic turncoat since he recently disavowed his former passion for Scribe.

VI. The Aesthete's Ambivalent Appraisal of Scribe's Comedy

If we turn to the aesthete's review of *The First Love* one is surprised at the number of pages the narrator spends on making hyperbolic comments on this one-act comedy. Indeed one begins to wonder if the aesthete is sincere in his appraisal of Scribe, when he starts his analysis by stating: "*The First Love*, however, is a flawless play, so consummate that it alone is bound to make Scribe immortal."[3] The narrator does not say that the comedy is a masterpiece because it contains extraordinary aesthetic qualities; it seems rather to be his choice of interpretation of Scribe's intention which decides its status as a great work: "If this is the intention, then *The First Love* is changed from a masterpiece to a

---

[1] Heiberg, "Om Vaudevillen," in *Prosaiske Skrifter*, vol. 1, p. 180, note. (This note and the next one were added in the reprinted version of the text in *Prosaiske Skrifter* and thus do not appear in the first edition.)

[2] Heiberg, "Om Vaudevillen," in *Prosaiske Skrifter*, vol. 1, p. 222, note.

[3] *SKS* 2, 241 / *EO1*, 248.

theatrical triviality."[1] Though the aesthete apparently argues that this is not the case, he does in his indirect way acknowledge the possibility of a deeply flawed play when analyzing the main female character: "If the play is interpreted in this way, then her concluding lines are even profound; whereas in the other case, to me at least, it is impossible to find any meaning in them."[2] Indeed, he does not even hide that its status as a masterpiece definitely rests on the interpreter's choice: "Therefore, since there is the choice between reducing Scribe's play to a triviality by insisting that there is something in it that cannot be established or delighting in a masterpiece by being able to explain everything, the choice seems easy."[3] Kierkegaard is more than insinuating that it is all up to the interpreter to decide for herself if *The First Love* is a masterpiece or exactly the opposite, which is the same as to say ironically that Scribe's text does not contain any literary quality at all.

It is also remarkable how insistent the narrator is on elaborating on the characters of the play. Heiberg wrote in *On Vaudeville* that the last thing one should search for in vaudevilles is "character portraits."[4] Scribe was famous in Denmark as a vaudeville writer and, except for its lack of music and songs, *The First Love* is very similar to Scribe's standard vaudevilles. It is part of the thesis of this article that Kierkegaard is scheming against Heiberg's resistance to critics who would want to subject the genre of vaudeville to character criticism by letting his narrator conduct an extensive analysis of the main characters as well as the minor ones.

It is, for example, not that difficult to hear the sarcasm of the author when the narrator states this about the main character: "Emmeline is infinitely silly, and she is just as silly at the end as at the beginning."[5] She "has not missed the opportunity to spin herself into a web of sentimentality."[6] Later in the text the narrator wants to emphasize this point of view about her: "Her old love for Charles is drivel, and her new love for Rinville is also drivel; her enthusiasm is drivel, and her

---

[1] *SKS* 2, 248 / *EO1*, 255.
[2] *SKS* 2, 251 / *EO1*, 258.
[3] *SKS* 2, 250-251 / *EO1*, 258.
[4] Heiberg, *Om Vaudevillen*, p. 47 (in *Prosaiske Skrifter*, vol. 1, p. 183).
[5] *SKS* 2, 250 / *EO1*, 257.
[6] *SKS* 2, 242 / *EO1*, 249.

rage is also drivel; her defiance is drivel, and her good resolve is also drivel."[1] Kierkegaard also seems to want to poke fun at the ludicrousness of the other characters: "The hopeful Charles becomes a debauched fellow, a black sheep, a failed genius."[2] The narrator names Charles' uncle a "simpleton"[3] and describes another character, Derviére, in a specific scene: "He stands there like an idiot who cannot comprehend a thing."[4] Read literally Kierkegaard wants to praise Scribe for his comical talent and funny characters, but read ironically he suggests that the French dramatist's cast is nothing but a parade of fools.

VII. Heiberg's Review of Either/Or

On March 1, 1843 Heiberg published a review of *Either/Or* in his journal *Intelligensblade*.[5] This review is crucial in understanding Heiberg's interpretation of Kierkegaard's hidden intrigue against him. First of all it should be emphasized that Heiberg was not just trying to ridicule the author of *Either/Or*. He was actually trying to hit Kierkegaard hard. This is especially evident in the passage where he writes of Kierkegaard's invention of Johannes the Seducer, the protagonist in "The Seducer's Diary":

> One hurries on to "The Seducer's Diary," for the title already suggests that this production must be more creative than critical. And in a way one is not disappointed with regard to this expectation, but one is disgusted, repulsed and incensed, and one asks oneself, not if it is possible that a human being can be like this seducer, but if it is possible that a writer can be constituted in such a way that he finds pleasure in imagining such a character and developing him in his quiet thoughts.[6]

---

[1] *SKS* 2, 268 / *EO1*, 276.
[2] *SKS* 2, 242 / *EO1*, 249.
[3] *SKS* 2, 243 / *EO1*, 250.
[4] *SKS* 2, 259 / *EO1*, 267.
[5] Heiberg, "Litterær Vintersæd," *Intelligensblade*, vol. 2, no. 24, March 1, 1843, pp. 285-292.
[6] Heiberg, "Litterær Vintersæd," pp. 290-291.

In a manuscript where Kierkegaard was trying to formulate his polemical answer to Heiberg's review, he refers to the insult in this ironic way: "Prof. Heiberg finds it necessary to be crude with me. Alas! Alas! Alas! Has it really come to this for me; for it must really be the case, I do not doubt it, when Prof. Heiberg says so."[1] It had really come to this for Kierkegaard that Heiberg insulted him publicly, but Heiberg thought he had good reasons for being angry. In another formulation Kierkegaard writes: "Prof. H. thinks that I have permitted myself to hold him up to ridicule—what a vile thought."[2] Kierkegaard is being ironical. He did want to ridicule Heiberg in his text on *First Love*. Heiberg's comment on the aesthete's dealing with this text contains hidden information:

> In order to have a positive starting point in this entire negativity, one decides to plunge oneself into a critique of Scribe's comedy *First Love*, but one finds that the author has transformed the positive given to his own pipe dream. He has wanted to make a masterpiece out of a beautiful little bagatelle thus attributing to it a tendency which is the opposite of what Scribe manifestly acknowledges for his comedies.[3]

By writing "He has wanted" Heiberg hints that he has not taken Kierkegaard's exhilarated aesthete's panegyric at face value. To complicate matters further Heiberg's use of the word "bagatelle" indicates something of fundamental importance to our understanding of Heiberg's interpretation of Kierkegaard's hidden satirical intentions with *First Love*. Heiberg is alluding to something he himself wrote in another article from 1842 in *Intelligensblade*: "To devote a trenchant critical analysis to an isolated bagatelle, which does not presume to be more than an improvised '*Lückenbüßer*,' exhibits a truly critical misery."[4] By alluding to this passage, Heiberg indirectly tells Kierkegaard that he has understood him to be scheming against Heiberg's critical point of view as it is formulated here. We know that Kierkegaard's text was on

¹ *Pap.* IV B 28, pp. 195-196.
² *Pap.* IV B 30, p. 196.
³ Heiberg, "Litterær Vintersæd," p. 290.
⁴ Heiberg, "Svar paa 'Fædrelandets' Replik," *Intelligensblade*, vol. 1, no. 10, August 1, 1842, p. 231.

his mind before the 1ˢᵗ of August, when Heiberg's article was printed, because of the letter Kierkegaard sent to Boesen, but Heiberg may have been thinking that Kierkegaard wanted to parody his objection against wasting critical energy on trifles, by letting the aesthete perform an extraordinary, penetrating, if highly ironic, analysis of a bagatelle whose Danish wordings Heiberg himself had fathered.

VIII. Heiberg's Hidden Polemics against Kierkegaard in "Lyric Poetry"

In this section I will argue that Heiberg in fact was so infuriated by Kierkegaard's text on *The First Love* that he chose to retaliate by producing some hidden polemical attacks against Kierkegaard in four articles in *Intelligensblade* in the spring and summer of 1843. It may seem surprising that these attacks have not been discovered before now, but that bears witness to the intense level of secrecy with which both Kierkegaard and Heiberg guarded their literary intrigues.

The titles of the four articles are "Lyric Poetry"[1] from April 15, 1843, "Contribution to the Philosophy of the Visible"[2] from May 15, "The Dramatic in the Lyrical"[3] from June 1 and "Orienting Oneself"[4] from July 1. The culmination of Heiberg's hidden polemics in each article has a defining common feature: Heiberg uses Kierkegaard's choice of title, *Either/Or*, to mock the author of this pseudonymous work.

In order to avoid a too complex line of argumentation in this article, I will present only Heiberg's first and last polemical attack.[5] Heiberg's hidden polemical strategy in "Lyric Poetry" is, on the surface of the text, to define the lyrical dialectically by distinguishing sharply between

---

[1] Heiberg, "Lyrisk Poesie," *Intelligensblade*, vol. 3, nos. 26-27, April 15, 1843, pp. 25-73.

[2] Heiberg, "Bidrag til det Synliges Philosophie," *Intelligensblade* vol. 3., no. 28, May 15, 1843, pp. 74-96.

[3] Heiberg, "Det Dramatiske i det Lyriske," *Intelligensblade*, vol. 3, nos. 29-30, June 1, 1843, pp. 97-118.

[4] Heiberg, "At orientere sig," *Intelligensblade*, vol. 3, no. 32, July 1, 1843, pp. 169-192.

[5] For a presentation of the second and third, see Jessen, *Tyvesprogets mester*, pp. 72-74.

authentic and false poets. Reading the article for the first time, the reader may wonder why Heiberg passes such harsh verdicts on the false poets. The reason for this is that Heiberg attacks Kierkegaard through these general observations of amateurism in the literary arts in Denmark. Heiberg's hidden polemics in "Lyric Poetry" culminates when he introduces a distinction between "two opposing phases of failed poetry." Notice how Heiberg uses the syntactical form "either-or" twice at the end of the passage:

> One phase [is] where the poet, lacking any personal feature, celebrates an abstract generality, a simple commonality, that he is not part of, at least not in regard to his own poetic personality, and here the poet varies his tone between the trivial and the bombastic; the second phase [is] where the poet, because of boredom in relation to the abstract generality and contempt for its triviality and bombastic nature, or in vain fear of the ridiculous, which is always part of such commonality, decides to deepen himself in his empty personality, which is only filled with nothingness, and exhibits it *in puris naturalibus*, and as such, though he avoids the Scylla of the former shortcomings, he falls into the Charybdis of either pettiness or impudence. However, taking a closer look, one does not avoid in either case the one rock because one hits the other; on the contrary, one must either avoid them both or be wrecked on both.[1]

In the third last and the last sentence Heiberg alludes to *Either/Or* by using this common syntactical form. Heiberg's denunciation of lyrical amateurism among Danish writers in general, turns out to have a hidden addressee alias Søren Aabye Kierkegaard. Heiberg insinuates that Kierkegaard has wrecked himself on both phases of failed poetry in *Either/Or*.

Kierkegaard did leave to posterity two material "pieces of evidence" that point to the fact that he was offended by Heiberg's article. First, Kierkegaard's copy of "Lyric Poetry" has survived, and in it he underlined certain passages.[2] Second, a manuscript exists, which consists of seven

---

[1] Heiberg, "Lyrisk Poesie," pp. 37-38.
[2] See *Pap.* IV B 50, pp. 205-206.

notes, in which he, in my judgment, is trying to formulate a response to Heiberg's hidden polemics,[1] a response that was eventually abandoned. In my dissertation I analyze these matters more fully.[2] Here I would like to highlight another passage from "Lyric Poetry": "For the lyrical is the immediate poetical, which ideally must be present, even in the forms of poetry where it is mediated. One, who is deficient in the lyrical, is not even a poet. It is exactly that which makes Scribe's reputation as a poet troublesome."[3] This should be taken, I think, as Heiberg's hint to Kierkegaard that he, by writing his hidden polemics in "Lyric Poetry," would not suffer Kierkegaard's provocative use of Scribe in *Either/Or* passively. When Heiberg on page 29 refutes that Scribe possesses a lyrical strain, and when he secretly on page 37 completely refutes the same in regard to the author of *Either/Or*, he is insinuating that it is Kierkegaard himself who is on the same mediocre and non-lyrical level as Scribe. Thus Heiberg, quite brilliantly, turns Kierkegaard's use of Scribe against him.

IX. Heiberg's Hidden Polemics against Kierkegaard in "Orienting Oneself"

In "Orienting Oneself" Heiberg introduces a clear-cut distinction between the good and the bad dilettante:

> Every age has distinguished between good and bad dilettantes, between careful and superficial ones. The good dilettantes are those who with lively interest and enthusiasm for a certain subject immerse themselves to a certain degree in it; the bad ones are those who have no enthusiasm for the subject except a vain interest in their own personalities. The careful ones know that they are but dilettantes; the superficial dilettantes begin to believe that they are masters or on the way to becoming ones.[4]

---

[1] *Pap.* IV B 51-57, pp. 206-207.
[2] Jessen, *Tyvesprogets mester*, pp. 64-66 and pp. 68-70.
[3] Heiberg, "Lyrisk Poesie," p. 29.
[4] Heiberg, "At orientere sig," p. 175.

Heiberg describes the duty of the good dilettante in the following terms: "In science the dilettante should pursue new discoveries; in the arts he should pursue new forms of art or strive for artistic originality."[1] This formulation plays a part in Kierkegaard's choice of subtitle to *Repetition*, a work which I will return to in the next section. First, the reader should note Heiberg's choice of words in referring to how the dilettante often experiences that his work goes awry. Heiberg is secretly addressing Kierkegaard in the following passage, where he once again uses "either-or" twice: "The dilettante will, by continuous work, often reach the result that his discoveries are either delusions or already familiar truths that were discovered many years ago; thus he will realize either that his originality was no good or the repetition of a manner which the history of arts already catalogued and judged to be ruined and forgotten."[2] Heiberg is secretly telling Kierkegaard that *Either/Or* has been written by a bad and unoriginal dilettante who has done nothing but repeat the styles of yesterday's art. What seems to be a rather straightforward criticism of dilettantism in the arts actually may contain the solution to the mystery surrounding Kierkegaard's sudden interest in the concept of repetition in his new work *Repetition* which was published on the 16th of October 1843.

X. *Kierkegaard's Choice of Title and Subtitle for* Repetition

First of all it is important to recognize the fact that Kierkegaard's use of the concept of repetition in *Either/Or* does not differ in meaning from Heiberg's use in his hidden critique of him in "Orienting Oneself." The aesthete, for example, reflects on the faithlessness of sensuous love: "But its faithlessness manifests itself in another way also: it continually becomes only a repetition."[3] The concept is used in a purely negative and traditional way. The ethical William apparently wants to remind the aesthete of a basic fact of life: "Thus, a person is born only once, and there is no probability of a repetition."[4] Here the concept basically means the

---

[1] Heiberg, "At orientere sig," p. 176.
[2] Ibid., p. 177.
[3] *SKS* 2, 98 / *EO1*, 94.
[4] *SKS* 3, 47 / *EO2*, 40.

same: a repetition with no notion of change involved, though in this case a repetition is impossible. Thus Kierkegaard must have undergone a radical change of opinion as to the value of the concept of repetition between the publication of *Either/Or* on the 20th of February and *Repetition* on the 16th of October 1843, because the pseudonymous narrator of the later work, Constantin Constantius, at least in the beginning, seems to be obsessed with the grandeur and extremely positive aspects of the concept of repetition. What ignited this complete revolution of perspective? Did Kierkegaard decide to entitle his new work *Repetition* and create the frame story of Constantius' wish to make an experiment in repetition under the influence of reading this very passage in Heiberg's article dating from July 1, 1843? Indeed so, and I will try to explain his new insight in this paragraph.

Kierkegaard did have other subtitles on his mind before choosing "A Venture in Experimenting Psychology." He crossed out the first four ideas for a new subtitle in his manuscript:

> A fruitless Venture.
>> A Discovery Venture.
> A fruitless Venture.
> A Venture in Experimenting Philosophy.
> A Venture in Experimenting ~~Philosophy~~ Psychology.[1]

In the sentence before Heiberg insinuates that *Either/Or* is nothing but a repetition he writes this: "But undoubtedly in most cases this striving for discoveries or originality turns out to be fruitless."[2] Kierkegaard alludes to this formulation in his first three ideas for a subtitle. Why did Kierkegaard not settle on these subtitles? Nobody can know for sure, but Kierkegaard may have worried that the allusions to Heiberg's article would perhaps be too easily discoverable by his contemporaries. By choosing the adjective "experimenting" Kierkegaard chose a more discreet allusion to the same pages of Heiberg's article, where Heiberg wrote: "In science the dilettante must aim at making new discoveries."[3] By

---

[1] *Pap.* IV B 97,1, p. 251. For a reproduction of this manuscript page, see *SKS* K4, p. 11.
[2] Heiberg, "At orientere sig," p. 177.
[3] Ibid., p. 176.

using this adjective Kierkegaard plays on his pseudonym's revolutionary scientific ambitions.

Frederic Bogel has reflected on "the unsettling fact of real and even necessary intimacy between satirists and readers, on the one hand, and satiric objects, on the other."[1] Kierkegaard is the master of this very real sort of satirical intimacy in Danish literature. The reader needs to bear in mind that Heiberg would be the only contemporary reader in Copenhagen who could easily catch the allusions of Constantius' title and subtitle. How would he interpret these allusions? This cannot of course be said with certainty, but it seems very plausible that Heiberg would be capable of understanding that he was about to read a work in which Kierkegaard would parody his formulations on the dilettante who wishes to do scientific research and make great discoveries for the good of mankind.

Turning to Constantius' description of his own scientific longings and trip to Berlin, Kierkegaard makes his narrator use a specific word: "But I must constantly repeat that I say all this in connection with repetition. Repetition is the new category that will be discovered."[2] Kierkegaard is alluding to Heiberg's formulation as quoted: "In science the dilettante must aim at making new discoveries." In the beginning of the narrative Constantius seems to be assured of success in making new discoveries: "I shall not dwell any longer on such examples but shall proceed to speak a little of the investigative journey I made to test the possibility and meaning of repetition."[3] The Danish phrase for "investigative journey" is "*Opdagelses-Reise.*" But as any reader of *Repetition* knows, Constantius' ambitions turn into farce, and he is not afraid of admitting it: "My discovery was not significant, and yet it was curious, for I had discovered that here simply is no repetition and had verified it by having it repeated in every possible way."[4] Kierkegaard's narrator admits that he is a bad dilettante in Heiberg's understanding of the concept whose discoveries inevitably turn out to be fruitless. What is so intriguing about these allusions is the fact that only Heiberg among

---

[1] Frederic V. Bogel, *The Difference Satire Makes: Rhetoric and Reading from Jonson to Byron*, Ithaca: Cornell University Press 2001, p. 32.
[2] *SKS* 4, 25 / *R*, 148.
[3] *SKS* 4, 26-27 / *R*, 150.
[4] *SKS* 4, 45 / *R*, 171.

Kierkegaard's contemporaries could possibly grasp them and see that Kierkegaard must have created this frame narrative after July 1 when "Orienting Oneself" was published. Only Heiberg could understand that Kierkegaard had invented the narrator in order to parody his point of view in regard to the scientific-minded dilettante. Seen from this perspective, Kierkegaard's invention of Constantin Constantius could be termed one of the most amazingly brilliant parodying inversions of another writer's polemics in the history of Danish literature.

XI. Kierkegaard's Letter to Boesen from Berlin

Kierkegaard traveled to Berlin on the 8th of May and returned at the end of the same month. He must have read Heiberg's "Lyric Poetry" before embarking on his trip. One could therefore assume that he chose to travel to Berlin in order to dedicate himself completely to the composition of a literary polemical reply to Heiberg. In a letter from the 15th of May Kierkegaard writes to his friend Emil Boesen: "In a short while you will see me again. I have finished a work that is important to me, and I am moving ahead with full speed with a new one, my library is indispensable to me, as well as a printing house."[1] Until now Kierkegaard philology has assumed that the first part of the manuscript of *Repetition* is the same as the work Kierkegaard finished in Berlin,[2] but this cannot be the case, since the manuscript contains allusions to Heiberg's "Orienting Oneself" from the 1st of July. Thus Kierkegaard must have composed the manuscript after that date when he was back in Copenhagen. He probably destroyed all the earlier manuscripts and kept only the final version which still exists today.

XII. Kierkegaard's Hidden Satire in Repetition

In this section I will argue that Constantius' denigrating comments on a young theater lover who turns to writing *posse* is to be read as

---

[1] *Breve og Aktstykker vedrørende Søren Kierkegaard*, vol. 1, pp. 120-121.
[2] See *SKS* K4, p. 20.

Kierkegaard's hidden analogous satire of Heiberg's career as a vaudeville writer. Kierkegaard mirrors Heiberg's hidden polemics where he uses the general concept of the bad and superficial dilettante to secretly insinuate something about a specific historical person.

In *Repetition* Kierkegaard begins to allude to Heiberg's manifesto for the vaudeville where Constantius informs the reader of the number of theaters in Berlin: "Berlin has three theaters. The opera and ballet performances in the opera house are supposed to be *großartig*; performances in the theater are supposed to be instructive and refining, not only for entertainment. I do not know. But I do know that Berlin has a theater called the Königstädter Theater."[1] Heiberg wrote in his work on vaudeville: "Any big city, where a court resides, should have at least three theaters; one royal for opera and ballet, and two more, preferably private enterprises, one for tragedy and larger comedies, the other for one-act comedies and vaudevilles."[2] Accordingly, Kierkegaard secretly confirms that Berlin fulfills Heiberg's seventeen-year-old demand. Heiberg also reflected on the phrase "not only for entertainment" in the same work:

> Our Danish scene, where not only comedies, but also tragedies, *singspiele*, and ballets are staged, has the common slogan: "not only for entertainment." However, if the audience interpreted this to mean that after each show they would be entitled to take home with them a certain moral lesson, then it would be better to delete the first word "not" from the slogan.[3]

When Constantius blatantly states "I do not know," Kierkegaard's indirect irony seems to be that Heiberg's point of view in regard of this slogan is of no importance to him whatsoever. On the other hand, the narrator is apparently truly thrilled by the Königstädter Theater: "The Königstädter Theater opened in 1828 and was situated at the corner of Alexanderplatz and Alexanderstraße. Until it was closed in 1845, the theater specialized in the burlesque comedies which in the French tradition are known as farces, in German as *posses*."[4] This commentary

---

[1] *SKS* 4, 29-30 / *R*, 154.
[2] Heiberg, *Om Vaudevillen*, p. 57 (in *Prosaiske Skrifter*, vol. 1, p. 195).
[3] Heiberg, *Om Vaudevillen*, p. 70 (in *Prosaiske Skrifter*, vol. 1, p. 211).
[4] *SKS* K4, pp. 99-100.

in *Søren Kierkegaards Skrifter* is slightly problematic. What in German is called "*posse*" were actually for Heiberg and his contemporaries the same as the French vaudevilles. For example, Heiberg in *On Vaudeville* refers to the *posses* as German vaudevilles: "All German vaudevilles remain backwards in comparison to the French vaudevilles."[1] Another problem is the English translations of *Repetition* where "*posse*" is translated into "farce." In the following quotations from *Repetition* I have therefore decided to interpose the word "*posse*" in brackets when it is used in the Danish original.

Kierkegaard begins his interpretation of Heiberg's non-career by letting Constantius come up with a digression on any young man's desire to play his part in theater life:

> There is probably no young person with any imagination who has not at some time been enthralled by the magic of the theater and wished to be swept along into that artificial actuality in order like a double to see and hear himself and to split himself up into every possible variation of himself, and nevertheless in such a way that every variation of himself is still himself. Such a wish, of course, expresses itself only at a very early age. Only the imagination is awakened to his dream about the personality; everything else is still fast asleep.[2]

Kierkegaard is alluding to Heiberg's use of the concept of imagination in the article "The Dramatic in the Lyrical":

> The artist is only obliged to study the ideal. When he has adopted the ideal, the bad and ridiculous deviations from the ideal turn out to be obvious. Daily life offers everybody the opportunity to study these deviations, so that he does not have to do the same when he is endowed with the imagination which is indispensable to any artist. If this is lacking, his knowledge of reality will not help him in any way.[3]

---

[1] Heiberg, *Om Vaudevillen*, p. 62 (in *Prosaiske Skrifter*, vol. 1, p. 201).
[2] *SKS* 4, 30 / *R*, 154.
[3] Heiberg, "Det Dramatiske i det Lyriske," p. 101.

Heiberg lauds the imagination in this article, and it is part of his polemics to insinuate that the author of *Either/Or* has no part in the glories of the imagination at all. Kierkegaard's satirical inversion consists in connecting the concept of imagination with the very first and very feeble desire for aesthetic originality in a young man. When this young man turns older he still feels the need to regress to his earlier experiences:

> Even though this element in the individual's life vanishes, it is nevertheless reproduced later at a more mature age, when the soul has integrated itself in earnest. Yes, although the art may not then be sufficiently earnest for the individual, he may at times be disposed to return to that first state and resume it in a mood. He desires the comic effect and wants a relation to the theatrical performance that generates the comic. Since tragedy, comedy, and light comedy fail to please him precisely because of their perfection, he turns to farce [*posse*].[1]

Kierkegaard is being perfectly ironical. It was of great importance to Heiberg to stress that his art of vaudeville was a completely independent genre which included the possibility of perfection just as any other genre of importance.[2] Kierkegaard underlines here in his secret satirical language that Heiberg in fact chose to reject the traditional high genres of the theater tradition precisely in order to practice the more than imperfect genre of vaudeville. When Constantius emphasizes that "No effect in farce [*posse*] is brought about by irony; everything is naiveté,"[3] Kierkegaard is sarcastically negating Heiberg's viewpoint in *On Vaudeville*, where the latter writes that vaudeville contains the "freedom to experience the comical in all its nuances and relations from the burlesque to the moving, through all the intermediary relations like the naïve, the gracious, the exquisite, etc."[4] Kierkegaard is basically saying that Heiberg's career has followed this extraordinarily ordinary and mediocre path from young worshipper of the theatrical imagination to elderly writer of naïve and nothing but naïve vaudevilles.

---

[1] *SKS* 4, 33 / *R*, 157-158.
[2] See Heiberg, *Om Vaudevillen*, p. 38 (in *Prosaiske Skrifter*, vol. 1, p. 169).
[3] *SKS* 4, 35 / *R*, 160.
[4] Heiberg, *Om Vaudevillen*, p. 48 (in *Prosaiske Skrifter*, vol. 1, p. 184).

Constantius also brings forth his evaluation of the audience at the Königstädter Theater:

> Farce [*Possen*] generally moves on the lower levels of society, and therefore the gallery and second balcony audiences recognize themselves immediately, and their noise and cheers are not an esthetic appraisal of the individual actor but a purely lyrical outburst of their feeling of well-being. They are not conscious of themselves as audience but want to be down there on the street or wherever the scene happens to be.[1]

Kierkegaard is parodying Heiberg's wish for greater refinement among Danish theatergoers with specific allusion to Heiberg's article "Expressions of Applause and Discontent in the Theater," in *Intelligensblade*, where the latter distinguishes between three possible expressions among the audience: "1) Applause with or without bravo, 2) booing, 3) whistling." [2] According to Heiberg, only category one and three contain an aesthetic value judgment, only applause and whistling "refer immediately to the performance."[3] Kierkegaard's analogous irony could be paraphrased to mean that Heiberg has to an extreme degree overrated his own audience; they are not by any means capable of any aesthetic judgment but only infantile outbursts of joy and exhilaration. Note how Kierkegaard uses the adjective "lyrical" against Heiberg just as Heiberg used the same word against him in "Lyric Poetry."

Constantius also elaborates on the question of what sort of actors the *posse* needs in order to become a hit. Notice once again how Kierkegaard alludes to Heiberg's use of the concept of the lyrical:

> A completely successful performance of a farce [*posse*] requires a cast of special composition. It must include two, at most three, very talented actors or, more correctly, generative geniuses. They must be children of caprice, intoxicated with laughter, dancers of whimsy who, even though they are at other times like other people—indeed, the very moment before—the

---

[1] *SKS* 4, 34 / *R*, 159.
[2] Heiberg, "Bifalds- og Mishags-Yttringer i Theatret," *Intelligensblade*, vol. 2, no. 21, January 15, 1843, p. 215.
[3] Ibid., p. 216.

instant they hear the stage manager's bell they are transformed and, like a thoroughbred Arabian horse, they begin to snort and puff, while their distended nostrils betoken the chafing of spirit because they want to be off, want to cavort wildly. They are not so much reflective artists who have studied laughter as they are lyricists who themselves plunged into the abyss of laughter and now let its volcanic power hurl them out on the stage.[1]

According to Heiberg, the lyrical is the fundamental positive aspect of poetry: "The lyrical is the immediate poetical."[2] Kierkegaard parodies Heiberg's use of the concept by implying that the lead actor in the art of vaudeville need only to be capable of a sort of completely non-reflective and purely expressive way of acting: "They know that they are able to sustain laughter the whole evening without its costing them any more effort than it takes me to scribble this down on paper."[3] Heiberg wrote in *On Vaudeville*, "I cannot approve of the opinion that vaudeville is the easiest branch of poetry for actors."[4] Here Kierkegaard insinuates that Heiberg is wrong. Their lyrical acting performances in vaudevilles are the easiest thing in the world.

Kierkegaard also wants to scorn Heiberg's view of the minor roles in vaudeville acting. Constantius deliberates on this aspect of the *posse*:

The rest of the cast need not be talented; it is not even good if they are. Nor do the rest of the cast need to be recruited according to standards of good looks; they should instead be brought together by chance. The rest of the cast may very well be just as accidental as the company that, according to a sketch by Chodowiecki, founded Rome. No one needs to be excluded even for a physical abnormality; on the contrary, such an accidental feature would be a splendid contribution. Whether a person is bowlegged or knock-kneed, overgrown or stunted—in short, a defective example in one way or another—he can very well be used in farce [*posse*] and can have an incalculable effect.[5]

---

[1] *SKS* 4, 36 / *R*, 161.
[2] Heiberg, "Lyrisk Poesie," p. 29.
[3] *SKS* 4, 36 / *R*, 161.
[4] Heiberg, *Om Vaudevillen*, p. 54 (in *Prosaiske Skrifter*, vol. 1, p. 192).
[5] *SKS* 4, 36-37 / *R*, 162.

In *On Vaudeville* Heiberg wrote that in "vaudevilles the minor roles can be acted by natural talents, without impairing the ensemble."[1] Heiberg is saying that people without any training or education in acting can play the minor roles without doing any harm. Kierkegaard comically misreads the adjective "natural" to mean people with some sort of physical disability. The younger writer is using Constantius to parody Heiberg's common sense point of view concerning the minor roles.

In Constantius' comments on the main actors who perform *Der Talismann* in the Königstädter Theater Kierkegaard once again alludes to "Lyric Poetry": "Beckmann is unquestionably a comic genius who purely lyrically frolics freely in the comic, one who does not distinguish himself by character portrayal but by ebullience of mood."[2] Constantius offers the other main actor Grobecker a rather ambivalent sort of praise: "Grobecker certainly is not as great a lyricist as Beckmann, but he does have a lyrical understanding with laughter."[3] On the level of fiction Constantius wants to use the concept of the lyrical to describe Beckmann and Grobecker's mastery of dramatic expressionism. On the level of hidden satire Kierkegaard is implying that the main actors in vaudeville are only capable of a completely thoughtless kind of acting.

XIII. Constantius at the Königstädter Theater

Something extraordinary happens to Constantius while he is present in the Konigstädter Theater. At the moment when the performance begins and Beckmann enters the scene he is overwhelmed by a memory of his own childhood nursemaid, which he renders by a sort of hilarious panegyric to her:

> My unforgettable nursemaid, you fleeting nymph who lived in the brook that ran past my father's farm and always helpfully shared our childish games, even if you just took care of yourself! You, my faithful comforter, you who preserved your innocent purity over the years, you who did not age as I

---

[1] Heiberg, *Om Vaudevillen*, pp. 55-56 (in *Prosaiske Skrifter*, vol. 1, p. 193).
[2] *SKS* 4, 38 / *R*, 163.
[3] *SKS* 4, 39 / *R*, 165.

grew older, you quiet nymph to whom I turned once again, weary of people, weary of myself, so weary that I needed an eternity to rest up, so melancholy that I needed an eternity to forget.[1]

Kierkegaard has invented this fictional scene in order to parody a specific passage in Heiberg's article "Orienting Oneself" where Heiberg discusses the "joy of orientation."[2] A master of orientation can use his power of memory to regain the joy of orientation; he is capable of "merely by memory returning to it like in a happy, but vanished childhood."[3] Kierkegaard is parodying this simile: "like in a happy, but vanished childhood" in Constantius' "homage" to his nursemaid.

The reader realizes that Constantius in fact is lying on the floor and chuckling:

> Thus did I lie in my theater box, discarded like a swimmer's clothing, stretched out by the stream of laughter and unrestraint and applause that ceaselessly foamed by me. I could see nothing but the expanse of theater, hear nothing but the noise in which I resided. Only at intervals did I rise up, look at Beckmann, and laugh so hard that I sank back again in exhaustion alongside the foaming stream.[4]

Once again Kierkegaard is parodying the next sentence from exactly the same paragraph in "Orienting Oneself." Heiberg urges the master to study other professions than his own: "But therefore he should seek the incentive in unfamiliar professions, since only by this strengthening bath will he keep his spirit unimpaired."[5] Where Heiberg is speaking of a spiritual bath, Constantius is experiencing a sort of psychical one in that he is swimming in the roaring laughter of the audience and his own. Then Constantius' attention is caught by a young female in the audience, and he cannot take his eyes away from her, thus forgetting all about the play: "If she had even suspected my mute, half-infatuated delight, everything would have been spoiled beyond repair, even with all

---

[1] *SKS* 4, 40 / *R*, 166.
[2] Heiberg, "At orientere sig," p. 178.
[3] Ibid.
[4] *SKS* 4, 40-41 / *R*, 166.
[5] Heiberg, "At orientere sig," pp. 178-179.

her love."[1] Kierkegaard is parodying the final sentence from precisely the same paragraph in "Orienting Oneself." Heiberg writes that a person who does not know about the positive aspects of an honorable dilettantism will never experience "the warm, indefatigable enthusiasm, stimulated by all obstacles, which, like the first love, is blind to everything except its object."[2] Kierkegaard makes a hilarious scene out of Heiberg's polemical use of the Danish cliché that first lovers are blind to everything except themselves.

Ronald Paulson has explored satirists' complex use of fiction in *The Fictions of Satire* from 1967: "To the extent that satire presents, and so represents, its "object," it is related to other mimetic forms. But to the extent that satire attacks, it is rhetorical—the *vituperation* of *laus et vituperatio*—and there is a persuasive end in sight. However much mimesis or representation is involved, the generic end is rhetorical."[3] Kierkegaard's use of fiction is fundamentally that of a satirist, though the rhetorical attack admittedly is almost impossible to become aware of if the reader has not studied the articles in which Heiberg's hidden polemics against him are to be found.

If the reader begins to study these hidden intertextual relations between Heiberg's articles and Kierkegaard's *Repetition*, he or she may begin to be convinced, like the author of this article, that Kierkegaard wanted to compose a work in which only Heiberg among Kierkegaard's contemporaries would be able to conceive how the fictional scenes were invented. Kierkegaard thereby succeeds in *Repetition*, and therein lies his satirical sublimity, in taking literary secrecy and intimacy to its extreme limit.

XIV. Heiberg's Hint in "The Astronomical Year"

Heiberg actually comments on *Repetition* in an article called "The Astronomical Year"[4] in 1844, where he terms the author's wish to substitute

---

[1] *SKS* 4, p. 42 / *R*, p. 167.

[2] Heiberg, "At orientere sig," p. 179.

[3] Ronald Paulson, *The Fictions of Satire*, Baltimore: The Johns Hopkins Press 1967, p. 3.

[4] Heiberg, "Det astronomiske Aar," in *Urania. Aarbog for 1844*, Copenhagen: H.I. Bing & Söns Forlag 1844, pp. 77-160.

the concept of mediation with the concept of repetition as a "delusion."[1] In this context Heiberg's judgment on a specific passage from *Repetition* is of particular interest: "What here is said is very true and very beautiful, when one understands it with the proper qualification and remembers that in *Repetition* one must know how to see and find something more and higher than itself."[2] Heiberg is hinting to Kierkegaard that he got the message. It is difficult to say exactly how Heiberg interpreted *Repetition*, but I think he, in reading the work, understood much more of Kierkegaard's hidden satire on him than we can understand today. A key ingredient in Kierkegaard's "thief language" is the twisting and turning of Heiberg's own wordings, and as such Heiberg would be the best reader to interpret Kierkegaard's allusions and hints.

When one is knowledgeable about Heiberg's hidden polemics against Kierkegaard in *Intelligensblade* it makes more sense that Kierkegaard spent time on writing a long reply to Heiberg's laconic "review" of *Repetition*.[3] Kierkegaard chose not to publish his reply. Again one passage is of special interest here. In referring to *Repetition* Kierkegaard writes in an apparently offhand manner: "The heavens and Prof. Heiberg must know under what star I wrote and published it."[4] Kierkegaard knew that Heiberg knew that he had written *Repetition* under the star of their secret and deeply antagonistic relationship.

XV. Conclusion

Heiberg was famous in his time in Denmark for his excellence in literary polemics, but he met his superior in Kierkegaard, who was fourteen years younger than he. Heiberg and Kierkegaard as literary-polemical writers need unpacking to a degree we have by no means reached today. To be sure, Heiberg did play a pivotal role in Kierkegaard's literary intrigues. Heiberg could have chosen not to be provoked by Kierkegaard's insinuations in *Either/Or* and remain silent, but polemics was part of

---

[1] Ibid., p. 97.
[2] Ibid., p. 100.
[3] *Pap.* IV B 101-124, pp. 255-312.
[4] *Pap.* IV B 120, p. 306.

Heiberg's personality, and a satirical challenge from an extremely talented young writer like Kierkegaard needed to be acted upon. The ramifications of the discovery of Heiberg's hidden polemics against Kierkegaard in 1843 remain to be explored. Indeed, it is very likely that Heiberg detected more hidden ironic negativity directed at him in *Either/Or* than we are capable of understanding today. Thus the extent of Kierkegaard's anti-Heibergian agenda in *Either/Or* needs further research. One could indeed argue that the scope and depth of Kierkegaard's literary intrigues in works like *Either/Or*, *Repetition* and *Stages on Life's Way* are still to this day not understood at all. This has something to do with Kierkegaard's use of fiction as an important building block in his hidden satires, but the main reason is the extremely difficult accessibility of his allusions.

Kierkegaard could not have written *Repetition* without Heiberg's hidden polemics against him. This literary masterpiece only came into existence through rather negative energies. Heiberg and Kierkegaard both understood that polemics could be very productive. Indeed, Kierkegaard's polemical power play with Heiberg in a way offered him the possibility of inventing radically new forms of literature. Thus the reader who would like to get a deeper understanding of the origins of some of the "golden" works of the Danish Golden Age needs to study and confront a rather fierce sort of literary aggression.

In *Fear and Trembling*, published on the same day as *Repetition* on the 16th of October 1843, Johannes de silentio, discussing Agamemnon, refers to vaudeville in a disparaging manner: "If he could say this by virtue of human reckoning, Iphigenia would very likely understand him, but as a result Agamemnon would not have made the infinite movement of resignation and thus would not be a hero; then the soothsayer's declaration is a sailor's yarn, and the whole event is a vaudeville."[1] One could also say that Constantius' trip to Berlin as an event turns out to be a vaudeville in the Kierkegaardian sense of the word: everything is farcical. Other disparaging comments on Heiberg's vaudevilles can be found in Kierkegaard's journals, but in the published works his secret satire of Heiberg as a vaudeville translator, canonizer and theoretician

---

[1] *SKS* 4, 203 / *FT*, 115.

culminates in the early phase of his pseudonymous authorship in *Either/Or* and *Repetition*. In terms of polemical substance there is not that great a difference between Heiberg's earliest critics in the late 1820s who denigrated his vaudevilles for being farces and Kierkegaard's mocking narrators in these two works, but in terms of literary quality there is of course a real difference. Kierkegaard made world literature out of his desire to ridicule Heiberg's poetics of vaudeville.

III. Theater and the Economy of Gender

Nina's Madness:
The Economy of Sentimentality in Heiberg's *Nina*

Gunilla Hermansson

I. Nina and her Sisters: A Preface

In *Nina, or the Madness of Love* (which was published in 1823 and premiered at the Royal Theater in Copenhagen in 1824), we seem to meet a different Heiberg from the one we are used to. Written in Paris and completed by the end of 1820 or beginning of 1821, this play strangely contrasts with those considered to comprise the real and more lucrative outcome of Heiberg's journey to Paris in 1819-22, namely, his vaudevilles. The story of Nina who literally went mad for love is part of a European Sentimental tradition that crosses the boundaries between arts and genres and extends from the mid-eighteenth century into the first decades of the nineteenth. *Nina* has attracted little attention from literary scholars. Morten Borup, in discussing its sources and predecessors as well as its performances in 1824 and later, sums up the work in one comment: "It is a rather thin play, not even original, and it has never had any success on the stage."[1] I argue that this lack of originality, or rather Heiberg's efforts to counterbalance the weight of the Sentimental heritage, actually provides an interesting key to the reading of *Nina*, and perhaps even to its lack of success with audiences.

The plot is not overly complicated: Nina and Germeuil love each other, but Nina's father, the count, supports another suitor, Blinval, who is

---

[1] Morten Borup, *Johan Ludvig Heiberg*, vols. 1-3, Copenhagen: Gyldendal 1947-49, vol. 1, p. 124. All translations from Danish and German are mine.

an officer in the same regiment as Germeuil but also a son of the count's old friend, the general. The young lovers plan to elope and Germeuil makes arrangements with some sailors, not realizing that they are pirates. These pirates are the most obvious new element in Heiberg's version. Blinval exposes Germeuil and Nina in the middle of the night; the two rivals duel but are separated by the count and the general. The general threatens to have Germeuil executed, and Germeuil throws himself into the sea in despair. Nina becomes mad and cannot bear the sight of her father, who now bitterly regrets his actions. Nina wanders out every night, decked in flower garlands, looking for Germeuil, believing that he will come to get her. In this state, she makes sure that love prevails in the more comic subplot of the play. This involves the gardener Victor, his beloved Colette, who is the daughter of Torcol, the estate manager, and the ludicrous official, Cauchon. When Germeuil finally returns alive and well from the sea and the pirates, Nina does not recognize him. She regains her sanity only when they reenact their first love scene and Germeuil kisses her, and she is subsequently reconciled with her father.

The basis of the story was created by Benoît-Joseph Marsollier (1750-1817) and Nicolas-Marie Dalayrac (1753-1809) for their opéra comique *Nina ou La folle par amour*, which premiered in 1786 at the Comédie Italienne in Paris. *Opéra comique* was a new theater genre that explored the space between comedy and tragedy and facilitated the self-reflection of the expanding middle class. In a preface to the libretto, Marsollier informs the reader that the inspiration of the story is drawn from Baculard d'Arnaud's (1718-1805) collection of anecdotes, *Délassements de l'homme sensible* (1783-86).[1] The anecdote was in turn based on a true story from a newspaper, according to d'Arnaud, but at the same time he thought it illustrated the *truth* in Samuel Richardson's (1689-1761) *Sir Charles Grandison* (1753-54), namely, the story of Clementina, who is struck by madness when she believes it impossible to marry Sir Charles, the man she loves.[2]

---

[1] See Stefano Castelvecchi, "From *Nina* to *Nina*: Psychodrama, Absorption and Sentiment in the 1780s," *Cambridge Opera Journal*, vol. 8, no. 2, 1996, p. 93.

[2] Castelvecchi has identified a crucial difference between the libretto and the anecdote, namely, the lack of a happy ending in the latter (cf. ibid., p. 93). This further illustrates the sentimental educating and harmonizing tendencies in the dramatic adaptations of the story, while it is obvious that the thrilling touch of authenticity played a role

Madame Dugazon (Louise-Rosalie Lefebvre, 1755-1821) was the first to play Nina in the French opera. Her effect on stage has been described in the memoirs of Elisabeth Vigée Le Brun (1755-1842) as an unequalled combination of virtue and passion that drew tears from every eye: "Nina, so upright and at the same time so passionate, so unhappy, so poignant; the mere sight of her was sufficient to provoke an audience to tears."[1] The opera quickly became a success and was reworked into both new operas and ballets. The best known of the operas was Giovanni Paisiello's (1740-1816) *Nina, o sia La pazza per amore*, which premiered in Caserta in 1789 and expanded to two acts in Naples in 1790.[2] In Denmark, Vincenzo Galeotti's (1733-1816) ballet *Nina eller Den Vanvittige af Kjærlighed* had its premiere on November 26, 1802; Margrethe Schall (1775-1852) danced the role of Nina, and the ballet attracted a large audience.[3] It was performed 61 times in over 20 years, the last performance being six days after the premiere of Heiberg's play on March 20, 1824.

Heiberg's main inspiration came from the ballet, not Galeotti's version, but the more famous staging by Louis J. Milon (1766-1845), *Nina, ou la Folle par Amour* (which premiered in Paris in 1813 with music by Louis-Luc Loiseau de Persuis, 1769-1819), in which Émilie Bigottini (1784-1858) performed a most celebrated Nina. It was a so-called pantomimic ballet, or *ballet d'action*, which focused on ballet as storytelling. Heiberg saw the ballet in Paris in 1820, the same year as did the young August Bournonville (1805-79). Bournonville debuted as a dancer for the Parisian Opera in 1826 with a part in *Nina*, and in 1834 he

---

in its reception. Even Borup claims, "a real incident lies at the root of the subject." Borup, *Johan Ludvig Heiberg*, vol. 1, p. 124.

[1] *The Memoirs of Elisabeth Vigée-Le Brun*, trans. by Siân Evans, London: Camden Press 1989 [1896], p. 55.

[2] Emilio Sala comments on the wide range of adaptations: "Even before Paisiello made his Italian setting of the subject (in 1789), *Nina* circulated throughout Italy not only with its original score [Marsollier/Dalayrac] but also as a straight play and even in the form of a ballet....Clearly, the adaptability of this subject to various forms (spoken play, opera, ballet), amply testifies to its cultural significance and its influence," Emilio Sala, "Women Crazed by Love: An Aspect of Romantic Opera," *The Opera Quarterly*, vol. 10, no. 3, 1994, p. 20.

[3] Cf. Thomas Overskou, *Den danske Skueplads, i dens Historie, fra de første Spor af danske Skuespil indtil vor Tid*, vols. 1-7, Copenhagen: Thieles Bogtrykkeri 1854-76, vol. 4, p. 43.

Margrethe Schall as Nina
(Engraving by G.L. Lahde, 1802,
Courtesy of the Theater Museum, Copenhagen.)

staged his own version, based on Milon's, in Copenhagen.[1] In his memoirs, he characterizes Milon's *Nina* as a masterpiece "in the more Sentimental style" that "touched the heart."[2] Whereas the operas started out with the mad Nina and let the characters around her fill in the background to her madness, the ballets included the first part of the story (in different versions).

---

[1] Interestingly enough, Bournonville chose to incorporate a romance from the French opera into his ballet. The first scene of the second act shows Nina awakening, distressed, in the garden and finding some consolation in the flower bouquet she will give Germeuil on his return, and she "expresses the content of the romance: *Quand le bien-aimé reviendra,*" from Dalayrac's *Nina* (*Nina, eller Den Vanvittige af Kjærlighed. Pantomimisk Ballet i to Acter af* Milon. *Musiken arrangeret af* Persuis. *Indrettet for den danske Skueplads af A. Bournonville,* Copenhagen: Schubothes Boghandling 1834, p. 9). This testifies to how well known the Nina tradition was in Denmark as well in the first decades of the nineteenth century.

[2] August Bournonville, *Mit Theaterliv,* vols. 1-3, Copenhagen: C.A. Reitzel 1848-78, vol. 1, p. 29.

When one considers the line extending from Richardson's Clementina to Nina of the opera and ballet, it is clear that, with *Nina*, Heiberg is most unusually placing himself in a tradition built on the tears and compassion of the audience. To be sure, *Nina* appears to represent much of what Heiberg was eager to distance himself from in his other writings. In the following reading, I will focus on Heiberg's handling of this Sentimental heritage and on the significance of feelings, desires, poetic imagery, and madness. I will then briefly comment on Heiberg's three attempts to make the work a theater hit and gain some economic profit by it in 1824, 1836, and 1839. I will do so by viewing these attempts in relation to the overlapping fields of Sentimentality, Romanticism, and Biedermeier.

II. Excessive Feelings: Father, Daughter, and Lover

It is hardly surprising that the Sentimental and melodramatic features were somewhat reined in under Heiberg's pen. Emotions rarely leave his characters speechless, for example, but this also means that the excessive feelings are thematized throughout the play. Nina puts her madness into words before it completely possesses her. As soon as Germeuil and she have announced their love for each other, she looks on the weeks passed as wasted time and now demands his presence every minute of the day, for she would die if he were forced to leave her:

> ...O, long
> Have I fought against this passion,
> Have fled you, and prayed to God in tears
> To save me from this madness!
> Now it has broken out, and now it knows
> No bounds. Therefore, grant me,
> That wasted is all the time, in which I fought;
> I should have surrendered at once
> To the power that was much stronger than I.[1]

---

[1] Ibid., pp. 37-38.

Scene from Bournonville's ballet Nina or the Madness of Love
(Drawing by Edvard Lehmann, 1834,
Courtesy of the Theater Museum, Copenhagen.)

This is not what would normally be considered a virtuous speech, but love is already madness, and for Nina it is an instinct that needs an outlet.

Tears, screams, and fainting are concentrated in Nina's role, while the rest of the main characters engage in expressions of humility and affection, such as throwing themselves at each other's feet and kissing each other's hands. Apart from the more comic parallel story, the young characters are Romantic dreamers and uncontrolled in a way that makes the fathers uneasy, if not repulsed. "Mr. Blinval, do rise, man! I beg you, rise!" says the count to Blinval, when he falls on his knees, kisses his hand, and shouts out "Triumph!" at the news that the count intends to support his proposal to Nina.[1] Blinval admits: "...Like a mighty river, / My joy

---

[1] Ibid., p. 51.

floods all banks, / And hardly notices the dam of the appropriate."[1] Germeuil's suicide attempt is an extreme expression of this lack of self-control. He comments later: "Good Heaven! / Forgive me this act! It was not / Myself, who chose freely; I was driven by / Unconscious, blind rage."[2]

According to Heiberg's stage directions in the 1823 printed edition, the actions take place at the count's manor house near Marseille. The time is set at the end of the reign of Louis XV, which would mean sometime around 1770, that is, a time of Enlightenment and/or Sensibility.[3] The prescribed set decorations are typical of both Sentimental drama and melodrama: a wrought-iron gate separates a garden from a country road and the sea. In the garden, one sees the house of the estate manager and an arbor where Nina and Germeuil declare their love for each other and where Nina finally regains her sanity. In the first scene, the two young couples are preparing a festive greeting for the general and his son. This would correspond to the typical melodramatic logic, in which, according to Peter Brooks, the villain arrives by road, makes his way through the gate, and undoes the innocence and sanctity of the intimate garden.[4] In Heiberg's drama, however, and in other interpretations of Nina, the visitors are only the catalyst for a clash of passions already existing within the seeming idyll.

Nina herself comments on the role of the gate, as she is about to elope with Germeuil:

> ...This narrow grille
> Is a vast partition. As of yet
> Nina's life is without any guilt;
> But once she has opened this gate and stands
> On the other side of this border,
> That separates her fatherly home
> From all of the unknown world out there,

---

[1] Ibid., p. 52.

[2] Ibid., p. 151.

[3] The nature and flexibility of the boundaries between these two fields or paradigms are disputed, but I will not go into this discussion here.

[4] See Peter Brooks, *The Melodramatic Imagination*, New Haven, London: Yale University Press 1995 [1976], p. 29.

Then she has already committed the first sin.
Forgive me, good Heaven, for this first one,
And do not tempt me to commit the other![1]

What is to be understood by the second sin is not very hard to guess, and Nina goes on to comfort herself with the thought that she and Germeuil will marry as soon as possible.

Nina's madness expresses itself in her relationships with both her lover and her father. Her first thought when she awakes after her fit is that her father, not Germeuil, has thrown himself into the sea and perished. When she realizes this is not the case, not having the strength to pursue the logic any further, she says about her father: "Then I will live to love him, / For I must love!"[2] In the next moment, she concludes that the father is the killer, a bloodthirsty animal that wants to kill her, too. The father is both murderer and victim, simultaneously hated and loved by Nina.

The main conflict in *Nina* is thus what usually constitutes the plot of a Sentimental drama or novel: the conflict between the bond of love and duty between father and daughter, and the bond of love and desire between two young lovers. This conflict often gives rise to self-contradiction in Sentimental literature between an economy of feelings and an economy in a more classical sense. According to Inge Stephan, the fact that the conception of the daughter as the father's property continued to figure prominently in the age of Sensibility must be understood in relation to the reformulation of patriarchal claims of power in the struggle of the middle class to define itself.[3] In attempts of the middle class to distance itself both upwards from the eroticized social play of the aristocratic salons and downwards from the material dependency and supposedly base instincts of the lower classes, the father figure seems to assume

---

[1] Johan Ludvig Heiberg, *Nina, eller Den Vanvittige af Kierlighed. Skuespil i fem Acter*, Copenhagen: Andreas Seidelin 1823, pp. 93-94.

[2] Ibid., p. 107.

[3] See Inge Stephan, " 'So ist die Tugend ein Gespenst.' Frauenbild und Tugendbegriff im bürgerlichen Trauerspiel bei Lessing und Schiller," *Lessing Yearbook*, vol. 27, ed. by Richard E. Shade, Detroit: Wayne State University Press 1985 p. 15. See also Albrecht Koschorke, *Körperströme und Schriftverkehr. Mediologie des 18. Jahrhunderts*, Munich: Wilhelm Fink Verlag 1999, pp. 15-16.

a new, double role as both a guardian of the new culture of sentiment (concentrated in the closed entity of the family) and a guardian keeping a more unsentimental watch over his own territory of power.

In Heiberg's play, both these aspects are actualized in the relationship between father and daughter: the father's almost incestuous desire to keep her for himself, ideally based on true love and sympathy,[1] and the need to control her choice of husband based on economic and social considerations. Love between man and woman is no more than a phantom, so a successful marriage builds on material comfort, the count explains just before Nina's attempted escape. The reason he gives is plainly that no love is constant—except for a mother's love for her child and, more specifically, his love for Nina.[2] Both he and the general represent a generation on the threshold between a feudal, aristocratic world, where marriage for love is nonsense and even counterproductive, and a new, middle-class understanding of family, virtue, and love. Consequently, the father becomes the true rival to young love, until *he* comes to his senses, according to the values of the play.[3]

Interestingly enough, even this love expresses itself in a need for physical presence and nearness. In the beginning, the count imagines that Nina will receive part of his estate as a wedding gift, but he will come to visit her every Sunday, wearing his "finest clothes." The finery suggests that he thinks of it as a kind of lovers' rendezvous.[4] During Nina's madness, this fantasy turns nightmarish, and he must avoid her

---

[1] See Stephan, " 'So ist die Tugend ein Gespenst.' Frauenbild und Tugendbegriff im bürgerlichen Trauerspiel bei Lessing und Schiller," p. 12, Koschorke, *Körperströme und Schriftverkehr. Mediologie des 18. Jahrhunderts*, p. 138.

[2] See Heiberg, *Nina, eller Den Vanvittige af Kierlighed*, pp. 86-88.

[3] See also the count's anger towards Germeuil, in which he characterizes Nina's disobedience as the first sign of madness: "You [Germeuil] loosened Nature's firm bond / Between the father and the child. She, / To whom I was as dear as life, / Forgot me because of you, she wanted to flee / Away from me, secretly, and leave / Me to the bitter sorrow. This was her first, / Her very first utterance of madness" (ibid., pp. 198-199).

[4] Heiberg changed this in later versions. The count now realizes that Nina's husband may take her far away, but he hopes that she will be able to visit him every summer; cf. *Nina, eller Den Vanvittige af Kierlighed. Skuespil i fem Acter*, in *Skuespil*, vols. 1-7, Copenhagen: J.H. Schubothes Boghandling 1833-41, vol. 5, pp. 129-30, and *Nina. Drama i fem Acter* in *Poetiske Skrifter*, vols. 1-11, Copenhagen: C.A. Reitzel 1862, vol. 3, p. 195.

by day, when she only sees him as the killer, and seek her company every night, when she does not recognize him but finds in him a dear father figure who comforts her when Germeuil fails to appear:

> Already they return, I must flee.
> I will hide, that she may not see me.
> Soon the night spreads its wings;
> Then first my life begins, when I hurry
> Back to the dear rendezvous.[1]

The count more or less monopolizes Nina's vain attempts to complete her nocturnal escape with Germeuil, and he nearly becomes a phantom himself, coming to life only at night for ghostly meetings with his just as ghostlike beloved.

There are indications of Heiberg's will to stress other elements in the socio-political complex of the rise of the middle class and the shift in the understanding of love and sentiment. Victor argues with Cauchon not with the pathos of a lover, but with that of an honest, hard-working peasant who is worth more than a corrupt official.[2] This is obviously part of a new rhetorical norm, and when the count arrives at the scene, even Cauchon goes on to speak of the farmer as the bone and marrow of the country, and the count gives a lecture on honor as the only nobility that should be considered when approving of a marriage. Neither Cauchon nor the count believes in their teachings, though. A little later, when Nina establishes that in "France, every soldier is of noble birth" to help Germeuil find the courage to propose, Heiberg links it even more obviously to a revolutionary theme.[3] However, this line of reasoning is soon overshadowed by the more acute question of love and its expression.

The same logic applies to the question of money. At the beginning of Nina's and Germeuil's first love scene, it seems that, with *Nina*, Heiberg is already employing the mercantile language and plotting of

---

[1] Heiberg, *Nina, eller Den Vanvittige af Kierlighed*, p. 184.
[2] See ibid., p. 16.
[3] Ibid., p. 30.

the vaudevilles, which recent studies have identified.[1] The lovers thus speak in terms of accounts, debtors, payments, and claims—up to the point at which Nina gives up, and her tears reveal the poorly concealed subtext. From now on, Heiberg concentrates on exploring the social and moral power of the father in relation to the question of what love is and does. This is underlined in the other love story. Victor receives an inheritance from an old aunt and, enriched with his new fortune, sees no obstacle to a quick escape with Colette. Colette is intimidated by Nina's example, however, and replies: "I will pray to God to save me. / But I would rather die than escape with you, / For Heaven punishes every disobedient child!"[2] The otherwise confident Victor accepts this interpretation, according to which disobeying the father is disobeying God, and they agree to give up. It is then no longer a question of money, but of something far more immaterial concerning the father and his jurisdiction.

The count and the general reject the passionate expressions of the young as inauthentic, childish role-playing. Nevertheless, the feelings and indomitable love that cannot bear physical absence or distance conquer as the behavioral norm after the suicide attempt and Nina's madness. In the remainder of the drama, the count is to be schooled in the Romantic concept of love and friendship and its Sentimental expressions. He actually does very well: his first action in the third act is to throw himself at the feet of his daughter, grab her hand, and beg her forgiveness. He even throws himself into the arms of Germeuil upon his return to the manor, exclaiming that he will hold on to him forever, and that they shall cry together like children over the loss of Nina's sanity.

---

[1] See Leonardo F. Lisi, "Heiberg and the Drama of Modernity," and Kirsten Wechsel, "Lack of Money and Good Taste: Questions of Value in Heiberg's Vaudevilles," both in *Johan Ludvig Heiberg: Philosopher, Littérateur, Dramaturge, and Political Thinker*, ed. by Jon Stewart, Copenhagen: Museum Tusculanum Press 2008 (*Danish Golden Age Studies*, vol. 5), pp. 421-448 and pp. 395-417 respectively. They refer to inspiration from Eugène Scribe as well as to contemporary political and economic conditions in Denmark, and they both question the image of Heiberg as purely conservative. Lisi pictures Heiberg as a writer who was very aware of the forces of modernity and at the same time eager to "domesticate" them and force them into his idealist and aristocratic world-view.

[2] Heiberg, *Nina, eller Den Vanvittige af Kierlighed*, p. 127.

His reward in the end is Nina throwing herself at his feet with regained sanity and a daughter's devotion and humility. He is then able to raise her, embrace her, and lead her to Germeuil, expressing one of the two morals of the play:

> ...You have both
> Deserved each other, for a love so strong,
> That it is able to first murder the soul,
> And then wake it from the dead,
> That love is worthy of the trophy.[1]

The second moral of the play concerns the difficult balancing of love, fantasy, death, and madness.

III. Desire, Virtue, and Fantasies: The Codes of Madness

Five years after publishing *Nina*, Heiberg accused Eugène Scribe (1791-1861) and other recent playwrights of false Sentimentality:

> In their work, duty is set in Sentimental contrast to love. A noble hero or heroine sacrifices his or her love for the will of the parents, especially when the latter are poor and he or she can help them by making a rich match. The authors forget more and more that even love is an absolute power, and that the promises one has given a beloved person may be just as sacred as the obedience one owes one's parents.[2]

However, the power of love very easily becomes a problem in Heiberg's poetic universe, and *Nina* seems to me an investigation of this absolute power, which in intricate ways glides between a Sentimental, a Romantic, and a more post-Romantic paradigm, namely, that of a Heibergian speculative idealism.

---

[1] Ibid., p. 248.
[2] Johan Ludvig Heiberg, "Scribe som Moralist," *Prosaiske Skrifter*, vols. 1-11, Copenhagen: C. A. Reitzel 1861, vol. 5, pp. 138-139.

From Marsollier/Dalayrac to Bournonville the most explicitly thrilling part of the play is Nina driven mad by love, *folle par amour, pazza per amore, vanvittig af Kierlighed*. The story draws on the traditional association between female insanity and sexuality, but transforms it into a picture of virtue. Sarah Hibberd has pointed out that the operas and ballets of *Nina* must be understood in line with the Sentimental interpretations of William Shakespeare's Ophelia.[1] Elaine Showalter sketches the background to this in an article on the varying representations of Ophelia in theater history: "On the Elizabethan stage, the conventions of female insanity were sharply defined. Ophelia dresses in white, decks herself with 'fantastic garlands' of wild flowers, and enters... 'distracted' playing on a lute with her 'hair down singing.'"[2] In Elizabethan and Jacobean theater, Showalter continues, disordered hair indicates either a lunatic or a rape victim, and in both cases suggests sensuality. This changes in the eighteenth century: "Late Augustan stereotypes of female love-melancholy were sentimentalized versions which minimized the force of female sexuality, and made female insanity a pretty stimulant to male sensibility."[3]

The white dress and the flowers also became emblematic of Nina. When she enters the scene in Marsollier's opera she is already insane and, according to the stage directions, "Her hair is unpowdered, carelessly bound; she is dressed in a white gown; she holds a bouquet in her hand; she walks unsteadily; she halts, she sighs, and goes to sit silently on the bench, her face turned toward the grating."[4] It is said that Madame Dugazon's performance made this look high fashion among the ladies in Paris. The opera employed the same codes as found in earlier theatrical conventions, but reformulated them in a Sentimental manner. The same

---

[1] Sarah Hibberd, " 'Dormez donc, mes chers amours': Hérold's *La Somnambule* (1827) and Dream Phenomena on the Parisian Lyric Stage," *Cambridge Opera Journal*, vol. 16, no. 2, 2004, p. 113.

[2] Elaine Showalter, "Representing Ophelia: Women, Madness, and the Responsibilities of Feminist Criticism," *Shakespeare and the Question of Theory*, ed. by Patricia Parker and Geoffrey Hartman, New York & London: Methuen 1985, p. 80.

[3] Ibid., p. 82.

[4] Cited from Emilio Sala, "Women Crazed by Love: An Aspect of Romantic Opera," p. 21.

appearance in white dress, disheveled hair, and staring eyes continued to be an unequivocal marker of female insanity in the European theaters of the 1820s and 1830s.[1]

When interest in Nina and the Sentimental Ophelia faded, other mad women took their place (creating new fashions) in the renewed interest in the insane in Romantic literature and theater, which further investigated the associations between madness, love, femininity, sexuality, and fantasy.[2] Emilio Sala's inventory of "women crazed by love" in Italian and French operas demonstrates that the Sentimental and the Romantic interpretations and adaptations of the subject thrived side by side in the 1820s and 1830s, but that Sentimental happy endings eventually gave way to the tragic endings of Romantic melodramas.[3] At the same time, scientific interest continued to increase in new medical and therapeutic treatments, and legal questions arose concerning responsibility and punishment—in a Danish context, one thinks of the Howitz controversy (1824-25), to which Heiberg also contributed. The girl driven mad by love continued to attract authors in Denmark, not least in those camps from which Heiberg was most eager to distance himself. In B.S. Ingemann's (1789-1862) wertheriade, *Varners poëtiske Vandringer* (from

---

[1] Hibberd finds 11 such plays running in Paris in 1827: "For eight months, then, Parisian theaters were overrun with entranced madwomen and sleepwalkers, presented in a similar fashion, with white robes, loose hair and staring eyes" (Hibberd, " 'Dormez donc, mes chers amours': Hérold's *La Somnambule* (1827) and Dream Phenomena on the Parisian Lyric Stage," p. 109). Hibberd's focus is on the sleepwalkers, and she finds that the madwoman rather than the sleepwalker represents a sexual threat to the audience and the social order (cf. pp. 122-123). An instance of the typical markers (dress and hair) of female insanity in the 1830s could be the stagings of Donizetti's *Lucia de Lammermoor* (Napoli 1835, Paris 1839, Copenhagen not until 1857); cf. Mary Ann Smart, "The Silencing of Lucia," *Cambridge Opera Journal*, vol. 4, no. 2, 1992, p. 125.

[2] See Showalter, "Representing Ophelia: Women, Madness, and the Responsibilities of Feminist Criticism," p. 83. In Romantic operas, a mad scene seemed almost *de rigueur* and was at times added to the subject (cf. Emilio Sala, "Women Crazed by Love: An Aspect of Romantic Opera," p. 35). Among Sala's French and Italian examples are operas from the 1860s and 1890s, which then depict a transition from a melodramatic "operatic Romanticism" to a more brutal "new school" in the age of "realist" poetics (ibid., p. 37).

[3] See Emilio Sala, "Women Crazed by Love: An Aspect of Romantic Opera," p. 22, p. 25.

Procne, 1813), which Heiberg ridiculed in *Christmas Jests and New Year's Fun* (1817), there is actually a Nina who haunts Varner's conscience.[1] The Romantics thus reinstate the erotic and demonic potentials of female insanity. However, it is quite clear from the examples of the first *Ninas* that the sentimentalizing of madness hardly managed to extinguish the subversive potential of her story altogether. If, as Albrecht Koschorke describes the culture of Sensibility (*Empfindung*), "the new lovers find each other only in the sign of a crossed out desire—which, furthermore, often leaves its traces on the stories in the fact that they go through a phase of renunciation towards a symbolic killing,"[2] then the Nina tradition represents a strand of Sensibility that explores and tests the limits of this norm or ideal. Koschorke understands Sensibility as an overall striving to spiritualize all instincts. This means transforming bodily streams (for example, blood, sweat, and semen) into streams of the human soul, and forgetting everything that has to do with sexual instincts by translating them into a kind of virtuous *anwesende Abwesenheit* (present absence), as in the fetish that allows desire to be lived out in excess but always in effigy.[3] Koschorke describes how this necessary absence in literature not only results in the sacrifice or even self-sacrifice of the protagonists, but in a sort of mild cult of death.[4]

In relation to this picture, it is quite clear that the Ninas will not be content with a fetish in this life, and claims that they should willingly sacrifice themselves in sensible marriages will have as violent an impact on them as would the sexual advances of a libertine. Yet, they become icons of a Sentimental-Romantic longing for the absent (dead) lover, that is, until the double resurrection in the finale of the comedy that sustains Nina's demands for fulfillment in the present. There is apparently such power in the symbolic killing of the young lovers that the story more or less triumphs over itself, insisting on the extraordinary combination of virtue and passion in the figure of Nina.

---

[1] See Nicolas Reinecke-Wilkendorff, "Paa Jorden Salighed er Brøde—Om B.S. Ingemanns 'Varners poëtiske Vandringer. Et romantisk Digt,'" *Danske Studier*, 2008, p. 119 and note 14, pp. 144-145.

[2] Koschorke, *Körperströme und Schriftverkehr. Mediologie des 18. Jahrhunderts*, p. 41. I thank Klaus Müller-Wille and Kirsten Wechsel for bringing Koschorke's work to my attention.

[3] Ibid., p. 140, cf. p. 143.

[4] See ibid., p. 146.

The emotional stress seems to have been greatest in the earlier adaptations. In Paisiello's opera, Lindoro (equivalent to Germeuil) lies in his own blood before Nina when her father insists on her marrying his rival and presumed killer (according to the résumé given in act one). In Galeotti's ballet, Germeuil is also killed in front of Nina, so it seems, but in the confusion around the fainted Nina and the wounded body, the rival simply flees the scene of the crime. In Milon's and Heiberg's (and Bournonville's) versions, Germeuil becomes a more Romantic desperado for love and freedom alike in his suicide attempt.[1]

Heiberg's Nina quite manifestly resists resignation, but at the same time, it is almost as though her new state of mind releases her from erotic pressure. When she meets Germeuil without recognizing him in the fourth act, she finds it almost tedious that he talks of love: "It is strange with men! They always lead / the conversation to love…It is because, / They think, we women only know / the one chapter of the book of life."[2] Heiberg is sparing of scene directions in the text itself and gives no indications for the costumes, but he had been quite specific in a letter to Jonas Collin (1776-1861), dated February 10, 1824, that all the characters should wear formal attire in the first and second acts (the soldiers should be uniformed), but that from the fourth act, Germeuil should wear a simpler frock and boots. As to Nina: "Nina may be clothed as one likes in the first and second acts, but in the third act, a light white morning dress is the most suitable for her. In the fourth and fifth acts she should also be dressed in white, but with more elegance, with short sleeves and a white veil."[3] Here we have the mandatory white dress, but in a more dignified version, that allows Nina somewhat to transcend the role of disorderly mental patient in a morning dress, attaining that of an elegant virginal figure.

---

[1] Vincenzo Galeotti, *Nina, eller Den Vanvittige af Kierlighed. Ballet i to Acter*, Copenhagen: B. Brünnich 1802, p. 8. Paisiello's libretto is cited by Castelvecchi, "From *Nina* to *Nina*: Psychodrama, Absorption and Sentiment in the 1780s," p. 92, and Milon's by Susan Leigh Foster, "Nina, ou la Folle par Amour (1813)," *Choreography Narrative: Ballet's Staging of Story and Desire*, Bloomington and Indianapolis: Indiana University Press 1996, pp. 188-189.

[2] Heiberg, *Nina, eller Den Vanvittige af Kierlighed*, p. 188.

[3] *Breve og Aktstykker vedrørende Johan Ludvig Heiberg*, vols. 1-5, ed. by Morten Borup, Copenhagen: Gyldendal 1946-50, vol. 1, p. 137.

I would suggest that Heiberg sends in the pirates from Tunisia to reemphasize the erotic aspect of Nina's madness while still containing it within the virtuous boundaries of a true loving woman.[1] Germeuil's attempt to elope with Nina is a threat to virtue in quite a harsher way than the count imagines. The pirates plan to sell her to a harem if she is beautiful, or use her as a sex slave if she is ugly. The pirate who hopes for the latter crushes his skull against a rock when he jumps into the sea after Germeuil to rescue his "merchandise," and his blood in the water makes the others assume that Germeuil is dead.[2] The pirates may then be understood as an attempt to sort out the chaotic and contradictory instincts of the main characters and to set a barrier against the low and materialist extreme. They function as a kind of lightning rod for the all-too-raw desires (i.e., for sex and money) and the all-too-melodramatic evil and sinfulness.

In the love scene in the first act, Germeuil wonders about Nina's exaltation, as he himself is calm. He regards the weeks of anxiety and doubt as an investment in their final happiness, and the preceding despair and torment becomes a measure of the extent and truth of their love.[3] He is a better lover at a distance, for he is better able to enjoy his happiness when he is not overwhelmed by sensual pleasure. He therefore prays to God for the strength to enjoy his happiness in full consciousness—that is, not to lose himself in passion as Nina has.[4] This is clearly the Heibergian ideal of love—full enjoyment but never with a loss of consciousness or some form of self-control—and Germeuil clearly has trouble living up to this ideal.

The interesting thing is that Germeuil gives the Sentimental logic of absence a typically Romantic turn. In the middle of his proposal, he declares that he did not love Nina at first sight, but was rather indifferent and cold. A Romantic fantasy made him love her; she had worn a dress white as snow and had playfully appointed him knight of the red rose:

---

[1] For some reason, the pirates have become Albanian in the later versions.
[2] It would obviously be possible to read the pirate as an externalization of Germeuil's instincts.
[3] See Heiberg, *Nina, eller Den Vanvittige af Kierlighed*, p. 37.
[4] See ibid., p. 64.

> ...You charmed
> Me into the days of old; I was a knight
> And you my lady; for you I hastened boldly
> To the battlefield; like the goddess of victory
> You hovered gloriously in my imagination; my rose
> Was a foretaste of the garlands of victory
> That awaited my head, if I fought
> Eagerly for the sacred on earth;
> And from that moment I have loved you.[1]

In this way, Heiberg also carefully transforms the white dress and flowers into a chivalrous-Romantic fantasy within the text.

Adding the pirates also shifts focus to a "men's" world outside the garden in a "wild forest by the coast,"[2] where a line is drawn between the civilized (Blinval, the Arab Ali, and Germeuil) and the brutal (the pirates). This allows Heiberg to make more room for Germeuil and his cultivated wavering between hope, doubt, and despair against this "wild" background. Germeuil thus continues operating in the same chivalrous paradigm when he believes that Nina is dead. He calls himself a pilgrim, and the manor with the presumed grave is simultaneously the Promised Land and buried hope. His new friend from the pirate ship, Ali, fits nicely into his fantasies, and he pictures himself as a Christian knight accompanied by a noble Moor.[3] In this way, Heiberg tightens the knot between Romanticism, passion, and madness, and it becomes more and more clear that the madness in his version of *Nina* is of a pronounced literary rather than theatrical kind.

Nina is never more Romantic than in her madness. She understands the sighs of the flowers, the simple songs of the birds, and she expects nature to transform itself at the arrival of the beloved.[4] She has seen Germeuil's rescue in a vision rooted in the Romantic–literary imagination: an angel caught him and brought him to a marvelous island, an earthly paradise with palms and date trees—just like the island of love in

---

[1] Ibid., pp. 40-41.
[2] Ibid., p. 146.
[3] See ibid., p. 168.
[4] See ibid., pp. 120-121, pp. 138-139.

Oehlenschläger's *A Midsummer Night's Play* (*Poems 1803*, 1802) or any other of the many Romantic islands of felicity.[1]

The doctor fails to understand and cure Nina when he falls back on morally condemning her unreasonable accusations against her father.[2] Yet, Germeuil's understanding of her madness is not unproblematic either. He is at first frightened out of his wits by her transformation. He would prefer to run away from "the dear corpse"—up to the point at which he is able to reinterpret her madness, fitting it into another set of Romantic imagery in which he can participate.[3] He, too, suddenly understands the flowers and their language of the heart, and he values the hall of quiet madness as more holy than the temple of reason.[4] At this point, he also submits to Nina's demands for total physical presence, and he swears never to leave her but to stay with her every single day. To the count, who thought Germeuil was about to flee the scene, he declares—for the second time in the play—that he did not really love Nina until now:

> I tell you: now at last I love Nina;
> My life is dedicated to her; constantly
> I will wander by her dear side,
> And dream with my dreamer, and forget
> What the world calls wisdom and reason.[5]

The count's dry comment on this pathetic exclamation is "You are a fine sophist!" Germeuil, however, prefers not to be reminded of the fact: "Do not tell a Sailor / That the anchor might break, do not mention / Your doubt in God to the dying."[6] This last, desperate remark did not make it into later editions of the play, and I wonder if it was ever spoken from the stage of the Royal Theater.

---

[1] See ibid., pp. 112-113. On this current of poetic imagination in Danish and Swedish Romanticism, see Gunilla Hermansson, *Lyksalighedens øer. Møder mellem poesi, religion og erotik i dansk og svensk romantik*, Gothenburg: Makadam förlag 2010 (*Centrum för Danmarksstudier*, vol. 23).

[2] See Heiberg, *Nina, eller Den Vanvittige af Kierlighed*, pp. 109-110.

[3] Ibid., p. 204.

[4] See ibid., p. 206.

[5] Ibid., p. 228.

[6] Ibid.

On a certain level, then, the drama shows the fathers to be right: the young do play roles they hardly see through themselves or understand the depths of.[1] Germeuil's attitude alters with every other feeling and impulse, and he is equally self-absorbed throughout. "Can you conceive the horrid substance that lies in the thought 'she is dead'?" he, jumping to conclusions about Nina's fate, asks Ali, who had previously actually witnessed the death of his own beloved.[2] It seems as though Germeuil too is possessed by forces and fantasies beyond his control. He even compares himself to the Aeolian harp. Once again, Heiberg displays a deeply ambivalent attitude towards the Romantic world of fantasy, dreams, and poetical ideals.

Nina keeps up her resistance to resignation up to the very moment when she regains her sanity. This is important. While the drama invests in the audience's hope and knowledge that everything turns out well in the end—Germueil rises from the dead and kisses Nina into being—the one question posed most frequently in the play is: what is best, madness or death? The answer is repeated like a mantra throughout the play: rather dead than insane. In the final scene, Nina herself declares that if she should survive Germeuil, she would rather be left to mourn herself to death, "With a full conscience of her lost happiness, / Than live happily in insane comfort!"[3] Although madness had saved her from death once, and shown that it contained a truth no one else could see, this is actually not to be wished for under any other circumstances.

It becomes clear that Heiberg has stretched the story of Nina well beyond the "ethics of feeling" of Sensibility.[4] Whereas the first moral of the play, spoken by the count, articulates the power of love both to kill and to resurrect the soul, the second moral subordinates this to the priority of consciousness, in the final words of Nina. A life of love and fantasy may lead to a living death, and Heiberg therefore chooses "real" death before unreason—not to reach for the "true" life and unity of lovers somewhere beyond, but to avoid madness/unconsciousness. In line with

---

[1] The count also plays more than one role, but he is more conscious of this fact (cf. ibid., p. 25, p. 44, p. 87).

[2] Ibid., p. 166.

[3] Ibid., p. 249.

[4] See Inger S. B. Brodey, "On Pre-Romanticism or Sensibility: Defining Ambivalences," *A Companion to European Romanticism*, ed. by Michael Ferber, Oxford and Malden: Blackwell Publishing 2005, p. 15 and p. 16.

the tendency Klaus P. Mortensen has recently identified in Heiberg's work as a whole, *Nina* could be considered an early attempt by Heiberg to write himself out of the luring but destructive sides of eros in order to secure self-knowledge and spiritual–intellectual power.[1] Certainly, Nina's resignation primarily represents a shift of agenda or focus from one "absolute" to another, a shift traceable in most of Heiberg's writings after his "Hegelian revelation," which took place some months after the premiere of *Nina.* The play, then, also indicates that he was indeed ready to receive the philosophical initiation.

IV. A Theater of the Heart: A Question of Economy?

When Heiberg published the play in 1823, he dedicated it to his father and described the piece thus:

> You will not behold great catastrophes,
> Not those, which form the destiny of nations and generations,
> Which crush the earth and storm the heavens.
>
> My whole theater is the corner of the heart,
> Its fine strings my only orchestra,
> Its feelings my only symphony.[2]

The play is lovely, simple and has a good and honest heart, he adds, all of which underlines the warm and idyllic-restricted trait common to both the literature of Sensibility and the so-called "small" genres often characterized by the word Biedermeier. There is no trace of irony in this poem, and this very nearly stands out as the most non-Heibergian part of the whole play.[3]

---

[1] Klaus P. Mortensen, *Stjernekiggeren. Johan Ludvig Heibergs "sande Biographie,"* Copenhagen: Gyldendal 2009. See in particular the readings of *The Fairies* (1835), *Fata Morgana* (1838), and *Day of the Seven Sleepers* (1840), pp. 100-122.

[2] See Heiberg, *Nina, eller Den Vanvittige af Kierlighed*, [pp. 2-3].

[3] The situation contains, however, a strange irony, since father and son parted in anything but love and friendship, according to Borup. Heiberg had so many debts upon his departure that his father, in helping him out, put himself in economic difficulties for a long time. Peter Andreas Heiberg broke off all contact with his

In a letter of March 1823, in which Heiberg tries to persuade C.E.F. Weyse to compose a romance and an overture for the performance, he uses similar expressions but in a semi-ironic tone, which is typical of their correspondence:

The overture could be spared in a pinch, but it would very much beautify the play if the great *musico* would glorify it with an introductory symphony that would express what is idyllic-Romantic-dreamy [*det Idyllisk-Romantisk-Sværmeriske*], the external lightheartedness and internal seriousness, which characterizes—I will not say "my play"—the fair subject, which almost already *is* music, and only needs a Weyse's support to become the most complete harmony ever heard by mortal ears.[1]

In this description, Heiberg opens up a small crack between the exterior and interior of the drama, discriminating between something playful and something serious.

Surprisingly enough, the romance gives the floor to Ali:

How slowly the day passes
For a sorrowful love!
Happiness knows no hours,
But sorrow every minute that yields.
There is no comfort in the bosom of the earth,
The waves of the sea are hopelessly blue!
Holy Prophet, thy moon
Coldly beholds my silent weeping.

Zulma, can you see my pain
From your happy Paradise?
Do you recall in earthly way
The promise I gave your heart?

---

son for five years, which means that the dedication (dated 1820—before the departure) was sent out to the public in the middle of this mutual silence (cf. Borup *Johan Ludvig Heiberg*, vol. 1, pp. 127-128).

[1] *Breve og Aktstykker vedrørende Johan Ludvig Heiberg*, ed. by Morten Borup, vol. 1, pp. 127-128.

C.E.F. Weyse, Romance af Nina (1823)
(Courtesy of The Music Museum, Music Historical Museum and
Carl Claudius' Collection.)

In my father's garden
I planted a small cedar;
The tree stands, as do my oaths,
Oh, but the gardener perishes![1]

---

[1] C.E.F. Weyse, *Romance af Nina for Pianoforte*, Copenhagen: C.C. Lose. The print
is not dated, but it must have been sometime between Heiberg's begging letter of
March 11, 1823 and Heiberg's comment that it had been published, made in a letter
to Jonas Collin of January 23, 1824; see *Breve og Aktstykker vedrørende Johan Ludvig
Heiberg*, ed. by Morten Borup, vol. 1, p. 137.

The key is G minor, the accompaniment resembles, according to Heiberg's own description, a plain guitar accompaniment,[1] and the tonal language colors the "lied" with exoticizing triplets, semitone intervals, etc.

Ali is a strange figure in the 1823 version. He has joined the pirates under false pretenses: he has no talent for looting, and instead he sings tender ballads of his deceased love. He was the one who saved Germeuil's life, spurred by the touching sight of Nina's despair. With Germeuil on the ship, he chooses to live for the next best thing, their elevating friendship, for he feels that Germeuil is educating him to greater thoughts and better feelings. He is, then, a representative of the Sentimental–Romantic friendship, but again in a way that verges on the ridiculous. He understands himself as the weak plant that needs to twine itself around the strong tree, and he resorts to physical measures to prove his point. He clutches his arms around Germeuil when the pirates want to separate the two, and he forces himself between the friend and the count when the count tries to takes his place at Germeuil's side.[2]

I do not know why Ali was rewarded with a romance by Weyse— maybe there simply was a musical "hole" in the pirate episode, an episode without precedence in the Nina tradition. Another explanation might be that Ali's romance is to be understood as a plain, poetical caesura in the play, a halt in the complicated turns of Nina's and Germeuil's love affair (contrary to Heiberg's later demands regarding the role of music in drama).[3] His sorrow is neither mad nor fancied, and not only does he languish because of an unmendable heartache, but he is a poet because of it. However, he is still a weak character in need of guidance and support, and almost a parasite on Germeuil's resumed business with the world. Ali would then be another double figure in the play, representing, on the one hand, the positively valued Romantic poetry and, on the other, the potential for ridiculous excess in Sentimental and Romantic expression.

---

[1] Ibid., p. 131.
[2] See Heiberg, *Nina, eller Den Vanvittige af Kierlighed*, p. 167, p. 158, p. 201. One cannot help thinking of Heiberg's further, comic elaboration on the need for physical closeness between lovers of opposite sexes in its modern form in the vaudeville *The Inseparables* (1827).
[3] Especially the criteria that the music should contribute to the dramatic element in "On Opera and *Singspiel*" (1834) and "Italian Opera" (1842); see Joachim Grage's contribution to this anthology.

Nina was the only complete literary work Heiberg carried with him on his return from Paris to Copenhagen in 1822. He had already submitted the play to the Royal Theater in 1821, and in the summer of 1822 it was approved on the condition that he make some "very necessary" cuts and corrections.[1] Heiberg had by then become associate professor (*Lektor*) in Kiel, and apparently had no desire to fiddle with the play himself, so he rather nonchalantly asked the theater managers to let someone else make the revisions.[2] When the production was finally set in motion in 1824, he could not supervise the rehearsals or even attend the performances himself.

The audience reaction in March 1824 was not so much tears as laughter, if we are to believe Thomas Overskou's theater history. Overskou talks of a fine psychological treatment, a natural and poetic expression of feelings, and a noble simplicity. However, the actors did not perform with sufficient delicacy and taste, and there were too many confusing episodes. Action that did not abide by the law of unity of time was clearly laughable in the eyes of the Copenhagen audience at that time: "Added to this, the audience could not keep up with the jumps in time between the acts, but burst into laughter, when they heard that several days had passed since they saw a person leave the stage."[3]

The worst blunder, however, was the costumes. For some reason, Heiberg's express wishes in his letter to Collin were not followed. The time indication was taken too literally, and the Sentimental–Romantic figures were sent on stage in powdered wigs, old-fashioned uniforms, and high, heavy boots, and this alone made the play a parody, Overskou reports. He even claims that the actors complained, but none of the

---

[1] *Breve og Aktstykker vedrørende Johan Ludvig Heiberg*, ed. by Morten Borup, vol. 1, p. 114.

[2] Heiberg's only former practical experience with the Royal Theater had been with the play, *Tycho Brahe's Prophecy*, which likewise was only performed five times in 1819. It had then taken him five years to make the cuts and changes requested by the Theater.

[3] Thomas Overskou, *Den danske Skueplads*, vol. 4, p. 733. In Galeotti's version from 1802, the problem of the unity of time was resolved by performing the first act of the ballet after the first act of the comedy of the evening—at the premiere, this was Jünger's *Ægtefolkene fra Landet*—and the second act after the comedy (cf. Galeotti, *Nina, eller Den Vanvittige af Kierlighed*, p. 4).

managers wanted to interfere, and he implies that the public assumed the costumes were intended to ruin the play.[1]

After the premiere, Heiberg entreated Collin both to shorten the play and correct the misunderstanding of the costuming: "I very well realize how much the old, tasteless costume must offend the audience's eyes—especially to us, who are not used to such accuracy on stage."[2] I would suggest that precisely the word "accuracy" indicates a problem inherent in Heiberg's text, namely, the historical distance. He not only set the action 50-60 years back in time, but also distanced himself from the culture of Sensibility by translating the ambivalences of the Sentimental drama towards excessive outbreaks of feelings into a more Romantic-modern ambivalence.

As mentioned earlier, Heiberg had made a laughing stock of Ingemann's sentimental figures in 1817 with *Christmas Jests and New Year's Fun*. Here he had Enrico and Blanca explain to the reader: "Sentimentality is our deity, we drown in sheer feelings, and we are Mohammedans in the sense that we worship the moon above all else; yes, we live practically on moonlight and skin of cream [*Maaneskin og Flødeskind*]."[3] Considering Ali's romance of the deceased love, the Holy Prophet, and the moon, the relationship between these two works, *Christmas Jests* and *Nina*, seems even more peculiar. Although it is unlikely that Heiberg meant to create a parody in *Nina*, it may not have been all that clear to the theater staff whether or not some of the parodic effects of the play were intended.

In any case, the play ran for only three performances, not the five that were necessary for the author to earn a percentage of the ticket sales. Heiberg had by then already spent the money he had counted on earning to cover one of his many debts.[4] He had no luck in selling the piece to

---

[1] See Overskou, *Den danske Skueplads*, vol. 4, p. 734.
[2] *Breve og Aktstykker vedrørende Johan Ludvig Heiberg*, ed. by Morten Borup, vol. 1, p. 146.
[3] Johan Ludvig Heiberg, *Julespøg og Nytaarsløier. Comødie*, Copenhagen: Boghandler Christensen 1817, p. 55.
[4] In 1821, *Nina* was already one of his weightiest arguments for receiving more money from the *Ad usus publicus* foundation so that he could travel on to Spain or at least afford to go home. The application was denied. Cf. Morten Borup *Johan Ludvig Heiberg*, vol. 1, pp. 108-109.

other theaters or publishers.[1] Nonetheless, he picked it up again in 1836 with the intention of scraping together a sum of money for a new trip to Paris with his wife, Johanne Luise Heiberg. *Nina* and a newly written vaudeville, *Nei*, were played for a single summer performance on June 1, 1836. Once again, in 1839, Heiberg staged *Nina* with Mrs. Heiberg in the title role, but this time it only received two performances before it was removed from the program. No matter how hard he tried, *Nina* never became a goldmine.

Why did he return to a theatrical fiasco, not once but twice? The summer performance in 1836 is easily understood as a spin-off of the success Bournonville's ballet had enjoyed in 1834 with Mrs. Heiberg in the role of Nina.[2] In his collection of plays, *Skuespil* (1835), Heiberg had shortened and altered the play quite effectively, and one can assume that the performances in both 1836 and 1839 followed this version, since there are no significant alterations in later editions of the text (1848, 1862). In the 1835 version, Germeuil creates a more resolute and firm impression, the count is less obdurate at the outset, Ali less clingy, Blinval no longer ridiculously excessive in his outbursts, and the dialogue as a whole a little less high flown. Most of the comic scenes between Victor and Cauchon have been erased, and so too the scene in which Nina understands the language of the flowers, the remarks on the equality of men, and some of the many invocations of God. Germeuil does not go so far as to worship Nina's soul in all its madness, but simply sees her flowers as a lovely poem with a clear and sacred meaning. The incestuous tones in the count's love for his daughter are diminished, he actively helps Victor and Collette, and he actually gets the final word: "And may every man, when the confusion of this life, / When the madness of our obscure plans ends,

---

[1] He tried in Berlin the same year with a shortened and reworked version; see his letter to Collin, dated March 26, 1824, *Breve og Aktstykker vedrørende Johan Ludvig Heiberg*, ed. by Morten Borup, vol. 1, p. 146.

[2] For Johanne Luise Heiberg, the ballet represented both personal and professional vindication; see her *Et liv genoplevet i erindringen*, vols. 1-4, ed. by Niels Birger Wamberg, 5th revised ed., Copenhagen: Gyldendal 1973-74, vol. 1, pp. 255-259. By the mid-1830s, the pantomimic ballet had gone out of fashion in Paris and had been replaced by a new, expressive Romantic style inaugurated by Filippo Taglioni's *La Sylphide* (1832); cf. John V. Chapman, "Jules Janin: Romantic Critic," *Rethinking the Sylph: New Perspectives on the Romantic Ballet*, ed. by Lynn Garafola, Hanover: Wesleyan University Press 1997, pp. 199-200.

/ Wake to the heavenly consciousness!"[1] Nina's madness has become an instance of common earthly confusion. The result is less Sensibility, less Romanticism, and what is left is a plot of rather ordinary complications with an added drop of mental derangement. While the 1823 version had too many agendas pointing in too many directions, the later versions presumably had too little at stake to be of interest.

Johanne Luise Heiberg comments on the 1836 performance in her memoirs; she thinks the play was well received, but to her the highlight of the evening was the vaudeville.[2] According to her, the spoken *Nina* could not compare with the ballet. She cites Heiberg's new dedication poem to her from the 1835 edition, in which Heiberg assigns a higher rank to Bigottini's and his wife's wordless images of thought than to his own play of words. She comments:

> Indeed, there are passions so deep and introverted that the word that explains almost weakens them. In the passionate expression of silence, accompanied by beautiful tones, there is somehow a larger scope for the fantasy of the audience. Passions such as these you could call musical; like music they have the greatest effect in their vagueness, into which anyone can set words according to his own feeling and wealth of fantasy; the fixed, clear word forces the fantasy to stay within the limits of the word. That is why the subject of *Nina* is probably better suited for the ballet or opera.[3]

Her argument is then that Nina should have stayed in the genres from which she originally came, because both passion and fantasy are

---

[1] Heiberg, *Nina, eller Den Vanvittige af Kierlighed. Skuespil i fem Acter*, in *Skuespil*, vol. 5, p. 294.

[2] The vaudeville is first and foremost a playful dialogue in which the "no" of the young girl comes to mean "no" to the wrong suitor and "yes" to the one she loves. Mrs. Heiberg's asessment is contradicted by W.H.F.A. Læssøe (1811-50, later known as Colonel Læssøe) in a letter to C.G. Andræ. *No* was entertaining but a trifle, whereas *Nina* was delightful: "You know the subject of *Nina* from the ballet; you have already admired Mrs. Heiberg's acting there; but imagine this perfected by the addition of the speech, and you will admit that the result could be a performance, worthy of the Théâtre-Français. Nina and her father (Ryge) are the most important persons; their acting was *non plus ultra* for a Dane. I have never seen anything superior" (Morten Borup, *Johan Ludvig Heiberg*, vol. 2, p. 73). To the best of my knowledge, neither Heiberg, his wife, nor Overskou commented on the performance in 1839.

[3] Johanne Luise Heiberg, *Et liv genoplevet i erindringen*, vol. 1, p. 271.

essentially nonverbal, and only as such can they reach the audience. Dedication or not, I very much doubt that her husband would fully subscribe to this poetics since it renounces the power and scope of the clear and distinct word.[1] Theater history proved her right, though, in the sense that Bournonville's ballet was more apt to survive, and played 27 times in the years 1834-51, though not achieving the same success as Galeotti's.

Heiberg had meanwhile launched his program of aesthetic education for public life, emphasizing politeness, decency, restraint, and integrity in public conduct. In this context, he also criticized the theater audience's inability to understand what they were seeing, not least, to "see" beyond the most raw, pathetic expressions on stage:

> When an actress enters the stage with a pale, deranged look and with fluttering hair, she may say whatever she wants; the effect has already been created and her lines are almost superfluous; this is not to imply that she might as well be silent; no, speak she must, but it is quite indifferent what she says as long as she speaks with passion....[2]

The true problem was perhaps obvious, namely, that Heiberg had painted himself into a corner by choosing Nina in the first place to represent his post-Romantic (or Romantic-conscious) warning against excessively Romantic-unconscious fantasy in 1820-23. In the 1835 version, he did his best to tame the pathetic-Sentimental legacy further. However, if Bournonville's *Nina* shows the ability of Sentimentality to fit into the harmonizing culture of Biedermeier, with its ambivalent fascination with and aversion to the dark sides of the human psyche (and the very taming effort of Biedermeier probably gives a renewed push for the women "crazed by love" in the arts), Heiberg's *Nina* of the 1830s shows its resistance to fitting into an idealistic, thought-provoking program.

So why, of all subjects in the world, *did* Heiberg choose Nina and her madness? The answer must lie in the effect on the audience he had

---

[1] This may be the reason why Heiberg—much to Johanne Luise's regret—omitted the dedication from the third edition of the play in 1848.

[2] Johan Ludvig Heiberg, "Hvad man seer, og hvad man hører," *Prosaiske Skrifter*, vol. 8, pp. 467-468.

experienced and witnessed in Paris in 1820, when he was out looking for a life philosophy and mission. Heiberg also wanted to captivate and educate his audience, and *Nina* can be regarded as an experiment in transforming the plot to his own purposes and to the taste of the Copenhagen audience at the same time. The experiment proved unsuccessful. The 1824 version (judging by the 1823 text) fluttered from image to image in a kind of middle-class confusion, from invocations of God and Heaven to the dying man's doubt in their existence, from a revolutionary agenda to that of excessive Sentimental expressions, further on to a frail, self-absorbed Romantic world of fantasy, and finally back to a more subdued, reason-based ethics. Heiberg in this way tripped back and forth between the two pitfalls he criticized and desperately tried to avoid in most of his writings: false idealism with its sublime, world-forgetting logic of absence (Heiberg's notion of Ingemann) and false realism with its materialist platitudes. In subsequent versions, the plot becomes more integrated, and many of the traces of Sentimentality are eliminated; at the same time, however, the madness loses much of its plot-driven force and *raison d'être*, becoming instead a picturesque excuse to pave the way for "consciousness."

Theater and Modernity:
Thomasine Gyllembourg's Novella *Near and Far*

Joachim Schiedermair

I. Near and Far *and the Theater: On the Marginality of Motifs*

That the topic "the Heibergs and the theater" should turn out to be profitable is not surprising. The two most important members of the family, namely, Johan Ludvig and Johanne Luise, bring together production and performance, theory and practice, institutional and artistic aspects of theater. But why talk about Thomasine Gyllembourg in this context? She is of course part of the Heiberg family and also wrote four rather unsuccessful plays, only two of which were actually performed. Although these plays faithfully adhere to the classical ideal of the unity of place, time and action, even Gyllembourg's own son Johan Ludvig doubted their dramatic character and said that these plays were really novellas in his foreword to the first printed edition in 1834.[1] If we bear in mind that Heiberg valued art based on its conformity to the ideals of its genre, this statement actually seems rather negative.

But I will neither direct my attention at any of these plays, nor will I undertake any doubtful attempts at rehabilitating Thomasine Gyllembourg as a dramatist. I have instead chosen one of her novellas,

---

[1] Johan Ludvig Heiberg, "Fortale til Skuespil af Forfatteren til en Hverdags-Historie," in *Prosaiske Skrifter*, vols. 1-11, Copenhagen: C. A. Reitzel 1861-62, vol. 4, p. 315: *"egentlig en Novelle."*

Near and Far from 1841,[1] which does not seem to have much to do with the theater at first glance. The core of this novella is a dispute between two brothers: Georg and Fredrik German, aged between 50 or 60 at the time of the action, were very close in their youth, but have grown distant due to an unhappy love triangle. Both of them were in love with Grethe, the daughter of a craftsman, who chose Fredrik. When the young woman became pregnant, Fredrik became aware of the disadvantages of such a socially inappropriate connection and broke up with her, but not without financially providing for her. His adherence to convention and social rules is what turned his brother Georg against him. This underlying conflict lies more than 25 years in the past when the plot of the novella commences, but it has led to a persistent communicative alienation between the two. Although the two brothers still love each other, even well-meant remarks are immediately interpreted as implicit accusations or even intentional disrespect for the other's feelings. This situation also explains the title, as the brothers are simultaneously *close and distant* (*Near and Far*).[2] Fredrik is especially hurt by the fact that Georg gives all his love to his adoptive son Fritz and thus prefers a stranger to his own brother.

The theater only enters this narrative via the figure of Alfred German, Fredrik's wayward son from his first marriage. He takes acting lessons in secret and has hopes of starting a career as an actor instead of following in his father's footsteps and becoming a merchant in the family firm. That his position is not to be taken seriously is illustrated by the fact that his favorite play is H.C. Andersen's *The Mulatto* (1840). What the Heiberg family thought of this play is well known: in Johan Ludvig's apocalyptic comedy "A Soul after Death" (in *New Poems*, 1841), which appeared in the same year as *Near and Far*, *The Mulatto* is performed in hell.

As far as the plot is concerned, the theater only plays a minor part. But for my approach to this novella, this marginality is not a disadvantage. I intend to investigate the discursive functionality of the theater motif in

---

[1] Thomasine Gyllenbourg, *Nær og fjern*, in *Samlede Skrifter af Forf. til "En Hverdagshistorie,"* vols. 1-12, 3rd ed., Copenhagen: C. A. Reitzel 1884, vol. 10, pp. 1-206.

[2] This reading of the title is proposed by Anni Broue Jensen in *Penge og Kjærlighed. Religion og socialitet i Thomasine Gyllembourgs forfatterskab*, Odense: Odense Universitetsforlag 1983, p. 43.

Gyllembourg's novella: which themes and discourses are brought into play by the fact that some characters are connected to the theater? If we ask such a question, even a marginal motif can acquire central importance because it imports a discourse into the text that is only indirectly connected to the motif itself. In saying this I follow the principle that literary texts—according to Sigrid Weigel—can function as "locations of culture," which "address the history of terms, theories and concepts, the conflicted creation of patterns of cultural interpretation as well as their enforcement in social interaction."[1] The advantage of literature over other forms of historical evidence is that it is not subjected to a specific purpose and thus presents different categories of meaning and their interconnections and overlaps simultaneously. This complexity can also be described as the concurrence of patterns of cultural interpretation which partially oppose and contradict each other. The following analysis of how a monetary and a gender discourse are developed in the novella merely by mentioning the theater and theatrical practices will show that these discourses are certainly conflicting and dissonant.

II. Symmetries

The general principle that apparently marginal themes can acquire a central significance for the whole text especially applies to Gyllembourg's prose: the most important element of her style is her "theoretically calculated conception," as Klaus Müller-Wille has put it.[2] The constellations of motifs and characters are established on the basis of mirroring, doubling and symmetry. The large number of interconnections in this delicate narrative architecture allows a seemingly marginal theme in a subplot to become relevant for the whole text because it is symmetrically related to a part of the main plot.

---

[1] Sigrid Weigel, "Zur Differenz von Gabe, Tausch und Konversion. Shakespeares The Merchant of Venice als Schauplatz von Verhandlungen über die Gesetze der Zirkulation," in her *Literatur als Voraussetzung der Kulturgeschichte. Schauplätze von Shakespeare bis Benjamin*, Munich: Fink 2004, p. 64.

[2] Klaus Müller-Wille, "Romantik—Biedermeier—Realismus," in *Skandinavische Literaturgeschichte*, ed. by Jürg Glauser, Stuttgart: Metzler 2006, p. 171.

Already the initial situation of *Near and Far* can be used as an example of Gyllembourg's systematic plot-construction. "The current owners of this trading house [German & Sons] are Georg and Fredrik German. These two brothers are connected by so many ties that their separation seems almost unthinkable."[1] The two brothers are obviously constructed as symmetrical characters and are thus defined by the balance of identity and difference. This reflexive doubling repeats itself in the next generation: Alfred, Fredrik's son, has his counterpart in Georg's adoptive son Fritz. At the beginning of the novella they are both afflicted by a vice; the rather ridiculous figure of Alfred is obsessed with the theater, while the sympathetic character of Fritz succumbs to the temptation of gambling over and over again. These symmetrical characters then become opposites as we learn how these vices are motivated and how they relate to them—I will address this later. Fredrik's pleasure-seeking and hardly domestic wife is defined against the background of her ward Pauline who represents ideal femininity. Accordingly, Pauline's harmonious betrothal to Fritz is a symmetrical contrast to Fredrik's unhappy marriage.

The symmetrical logic of the narrated world also appears in the psychological motivations of the characters and their actions. When a Norwegian woman called Thora Muk appears on the scene and claims to be betrothed to Fritz as well, Georg and Fredrik both painfully recognize this constellation as a recurrence of Fredrik's infidelity to Grethe. This recursive mirroring of their fate leads to the collapse of the hermeneutics of suspicion between the two old men and allows them to establish a new bond of trust.

At the end of the narrative Georg reveals to his brother that his adoptive son Fritz is in fact Grethe's and Fredrik's child and that all the love that Georg devoted to the young man was indirectly felt for him, his brother. This plot twist shows that Fritz is the cardinal point of the narrative construction around which the symmetrical and counter-symmetrical elements are organized. In his character the processes of doubling and mirroring are at peace: a) he neutralizes the differences between the brothers and even applies the same role, namely, that of the father, to both of them: Fredrik is his biological father, Georg his father

---

[1]   Gyllembourg, *Nær og fjern*, in *Samlede Skrifter af Forf. til "En Hverdagshistorie,"* vol. 10, p. 3.

by adoption. Fredrik finally says about him: "I shall love him twice as much, considering that, in a way, we are *united* in him."[1] b) Through his double status as a son he even reconciles Grethe and Georg, whom she rejected, because they now have a child via the adoption of Fritz. c) Fritz's acceptance into the family mends the breach of trust Fredrik committed when he made Grethe pregnant and then shied at the responsibility. d) A generation later, Fritz's marriage with Pauline also balances out Fredrik's failed marriage, since Fritz comes from the German family and Pauline is a relative of Fredrik's wife. e) Finally, Fritz also re-established the firm's initial unity. After having been in the hands of German senior alone, the next generation saw a split of the firm between Georg and Fredrik, and now it is reunited in Fritz's possession. The figure of Fritz makes the novella a narrative about the re-establishment of order on all levels and about harmony through order.

One of the strands in this web of mirror images is the theater. I will now address two moments in the text where the motifs of the theater and of acting unfurl a specific cultural pattern of interpretation.

III. Gender Discourse

First I will investigate a scene with a lot of melodramatic potential situated roughly in the second third of the text. The scene in question features the first appearance of Erik and Thora Muk at dinner in the German household. The whole situation is precarious, because Thora claims that she became engaged to Fritz during his business trip to Norway. The reader quickly realizes that Fritz is not really to blame for this embarrassing situation; Fritz's promise of marriage was intended as a joke and given under the influence of alcohol; no one present on the occasion had taken the engagement seriously and Fritz apologized to Erik for his behavior the following day. But Thora is highly emotional and performs a whole repertoire of emphatic theatrical gestures which she could have learned from Iffland or Kotzebue. I cite this passage in full to allow the reader to follow the theatricality of her behavior:

---

[1] Ibid., p. 204. My emphasis.

Thora Muk gripped his arm and sobbed: "Is it really true, Fritz? Is it really possible? You're refusing me! Do you see this ring on my finger? This is the ring you gave me on the evening you begged for my love and pledged loyalty to me….I prostrate myself before you." …This whole reply and all the previous ones were uttered by an utterly confused Thora, with shaking lips and a quaking voice. She now made a move, as though she was about to kneel before Fritz; but he prevented that by holding her upright while saying: "For the love of God! You don't know how unhappy you are making me."

"Kill me!" screamed Thora: "Say that you break our bond."

"Oh God! For me there never was any bond between us."

"Say that you despise me!"

"Honestly! I do not love you. I love another woman. My fiancée is sitting over there…"

Thora jumped up in desperation and declaring: "So now it is time to die," she took a knife from the table and pointed it at her neck. Georg, who was closest to her, lunged at the knife and gave the thrust a different direction; but he could not prevent her from wounding herself. The blood blossomed on her white collar, and she fell into Georg's arms, all pale and unconscious…. Erik lamented and moaned. They loosened her clothes, and everyone was very busy helping her when Fritz came with a doctor a few minutes later. The doctor smiled when he saw the wound, cleaned and bandaged it and reassured them that she would be fine in a few days. Thora was very weak.[1]

It is quite obvious that Thora's behavior is influenced by contemporary theatrical conventions and that Gyllenbourg rejects these conventions as overly dramatic and overstrung. Fritz's exclamation, "All this is a wretched comedy,"[2] which is repeated by another character shortly afterwards, points the reader to the theater discourse—although of course its meaning is only metaphorical at first. The doctor's smile also illustrates that Thora's attempted suicide probably only has a very limited claim to authenticity and is little more than a flashy performance. At this point the characters (and the readers) do not know yet that Thora is in fact an amateur actress. A few days later Erik relates that his sister possesses

---

[1] Ibid., pp. 129-131.
[2] Ibid., p. 129: "*Det Hele er jo en elendig Comedie.*"

an unrivalled talent for acting.[1] "She had often charmed the audience in private theaters, and her many admirers shared the opinion that she could have a brilliant career, if only she would devote herself to the art and accept a profitable engagement which a public theater would offer her."[2] She soon demonstrates her skill: every afternoon she transforms her sick room into a stage, where she shows off her talent with Alfred as a partner. It is only consistent that the group of theater-lovers also interprets Thora's suicide attempt as part of her stage performance: Thora "and her new friends [had] agreed that this scene, which her appearance in the German household had entailed, was so beautiful and touching that it was worth including in the most magnificent tragedy."[3]

This quotation is crucial. The conventions of the theater shape the way the theater-lovers perceive the world in such a way that ordinary life appears as a theater play. Gyllembourg thus incorporates the central point of one of the most famous eighteenth-century polemics of the theater into her narrative. I am of course referring to Rousseau's *Lettre à M. d'Alembert* (1758). According to him, the danger of acting is that it could transfer its logic to the world outside the theater:

> What is the actor's talent? The art of feigning, of assuming a character other than his own, to appear different from what one is….I know that the actor's performance is not the game of a rogue who is trying to trick someone…. Nor do I accuse him of being an imposter, but rather of cultivating the art of deceiving others as well as possible.[4]

That Gyllembourg, who greatly admired Rousseau, does not use the theater-lover Alfred to introduce this problem, but creates an extra female character, Thora, shows how closely she read Rousseau. Rousseau draws a connection between this danger of unreality and his own

---

[1] Ibid., p. 138.
[2] Ibid., p. 138.
[3] Ibid., p. 147.
[4] Jean-Jacques Rousseau, *Lettre à M. d'Alembert*, ed. by Michel Launay, Paris: Garnier-Flammarion 1967, pp. 163f.: "*Qu'est-ce que le talent du Comédien? L'art de se contrefaire, de faire revêtir un autre caractère que le sien, de paroître différent de ce qu'on est….Je sais que le jeu du Comédien n'est pas celui d'un fourbe qui veux en imposer…. Aussi ne l'accuse-je pas d'être précisément un trompeur, mais de cultiver pour tout métier le talent de tromper les hommes…*"

construction of gender. According to his conception, a woman who has
not been twisted by culture is utterly incapable of dissimulation; unlike
the man, her body and her behavior are transparent and let her soul shine
through at all times.

> As regards the true inclinations of their sex, even when they lie, women are
> not false at all. Why do you look at their mouth, when it is not the mouth
> that does the talking? Look at her eyes, her color, her breathing, her fearful
> air, her reluctance: that is the language nature gives them to answer you. The
> mouth always says no and ought to do so. But the tone she gives to it is not
> always the same, and this tone cannot lie.[1]

But if a woman assumes a role, lets this role take over her whole behavior
and uses the body at her disposal, thus making her a good actress, then
this behavior would cause her to reject her natural disposition. Acting
does not agree with femininity. The two concepts oppose public and
private, role and nature, performance and transparency. Accordingly,
Thora Muk's function in the architectural economy of the novella is to
contrast the "true" femininity represented by Pauline, as she is essentially
characterized by her inability to dissimulate. Thus Fritz is positioned
between two women who are reciprocally related to each other.

That Pauline's opposite is an actress has its own intricate implications.
For with the problem of gender being infected with the topic of
theatrical pretence, the conception of femininity is linked to the problem
of modernity: in her interesting article "Die Frau als Schauspielerin.
Auskünfte einer Metapher" Ursula Geitner investigates the importance
of the profession of actress (as an exception and anticipation) for
"woman's entry into modernity"[2] during the eighteenth and nineteenth

---

[1] Jean-Jacques Rousseau, *Émile ou de l'éducation*, ed. by Michel Launay, Paris: Garnier-Flammarion 1966, p. 505: "*[D]ans les vrais penchants de leur sexe, même en mentant, elles ne sont point fausses. Pourquoi consulter leur bouche, quand ce n'est pas elle qui doit parler? Consulter leurs yeux, leur teint, leur respiration, leur air craintif, leur molle résistance: voilà le langage que la nature leur donne pour vous répondre. La bouche dit toujours non, et doit le dire; mais l'accent qu'elle y joint n'est pas toujours le même; et cet accent ne sait point mentir.*"

[2] Ursula Geitner, "Die Frau als Schauspielerin. Auskünfte einer Metapher," in *Schauspielerinnen. Der theatralische Eintritt der Frau in die Moderne*, ed. by Ursula Geitner, Bielefeld: Haux 1988, pp. 252-284.

centuries. One of the key features of the transition from a stratified to a modern, functionally organized society is the differentiation between private and public space.[1] This separation can be applied to the pair of metaphors "on stage"/"off stage." In public an individual plays various social roles; the private space, on the other hand, is conceptualized as a space in which the repertoire of possible actions is not defined by role, but by the natural motivations. Geitner sees the private sphere and its non-functional organization as a remnant of the pre-modern feudal society. That this differentiation is affected by gender is quite obvious. For unlike the man, the woman is exempted from public role-playing, as she is excluded from public efficacy—she is only private and thus completely natural. This preconception explains why people in the eighteenth and nineteenth century were so skeptical about the profession of actress. On stage, a woman would have to act within a functionally defined role and thus subject herself to the pattern of modernity. In Geitner's argument, Rousseau's letter to *M. d'Alembert* is one of the central documents of this connection between the definition of gender and of modernity.

So the function of the theater discourse in this novella is to connect the gender discourse and the modernity discourse like a relay. Gyllembourg embeds her narrative about the re-establishment of order into a modernity discourse which has political, technical and economic features. The first lines of the novella are as follows:

> Everyone who knows the established trading house "German and Sons" must wish that our country had many of its kind: wealthy but not enormously rich, industrious but not unsettled, hospitable but not pompous....It had the good fortune of having remained untouched by the tempestuous

---

[1] See, for example, Karin Hausen, "Die Polarisierung der 'Geschlechtercharaktere.' Eine Spiegelung der Dissoziation von Erwerbs- und Familienleben," in *Seminar. Familie und Gesellschaftsstruktur. Materialien zu den sozioökonomischen Bedingungen von Familienformen*, ed. by Heidi Rosenbaum, Frankfurt a. M.: Suhrkamp 1978, pp. 161-191. Jürgen Habermas, *Strukturwandel der Öffentlichkeit. Untersuchungen zu einer Kategorie der bürgerlichen Gesellschaft*, 4th ed., Neuwied/Berlin: Luchterhand 1969, pp. 55-63. Niklas Luhmann, *Liebe als Passion. Zur Codierung von Intimität*, 5th ed., Frankfurt a. M.: Suhrkamp 1999, pp. 13-39. Ute Frevert, *'Mann und Weib, und Weib und Mann.' Geschlechter-Differenzen in der Moderne*, Munich: Beck 1995, pp. 133-165.

changes of time for a large number of years, partly due to the fact that it
had not only dealt in speculative trading, but also actively engaged itself in
building remarkably well-constructed new [ships] in its own shipyard. All
these enterprises were pursued with the determination and zeal that the
Zeitgeist of our time has evoked to make life more happy and its burdens
more bearable.[1]

The narrative develops before a background of social modernization,
and the theater discourse draws the problems of gender roles into this
vortex of "tempestuous changes" ("*stormende Forandringer*"). The theater
makes the gender discourse readable as a discourse of modernity and
vice versa. Only as an actress can woman leave the pre-modern space
which is conserved in the private sphere. Applied to the text, this means
that one would have to read the devaluation of Thora Muk in favor of
Pauline's natural state as an expression of conservative social analysis, or
if we assume that every expression also has a function, as an expression of
conservative social analysis with the intention of stopping social mobility
("changes"/"*Forandringer*") and thus the mobility of gender positions.

But this novella does not limit its presentation of the negative effects
of the theater discourse to the middle-class model of femininity, but also
makes the concept of masculinity appear ambiguous. Being an actor was
not problematic for a man, since masculinity was modeled as a socially
defined existence in various roles. But one must pay attention to the fact
that Thora Muk's Norwegian nationality significantly modifies the theater
discourse in the novella. For as far as the development and acceptance
of the theater were concerned, Norway was still very provincial even in
the second half of the nineteenth century. Admittedly, the completion of
the Christiania Theater on Bankplassen in 1837 did provide the country
with a theater that was both larger and better equipped than Dramaten
in Stockholm and the Royal Theater in Copenhagen.[2] But the manners
and behavior of the audience as well as the performance of Norwegian
actors were far from acceptable by Danish standards: Johan Ludvig

---

[1] Gyllembourg, *Nær og fjern* in *Samlede Skrifter af Forf. til "En Hverdagshistorie,"* vol.
    10, p. 3.
[2] Lise Lyche, *Norges teaterhistorie*, Asker: Tell Forlag 1991, p. 98.

Heiberg, for example, had led a journalistic charge in Denmark against loud clapping and booing. In Norway wild brawls in the auditorium were still not uncommon.[1] As far as actors were concerned, Norwegian theaters were forced to import competent personnel from Denmark as late as the middle of the nineteenth century. Formal training was virtually non-existent in Norway. But above all, the lack of professional theaters was responsible for the fact that most acting took place in the semi-public space of private parties and amateur performances. So as an amateur actress, Thora Muk has not been completely absorbed into the (male) public sphere, and is thus at least partly rehabilitated from the perspective of a concept of femininity based on naturalness. For Alfred on the other hand, the semi-public character of the Norwegian theater scene has a completely different consequence. At the end of the novella, he elopes to Norway with Thora who wants to "introduce him on the Norwegian stage, the pearl of which she herself will become."[2] For him, this step is a step out of the public space that he should occupy as a man. One could argue that Alfred's escape from the public function of a merchant, which his father had intended him to fulfill, into the semi-public sphere of the Norwegian theater amounts to an effeminization of his character.

IV. Money and Modernity

We have established that the theater discourse causes gender problems, which in turn links the novella to a negatively connoted discourse of modernity. But the text contains another evaluation of modernity which paradoxically turns out to be positive. The passage quoted above makes

---

[1] Ibid., pp. 100-107. We also know from a letter Gyllembourg wrote to her daughter-in-law Johanne Luise Heiberg, who was performing in Kristiania at the time, that Gyllembourg did not think much of the Norwegians' taste in art. This letter is included in Johanne Luise Heiberg's autobiography: Johanne Luise Heiberg, *Et Liv gjenoplevet i Erindringen*, vols. 1-4, ed. by Aage Friis, 4th ed., Copenhagen: Gyldendal 1944, vol. 1, pp. 95f.

[2] Gyllembourg, *Nær og fjern*, in *Samlede Skrifter af Forf. til "En Hverdagshistorie,"* vol. 10, p. 167.

clear that the reasons for the "tempestuous changes of time" are economic. When Gyllembourg explicitly mentions the advantage of having invested the firm's money not only in the speculative finance transactions but also in real values, she is probably referring to the national bankruptcy of 1813 and all its consequences for the redistribution of capital and the resulting restructuring of the Danish society. What Gyllembourg establishes for Denmark in her novella agrees with the well-known theories used to describe the process of modernization by Georg Simmel in his important work on the cultural impact of money, and the system-theoretician Niklas Luhmann. In Luhmann's *Die Wirtschaft der Gesellschaft* one can read that "the transition to the money economy played an important, some even say a decisive, part in the development of modern society."[1] And Simmel says that the money economy causes the "separation of the personality from its individual accomplishments,"[2] meaning that the money economy is essential to the production of the functionally organized society with its role identities, which was outlined above.[3] This means that the logic of the monetary discourse would be the motor powering the theatrical discourse of performed identities. In order to investigate further, I want to look at a second scene in the novella where there is also a tangible connection between theater and modernity. In this case, however, the theater is presented as an opposite of modernity,

---

[1] Niklas Luhmann, *Die Wirtschaft der Gesellschaft*, Frankfurt a. M.: Suhrkamp 1988, p. 43.

[2] Georg Simmel, *Philosophie des Geldes*, ed. by Otthein Rammstedt, Frankfurt a. M.: Suhrkamp 2000, table of contents.

[3] Instead of medieval face-to-face communities in which most economic exchange took place within a limited social network, in which one knew one's partners personally and was thus also subject to various non-economic dependencies, the money economy creates abstract relations, because all accomplishments are transmitted via the abstract medium of money. A merchant, for example, only knows his supplier in this specific function and not personally. Thus he can replace him in his completely non-individualized function with other contractors. "The significance of the individual social element has been transformed into the one-sided practicality of its performance. This can also be produced by other and personally different people to whom we are only connected by an interest which is completely expressible in money." (Georg Simmel, "Selbstanzeige von 1901," in *Philosophie des Geldes*, ed. by Otthein Rammstedt, Frankfurt a. M.: Suhrkamp 2000, pp. 721f.) So for Simmel, the rising money economy is the driving force behind the transition of social existence into theatral role-identity.

as a metaphor for an outdated reference to the world. It is confronted with the logic of the monetary discourse as the true motor of modernity in a surprisingly affirmative way.

One does not need a lot of imagination to notice that money is an important topic in the novella. Money, or the lack of money, is repeatedly the subject of conversation between characters. Thora Muk is persuaded to drop her claims to Fritz with a large sum of money, Pauline is forced to work as a governess due to her poverty and consequential lack of a dowry, Fritz and Alfred are never solvent for various reasons: Alfred's father does not give him much, and Fritz succumbs to his gambling problem again and again—and there are many more such incidents in the text.

But lack of money is not only a motif. It, or rather the circulation that maintains it, becomes a metaphor of a model of the world in the same scene that introduces the topic of the theater into the novella. Alfred is low on funds once again and asks Fritz for money, who himself has just lost all his at a game of cards. This communicative situation allows Gyllembourg to contrast these two figures and especially their specific weaknesses. Both of them are driven to their passions by boredom. "God give that I could close my eyes and ears to all the sensual experiences in this boring world and could rise far above the petty, every-day interests!"[1] Alfred moans and employs a dualistic rhetoric in doing so: the surface and the true nature, purposeful every-day life and the disinterested pleasure of art. He justifies the theater as the realm of truth which can only be found beyond the world of sensually perceivable phenomena. Fritz's justification of his passion for gambling reads quite similarly:

I do not play in order to win money; no, it is about the tingling pleasure of permanent excitement and of hovering between hope and fear; it is about this bold glance under the secretive blanket hiding the machinery of chance, and about how the wheels of fate which whirl so quickly, grind so slowly in life as though they had stopped all together. This suffocating boredom which we have to fight if we want to fulfill our wishes and plans, is

---

[1] Gyllembourg, *Nær og fjern*, in *Samlede Skrifter af Forf. til "En Hverdagshistorie,"* vol. 10, p. 20.

the worst thing here on earth in my opinion. But in the game, every minute creates a new fate; it is as if one were in a new existence; no heartbeat passes without movement in the soul; everyday life is quite different; there the precious circulations of blood and thought are wasted without gain or gratification.[1]

The first phrase I want to highlight is the "bold glance under the secretive blanket hiding the machinery of chance" ("*Titten ind under det hemmelige Dække, som skjuler Tilfældets Værksted*"), because it shows that Fritz argues in a way similar to Alfred. Put more abstractly, one might say that both positions are ways of handling experiences of contingency. Both justify their passion by saying that it provides them with meaning. They want to reduce the contingency of life by ignoring the confusing surface (in the case of the theater), or by finding the general rule behind everything (in the case of gambling).

But despite all functional similarities between the passion for the theater and the passion for gambling, the ways in which they fulfill these functions differ greatly. They both make it possible to handle the contingency of the world by providing a framework for differentiating between relevant and irrelevant contingency; but these frameworks have significant differences. Following Luhmann, one might say that Fritz and Alfred apply different contingency formulas to the world. In system theory, this term means the reduction of the stunning complexity of the world to a more manageable degree of complexity, which in turn makes (individual and social) action possible in the first place.[2] In other words, the contingency formula is a screen with a hole in it that leaves only a small amount of contingency which can then be dealt with.

Alfred's contingency formula is finitude: he solves the problem of unintelligible complexity by reducing all phenomena to an either/or: either they are sensual/perishable/finite, or they are mental/permanent/infinite: "God grant that I could close my eyes and ears to all the sensual experiences in this boring world and could rise far above the petty,

---

[1] Ibid., pp. 26f.
[2] See, for example, Luhmann, *Die Wirtschaft der Gesellschaft*, p. 181.

everyday interests!"¹ In saying this, he employs a rhetoric that draws upon the repertoire of (secularized) Christianity: he speaks about a "calling" to the theater ("*Kald*") and that he wants to "devote" (or even "hallow") all his strength to the theater ("*vil hellige alle mine Kræfter*").² In one of his letters he explicitly writes that art is "the true religion for those who understand it."³ So the theater (at least its negative form which Alfred represents) appears as religion's heir.

The model of gambling, however, does not differentiate between this world and another world, but operates with the principle of circulation in a closed system, where the total remains unchanged. The money of a player changes hands from one moment to the next without causing any change in the quality or quantity of the total money staked. It is important to observe that Fritz emphasizes that the world works in the same way, albeit at a different speed. According to Luhmann, the contingency formula "shortage" with the code have/have-not defines the economic system. In other words, in the case of Fritz, these two constituents (shortage with its code) with their monetary logic seem to function as the general model for the whole society. This becomes clear when Fritz speaks of the "circulation of blood and thought." It is obvious that the metaphor of the cash flow is derived from the circulation of blood. But in the passage quoted above, the opposite happens: the circulation of money makes the blood flow. I repeat, "But in the game, every minute creates a new fate; it is as if one were in a new existence; no heartbeat passes without movement in the soul; everyday life is quite different; there the precious circulations of blood and thought are wasted without gain or gratification." In other words, the circulation of money ("every minute...a new fate") is more effective than the circulation of blood.⁴

---

¹ Gyllembourg, *Nær og fjern*, in *Samlede Skrifter af Forf. til "En Hverdagshistorie,"* vol. 10, p. 20.
² Ibid., p. 22.
³ Ibid., p. 167.
⁴ I am grateful to Jon Stewart for pointing out that there is a quite similar justification of gambling in the works of Johan Ludvig Heiberg. In his article "Nemesis" (1827) he writes: a defender of gambling should use the argument "that for any participant gifted with imagination it is interesting to see the large number of contingent events, hardly fewer than those normally encountered in an entire lifespan, let loose in the course of an hour as a matter of course....For games of chance symbolize life

But in this quotation the circulation of money also becomes the general metaphor of a life without transcendence: precisely because money has no quality of its own, it can function as the medium that makes everything in the world comparable and thus replaceable. This is also what makes body and spirit replaceable in Fritz's model: "[N]o heartbeat passes without movement in the soul," and blood and thought are two different currencies which can be exchanged into each other in the same cycle. Another characteristic point is that Fritz loves mathematics and Ovid's *Metamorphoses*,[1] because they both feature transformations, in the case of mathematics even transformations with equal sums on both sides of the equation.

A look at Luhmann's work shows that this inflation of the monetary logic, which we have traced in Fritz's exclamations, is a specific characteristic of the eighteenth and nineteenth century: the statement, "Only the creation of a middle-class society replaces the omnipresence of god with the omnipresence of money,"[2] is one of the few phrases in his work which is immediately intelligible. One could claim that Gyllembourg analyzes two specifically middle-class models of coping with contingency in Fritz and Alfred: we have, on the one hand, the role of art (theater in this case), which is to establish transcendence and to take over the functions of religion, thus trying to conserve a pre-modern society, and, on the other hand, the role of money, which is to create immanence and thus produce modernity.

But this means that Gyllembourg assigns quite different functions and connotations to the theater here than in the case of Thora Muk. First, the theater was the model representing the fragmentation of the individual into a role-identity, whereas we are now in the situation that the theater discourse—unlike the monetary discourse—provides an order

---

insofar as life depends on contingency."). Johan Ludvig Heiberg, "Nemesis," in *Johan Ludvig Heibergs Prosaiske Skrifter*, vols. 1-11, Copenhagen: C. A. Reitzel 1861-62, vol. 2, pp. 213f. (English translation quoted from *Heiberg's Contingency Regarded from the Point of View of Logic and Other Texts*, ed. and trans. by Jon Stewart, Copenhagen: Museum Tusculanum Press 2008 (*Texts from Golden Age Denmark*, vol. 4), p. 116.)

[1] Gyllembourg, *Nær og fjern*, in *Samlede Skrifter af Forf. til "En Hverdagshistorie,"* vol. 10, p. 21.

[2] Niklas Luhmann, "Knappheit, Geld und die bürgerliche Gesellschaft," *Jahrbuch für Sozialwissenschaft*, vol. 23, 1972, p. 191.

intended to guarantee transcendence, a kind of ghost in the machine. I think that this opposition cannot be broken down. On the contrary, these conflicting evaluations of the same discourse show the concurrence of different patterns of cultural interpretation in the same literary text which I mentioned at the beginning. But what is even more surprising is that the reader's sympathies are so clearly directed, for Alfred's rhetoric of transcendence is exposed as an act itself. At the end of the novel he elopes with Thora Muk, but not before extorting a check for 500 Rigsbankdaler from his father. In doing so he gives up his contingency formula of "art as religion" for the contingency formula of money. Fritz, on the other hand, reconciles all loose ends of the plot at the end of the narrative, as I related at the beginning.

One could object that Fritz changes in the course of the novella. He gives up his gambling and becomes a responsible member of middle-class society through his connection with Pauline. One would assume that this conversion is a denial of the monetary contingency formula which he expounds at the beginning of the novella. Gambling and the logic of money would remain just as negative as Alfred's passion for the theater. But precisely this interpretation is not supported by the novella. For when Fritz's hope that Pauline would marry him is fulfilled, he exclaims: "The wheel of fortune no longer tempts me, since I have bet on higher odds and won."[1] Fritz promises to stop gambling, but the logic of his betrothal also follows the rules of the lottery. The contingency formula of shortage, which we have reconstructed as monetary, is thus preserved and dominates even Fritz's erotic and matrimonial discourse.

This leads to my final argument. The two cornerstones of the monetary system—shortage and stability of the total sum involved—determine not only Fritz but also the other characters. (I limit myself to one example: Fredrik feels that his brother's love has passed over to Fritz. Thus he imagines love in the sense of shortage and stability of the total sum involved: if someone has it, someone else lacks it.) But I want to go further still and claim that Fritz has exposed the general model of the fictional world of the novella. I have shown earlier that the plot obeys a strict structure, namely, the principle of symmetry. Fritz is *the* value that

---

[1] Gyllembourg, *Nær og fjern*, in *Samlede Skrifter af Forf. til "En Hverdagshistorie,"* vol. 10, p. 104.

fills all vacant positions in order to guarantee a stable balance. This means that the structure of the novella which is so typical of Gyllembourg's work itself obeys the principle of the stability of the total sum involved. If this is true, the idealistic Biedermeier harmony that is so characteristic for the *Hverdagshistorier* is not the result of a search for transcendence or art as religion but the result of a favorable balance.

V. Theater as the Intersection of Discursive Conflicts

Although *Near and Far* is only about the theater in a few passages, I hope to have made clear that these passages are essential for a reconstruction concerned with discourse analysis. In the context of Alfred's passion for the theater, the novella discusses the question of naturalness with all its gender connotations and the question of the possibility and conditions of meaning. I also hope to have made clear that both questions are combined with a discourse on modernity. In the case of the first theme, the theater (as a place of dissimulation) is part of a metaphor for the constitution of the *modern* individual; in the case of the second, it is the location of a *pre-modern* assignment of meaning. In other words, in the first discourse, the theater represents modernity, in the second pre-modernity. It is surprising that the theater is negatively connoted in both cases, since this leads to the paradoxical conclusion that modernity is evaluated pejoratively and positively in the same text. This inconsistency illustrates the fascinating complexity of literary texts which reflects the "conflicted creation of patterns of cultural interpretation," to recall the words of Sigrid Weigel, quoted above.

Translated by Henry Gordon-Heitmann

The Ethics of Performance in Johanne Luise Heiberg's Autobiographical Reflections

Karin Sanders

It takes Johanne Luise Heiberg (1812-90) some fifty printed pages to provide her readers with an answer to the question posed in the title of her essay "Er Skuespilkunsten en Moralsk Berettiget Kunst?" or "Is the Art of Acting a Morally Justified Art Form?" The essay, found toward the end of the fourth and last volume of her posthumously published autobiography *A Life Relived in Memory* (1891-92), serves as a kind of testament and treatise on her art form. She reflects:

> My work as an actress was now forever finished. Everything now lies in front of me like a book with densely written pages on which my account has been tabulated and thought over in many an earnest, restless hour, in many a sleepless night, and the result has been the recurrent question to myself: Is the art of acting a morally justified art form?[1]

The question seems to call for a straightforward answer: *either* the art of acting is morally justified *or* the art of acting is not morally justified. It turns out, predictably, that no such simple answer is to be found. Johanne Luise Heiberg's response to her own query is strikingly ambiguous: an explicit and resounding "no" *and* a surreptitious and rhetorically embedded "yes."

---

[1] Johanne Luise Heiberg, *Et liv genoplevet i erindringen*, vols. 1-4, ed. by Niels Birger Wamberg, 5th revised edition, Copenhagen: Gyldendal 1973, vol. 4, p. 209. All translations to English are my own.

There are a number of questions to consider here, not only the one addressed deliberately by Mrs. Heiberg, as she was known in her time and since, regarding the morality of the art of acting, although this question is far richer and more complicated than we may expect at first glance. We need also ponder the ramifications of her narrative strategy, the placement of the "theoretical" treatise on the morality of acting within her autobiography, and with it the "actual ethical effects," to borrow Wayne Booth's words, on the intended readership.[1] An analysis of her ethics of performance must, therefore, I propose, encompass both questions of acting and questions of writing about the morality of acting. To do so, the difference between Mrs. Heiberg's somewhat restricted query (about what is morally justified in one specific art form: stage acting) needs to be considered vis-à-vis reliability in a larger sense of the word (including the ethics of writing, reading, publishing). The appeal of Mrs. Heiberg's treatise for an analysis of the ethics of performance is not only that she addresses the morality of aesthetics head-on, but also that the treatise itself is couched in a myriad of indirect communication and strategic co-signers.

The autobiography in its totality gives us a way to understand how Mrs. Heiberg navigated the aesthetic-ethic divide. It starts and ends with a description of shame, "*Skam.*" Shame is linked to her social heritage, surrounded by alcoholism, poverty, sickness, sexuality and religious otherness as half-Jewish and half-Catholic in a Protestant state. Shame is also linked to her artistic legacy in the theater, surrounded by actors in a world of vanity and self-importance. Her reflections offer a psychological, a social, a philosophical and finally a religious explanation of and response to the experience of shame. She couches her rescue from the humiliation of her origin in psychological terms and sees herself as saved by an inherent naïveté, incorruptibility, lack of self-consciousness

---

[1] Booth elaborates: "the serious ethical critic is always faced with two tasks, not just the one that earlier ethical critics performed in describing the moral health or disease of any one work. To talk about the ethical powers of a work as being actually in the work, regardless of readers' differences, is one thing. To talk about a work's actual ethical effects is quite another. Can the two tasks in any way be reconciled?" Wayne C. Booth, "The Ethics of Forms: Taking Flight with *The Wings of the Dove*," in *Understanding Narrative*, ed. by James Phelan and Peter J. Rabinowitz, Columbus: Ohio State University Press 1994, p. 102.

and self-reflection as well as a deep connectedness to forces of nature. In social terms she essentially erases her biological family from the fabric of her life story as she transforms herself from Jomfru Pätges to Fru Heiberg. In philosophical terms, she moves herself from immediacy into reflection (to use Kierkegaard's terms), a move that is finally connected to a series of ethical principles and to religious reflections in the treatise. The problem with the aesthetic, in Mrs. Heiberg's view, is that it tends toward the self-serving. Because aestheticism potentially constitutes self-indulgent escapism, and with it decadent evasion of proper sociability, it lacks the commitment and responsibility that she sees as *sine qua non* for her art. We detect Kierkegaardian undertones here, because she, on this matter, sees eye to eye with Søren Kierkegaard. To both the philosopher and the actress, lack of ethical commitment translated to failure in acknowledging one's social debt and with it one's collective public reality.[1] Kierkegaard's insightful reading of her art form in "The Crisis and a Crisis in the Life of an Actress" from 1848 and his distinction between *being* and *performing* a role (the first does not require artistic skills, the latter does) resonated with her own views on performance.[2] But Kierkegaard also threw coals on a fire that already had made her anxious about the ethics of performance. He gives numerous examples of the potentially destructive attention that actors have to endure from the public.

In "Is the Art of Acting a Morally Justified Art Form?" we can therefore locate Mrs. Heiberg's efforts to formulate something close to what Bruce Kirmmse has called "an aesthetic analogue to the ethical acquisition of the self."[3] The analogue, we are supposed to imagine,

---

[1] See also Bruce Kirmmse's chapter on Johanne Luise Heiberg in *Kierkegaard in Golden Age Denmark*, Bloomington and Indianapolis: Indiana University Press 1990, pp. 329-330.

[2] Søren Kiekegaard's "Krisen og en Krise i en Skuespillerindes Liv" was originally published in *Fædrelandet*, vol. 9, July 24, 1848, no. 188, columns 1485-1490; July 25, no. 189, columns 1493-1500; July 26, no. 190, columns 1501-1506; July 27, no. 191, columns 1509-1516. (Reprinted in Kierkegaard's *Samlede Værker*, 1st ed., vols. 1-14, ed. by A.B. Drachmann, J.L. Heiberg, and H.O. Lange, Copenhagen: Gyldendal 1901-1906, vol. 10, pp. 323-344. English translation in *Christian Discourses. The Crisis and a Crisis in the Life of an Actress*, trans. by Howard V. Hong and Edna H. Hong, Princeton: Princeton University Press 1997, pp. 303-325.)

[3] Kirmmse, *Kierkegaard in Golden Age Denmark*, p. 330.

is not just one that pairs aesthetics and ethics in general or abstract terms, but one that speaks very directly to the challenges faced by the individual practitioner of stage art. She uses a circuitous way, however, to describe her (often provocative) views. One characteristic feature is that she allows others to speak on her behalf, a kind of adaptation of indirect communication. While she uses this strategy throughout the four-volume autobiography, the ways in which it is used in the treatise are particularly noteworthy.

To show how this works, it helps to start reading her treatise from the back first. This reveals that her spiritual mentor, the Hegelian bishop Hans Lassen Martensen (1808-84), for all intents and purposes serves as a designated co-signer of her ethical-religious reflections on the morality of performing. In fact, in numerous ways the treatise functions as an indirect dialogue with Martensen. She goes so far as to enclose a letter from him, in full, and with the blessing of the bishop himself, in which he clearly endorses her moral judgment of the theater and its actors. On the very pages of the treatise, from *within* the text on which he comments, Martensen lends his considerable weight as arbiter of taste and morals:

> …these reflections…have a great and exacting value in that they are also self-reflections and confessions. They are surely the first I have read or heard in regard to such *ethical* questions, something new and extraordinary. In my view they ought to be published one day and will be of lasting value not just in the literature of our fatherland but also in all literature, and will not just be of interest, but call forth deep and serious reflections. For me they have served greatly to sharpen the problem in regard to individual ethics. Yet seen from the standpoint of social ethics I have never doubted and do not doubt that the theater is necessary on a certain level of the society's development. And no one will here be able to deny its ennobling and educating influence. The difficulties arise in regard to the individuals who as artists have to sacrifice themselves, so to speak, for society. And these difficulties, particularly in regard to men, you have placed under a sharp light of truth, so that the full question—so it seems to me—gets a new and sharper edge.[1]

---

[1] Johanne Luise Heiberg, *Et liv genoplevet i erindringen*, vol. 4, p. 261.

The salient point here is that societal ethics (*samfundsetikken*) finds an aesthetic equivalence in the theater institution. The ethical problems, as the readers have already culled from Mrs. Heiberg's reflections throughout her autobiography, and now again from Martensen's letter, do not concern the theater as an institution, since it, in-and-of-itself, is cultivating and edifying. There is, as Martensen argues, no doubt that the theater is necessary on a certain level of society's development; no one will be able to deny the institution its "ennobling and educating" influence. The problem is the individual actors, who, in Martensen's optic, must sacrifice themselves on the sacred alter of this institution. This places them in peril and calls for stalwart personalities. The principal mission of stage actors is to serve as a receptacles for and executors of the words and vision of the poet's creative mind. The dramatic texts, in other words, could or should be regarded as quasi-sacred texts. Particularly the male actors, as both Mrs. Heiberg and Martensen seem to agree, fall short in regard to submitting themselves to the texts and to their authors. Female actors are naturally responsive to be filled with words, while male actors, already full of themselves, are in danger of mismanaging their "God-given" mandate as vessels for the theater's mission and for the charge of its writers.

The placement of Martensen's endorsement at the end of the treatise is inspired, in that it permits Mrs. Heiberg to use the bishop's letter as a stamp of approval, a co-signing of sorts, from one of the most powerful men of her day—one, whose friendship with her husband Johan Ludvig Heiberg and the Hegelian affinity the two men shared, only added extra weight to her reflections. Yet the religious language used to describe the theater differs on key points from Johan Ludvig Heiberg's deliberations. To him, the theater was analogous, not to the church, but to the state. "Theater is a state," he noted in his essay "On Theater," and he goes on to say that in this theater-state, "the poet represents the legislative branch, the actor serves as the executive branch, and the public constitutes the judiciary branch."[1] More importantly, Johan Ludvig Heiberg adds a

---

[1] Johan Ludvig Heiberg, "Om Theatret," in *Prosaiske Skrifter*, vols. 1-11, Copenhagen: C.A. Reitzel 1861-62, vol. 6, p. 194. See also Kirmmse, *Kierkegaard in Golden Age Denmark*, p. 157.

critical level to this model in that above it all, at the pinnacle of the pyramid of power, he places the theater management. The management is not only beholden to the economics of the theater, although Johan Ludvig Heiberg spends most of his eight-part essay on the practice, architecture, and economics of place, but he also sees the management as arbiter and controller of what transpires in the theater at all levels. Most importantly the director must oversee and implement a practice that not only instructs the audience (*publikum*) in a sense of propriety and ethics, but also teaches it how to balance its inclination toward subjective judgment with a more refined objective judgment. As mentioned, for Johan Ludvig Heiberg, the theater was not, as it would later be for his wife, analogous to the church. His pantheistic Hegelianism and belief in the power of human agency and in the authority of ideas made him regard religion as a childhood sickness for the uneducated. Mrs. Heiberg, on the other hand, never outgrew her childhood sickness; to her, the church offered a valuable parallel to the theater and presented a foil for her reflections on the ethics of performance. Thus Bishop Martensen's co-signature on the treatise is both a gesture toward her dead husband and, on this point, a break from his stronghold.

If Johan Ludvig Heiberg was primarily interested in articulating a model of aesthetic value that was not divorced from, but rather reinforced by political, social and economic concerns, and if his aesthetic morality (*æstetiske moral*) can be seen as sewn up with this model, Mrs. Heiberg, for her part focused more directly on the implied ethics in the concept of good taste and all that comes with it. The reason is obvious and simple: as a member of the "executive branch," Mrs. Heiberg, along with her fellow actors, were placed and pressed in the middle, between implementing the legislation (i.e., the words of the dramatists and decisions of the administration) and satisfying the judiciary (i.e., the cravings and judgment of the public). Actors had to carry out the instructions, and enjoy or suffer (sacrifice themselves to, as Martensen puts it) the verdict of public opinion and prevailing tastes.

Mrs. Heiberg's analysis of this potentially precarious position takes the form of a defense and an attack. It reads like a vacillation, an often incongruent back-and-forth, where she uses the strategy of attack ironically, as an indirect defense. We recognize this pattern from her contemporaries, not least Kierkegaard, and recall the tactic that he

had employed on Johan Ludvig Heiberg amongst others. She sees the ethics of performance as one of self-control (*selvbeherskelse*). This control is articulated in her honing of an aesthetic of distance in which she distinguishes sharply between her personal and professional life. She turns the question of ethics to a question of religion as she moves herself from the eye of the audience to the eye of God, and from the judgment of the audience to the judgment of God. Her growing disillusion with spectatorship and her difficulties with the fleeting nature of acting make her want to bestow some grace on her art form by comparing the theater with the church: "here everyone is equal and where do we find this except in the temple of art and—in the church."[1] The theater, she goes on, prepares the spectator to be "receptive" to the highest truth.

Not surprisingly, she adopts a dialectical model to explain this. However, in her optic the dialectical theater model is configured very differently from her husband's state analogy. To her, the actors and the public constitute an interdependent dynamic where the actor serves as a mirror of a higher reality for the public. This dynamic between actor and public can only escape corruption and the unethical, she posits, if the actor is true to the word of the poets and thus gives to the public the vision and hope of an ideal world. In her triangle, then, the text, and the intention of the poet serve as the highest unassailable law. The word of the poet is not unlike the word of God. You must obey it. Johan Ludvig Heiberg, we should recall, places the administrator (i.e., himself) at the highest level, and Mrs. Heiberg seems to agree, but in doing so, she uses a religious argument. Either way, as administrator or as poet-god, Johan Ludvig Heiberg maintains his pride of place.

When her husband's position is threatened, Mrs. Heiberg minces no words. Her attack on the so-called new realistic acting school, started by the actor Frederik Høedt (1820-85), can serve as case in point. The fact that Høedt was a fellow actor gave her license to admonish his hubris: "Actors," she lectures, "are only a [sic] kind of poet at a secondary level, and can only be reformers in the art of acting through the poets, who are the true reformers at a first level."[2] And, she continues, since this

---

[1] Johanne Luise Heiberg, *Et liv genoplevet i erindringen*, vol. 4, p. 211. For more on this, see also Karin Sanders, "Staging the Invisible: From the Scene of Theater to the Scene of Writing," *Scandinavica*, vol 32, no. 1, 1993, p. 16.

[2] Johanne Luise Heiberg, *Et liv genoplevet i erindringen*, vol. 4, p. 77.

reformation has already been successfully completed by her husband, "Mr. Høedt, consequently, arrived much too late as reformer"[1] He did not understand that "faithfulness to the poet is the main point and serves as the actor's theatrical conscience."[2]

If we place this attack on Høedt vis-à-vis Mrs. Heiberg's treatise on the morality of acting, Høedt's new school and his advocacy for realism in acting is seen not only as aesthetically misguided and misguiding but in fact, as ethically suspect. Add to that her strike at Høedt's, in her view, unfortunate appearance: a large head on a thin frame, a dry and flat voice that suffered from a strong nasal sound, and it seems that even his lack of ideality becomes, in a word, ethically visible. Immediately following her description of Høedt's appearance, she muses on Judas' appearance and agrees with Johann Kaspar Lavater's (1741-1801) call for beauty in the portrayal of all things, even of betrayers. A stipulation that, she writes, could and should be directed at all naturalistic artists. The implication is clear: if Johan Ludvig Heiberg is the Messianic savoir of good taste, Høedt becomes Judas, who betrays good taste in art. This is the ultimate treachery: "if art sinks so low as to only depict *reality*, whose dirt has not been sifted through a sieve, then we yell with the poet (Goethe): *Das haben wir besser und bequemer zu Hause!*"[3] That the state, under such conditions, should withdraw funding from the theater, is, she concludes, only appropriate. In other words, the charge of the new realistic school of acting not only challenges the aesthetics and the ethics of the theater, but also the theater's role as a service for the state.

The ethical dilemma for the actors, she goes on, indeed, the danger they face *as* actors, is that they build their feelings and emotions on the aesthetic. That this should be a dilemma would seem counterintuitive since we are dealing with aesthetic production. But feelings of the heart, she warns, cannot or ought not be "built on aesthetics,"[4] but only on the law and on scripture. Since actors are often blinded by the illusions they produce, "the footprints, they make on their life-journey, are immediately erased behind them."[5] Lack of self-awareness, of shame, and regret, and

---

[1] Ibid., p. 77.
[2] Ibid., p. 83.
[3] Ibid., p. 91.
[4] Ibid., p. 218.
[5] Ibid.

not least lack of the ability to remember binds them to the moment and makes them soft jellyfish (*"bløddyr"* and *"vandmænd."*). The soul of an actor is therefore damned to misery and agony, unless he or she belongs to the select few whose personalities are firm and fixed enough to resist placing "the artistic self over the moral self"[1] and hence able to resist the temptation to sell one's soul to please the audience.

Some four decades before Mrs. Heiberg wrote these reflections, her husband's 1840 apocalyptic comedy "A Soul after Death" presented an actor, who lives in immediacy, unreflectedness and lack of fixed identity. In Johan Ludvig Heiberg's vision, hell is populated with actors who are synonymous with their roles and whose religious beliefs are as shifting as the roles they perform, as illustrated when an actor declares his faith to many different deities, Christ, Jupiter, Mohammed, Brahma, Odin and Thor in one fell swoop.[2] To Mrs. Heiberg, the problem of such religious inconsistency is linked to a question of the individual's goodness. In her optic, the theater, the state and the church are implicitly good. The individuals, on the other hand, are implicitly not. They are sinful, fighting daemons of numerous kinds. Her strategy is to save the soul of the actor by breaking it down. A Phoenix-like destruction, described as a necessary cleansing ritual from which acting as an art form can be resurrected, replenished and cleansed from the corruption and vanity of man.

Tragedy is particularly dangerous because it lacks the "purification salt" of comedy.[3] In tragedy, Mrs. Heiberg posits, the emotive rules and allows for a conflation of person with role and as a consequence produces an unhealthy and unjustified sense of omnipotence in the actor. Only the cold plasticity in ancient Greek tragedies and in some French tragedies does not call for the comical element as moderator. Most other tragedies, however, and in particular bourgeois tragedies risk that actors fall into deep "softness" (*blødhed*) and sick sentimentality. Elements of the comical therefore should be injected into the tragic in order to create an aesthetic of distance that in turn offers protection of an ethical nature against

---

[1] Ibid., p. 221.
[2] Johan Ludvig Heiberg, "En Sjæl efter Døden" in *Nye Digte*, Copenhagen: Det danske Sprog- og Litteraturselskab, Borgen 1990, p. 72.
[3] Johanne Luise Heiberg, *Et liv genoplevet i erindringen*, vol. 4, p. 227.

the corruption of the individual actor. We may recall Hegel's definitions of tragedy and comedy, here parsed by Hayden White: "Hegel regards Tragedy and Comedy, not as opposed ways of looking at reality, but as perceptions of situations of conflict from different sides of the action. Tragedy approaches the culmination of an action....Comedy looks back upon the effects of that collision."[1] Mrs. Heiberg is clearly in sync with Hegel's distinctions between the tragic and the comic in that her use of comedy as regulator creates a distance to the culmination of the tragic action. The comic is vital, in other words, to maintain proper distance and dissuade the potential sinking, of the individual actor, into the lure of tragic absorption and its corruptible "*blødhed.*"

The ethics of performance, then, can be seen both as a kind of economy (the necessary commodification that comes with performing for a price in order to produce pleasure) and as a venue for individuation, used here generically as a term that connotes the ordering and subjugation of the "chaos" that public space and public desire project at the executor-actor. That is, the individual actor must gain, not lose, a sense of self. Yet loss of self is a danger that is very much on Mrs. Heiberg's mind. For all intents and purposes, her use of aesthetics of distance in her writing strategy is commensurate with her concepts of performance ethics.

Kirsten Wechsel has offered a persuasive analysis of the economics of props in Johan Ludvig Heiberg's vaudevilles.[2] She argues that the props are multifunctional and over-determined in Heiberg's aim for aesthetic unity. The props, in other words, served as a link between funfair visitors and their inclination toward commodity fetishism and traditional theater aesthetics, i.e., good taste. Heiberg's inclusion of the authentic (in particular in *The Reviewer and the Animal* from 1827 with the notorious use of the authentic Dyrehavesbakken tent that belonged to his future mother-in-law, Madame Pätges), Wechsel's argument goes, served as a trick that turned the tables on illegitimate entertainment and allowed the spectators to understand the nature of bad taste.

---

[1] Hayden White, *Metahistory: The Historical Imagination in Ninetieth-Century Europe*, Baltimore: The Johns Hopkins University Press 1975, pp. 94-95.

[2] Kirsten Wechsel, "Lack of Money and Good Taste: Questions of Value in Heiberg's Vaudevilles," in *Johan Ludvig Heiberg: Philosopher, Littérateur, Dramaturge, and Political Thinker*, ed. by Jon Stewart, Copenhagen: Museum Tusculanum Press 2008 (*Danish Golden Age Studies*, vol. 5), pp. 395-417.

Comedy in many ways serves the same purpose. The aim was, in both Johan Ludvig Heiberg's and Mrs. Heiberg's assessments, to move without being portentous, and to amuse without producing caricature.[1] In a number of ways, Mrs. Heiberg's predicament and her ongoing negotiation of the aesthetic and the ethical looks like an attempt to come to terms with the necessary intoxication and transport of desires in a Dionysian sense in order to find the "proper" ethical order in Apollonian terms. She understands intimately the tension between the two. Interestingly, at the time when she was deep into finishing her writing process, in 1872, Friedrich Nietzsche articulated a variation of this problem in his conflation of Dionysian dismemberment and Apollonian individuation in *The Birth of Tragedy*. But instead of giving in to the uneasy synthesis in the creation of tragic art (as Nietzsche will have it) she, like her husband, calls on the comical to create a sense of balance and stability.

Yet while she chastises the art of acting, she also offers an apology. The motivation behind the need to act, if not driven by vanity, is equivalent to the need to experience the divine. At the same time, the artistic reach for the divine is problematic because it functions as a shortcut to the ultimate realization of the self, which cannot or should not occur here, but belongs in the hereafter: She writes:

> But what do we want? Reveal oneself, animate one's individuality for others, and stress the I, of which one exists, as an autonomous image that differs from the masses by the singularity of its soul. There is a certain impatience in us humans in that we want to be revealed already here on earth; we ought to wait until we are made fully transparent in the hereafter, but we cannot.[2]

What, then, awaits the poor actors? The list is long and gruesome. To sum up from just one of Mrs. Heiberg's pages, consequences include: depression, insanity, low desires and dumb inclinations, despair, disfavor, indecision, misery of the soul, depravity and drunkenness. "Isn't it

---

[1] Johanne Luise Heiberg, *Et liv genoplevet i erindringen*, vol. 4, pp. 77-80.
[2] Ibid., p. 232.

terrible," Mrs. Heiberg asks. And who can but answer "yes" and shudder at such prospects? It is, in short, a death sentence to mistake oneself for one's masks, as she phrases it. The individual actor needs to be aware that he or she owes a great debt to the state, and if this is not paid voluntarily, through proper artistic and personal conduct, the violator could wake up one day from the illusion caused by admiration and applause and find himself or herself in "a penitentiary, amongst the despised, those who have been hit by the long arm of the law, those dressed in the coarse, humiliating prison garment, stuck with hard forced labor in order to repay the state a little of what [his] dreadful deed has cost it."[1] The conclusion seems obvious: acting is immoral. Yet, just as Martensen helped "sign" her treatise and offered his blessing, so she finds help, it seems, from the hereafter, in the form of the spirits of dead dramatists who address her at the very moment when she has passed her harsh ethical judgment and drawn the sad conclusion that her life's work had indeed been immoral. The spirit laments:

> Do you intend to destroy us? Will you rob us of the aid without which we cannot come to a full understanding [with the audience]…and you will annihilate the voices that our works cannot do without if they are to penetrate the people, educate them, lift them into a sphere that they would otherwise have difficulty in reaching! You are confessing to views that would result in the elimination of the mother tongue from the stage? The mother tongue that is so extraordinarily attached to the inner core of the nation and on which our national feelings rest….The stage is the grand mirror in which the nation can contemplate its own features and learn to know its own physiognomy; the dramatic poets are like those divers who fetch pearls from the depths of the ocean; the poets dive into the souls and bring to the light of day that which these souls only dimly suspect is hidden down there. The actor must exist as an organ for the poet and the poet as an organ for the people.[2]

Notice again the clever and ironic twist that forms an act of rescue for herself and her profession. This rescue from the hereafter is dramatic

---

[1] Ibid., p. 223.
[2] Ibid., p. 253.

in the theatrical sense of the word. We are meant to imagine, of course, that the voice of the dead dramatist is that of her husband, arguing from beyond the grave, the same way he did when he was alive, that the theater serves as an edifying and therefore ethical institution essential for the health and progress of the nation. The actor's duty, then, is to be the instrument with which the nation, by way of the dramatic poets, can save itself from itself.

With this endorsement and command from her dead husband, Mrs. Heiberg manages to produce two "truth witnesses": Martensen and Johan Ludvig Heiberg, who each in his way transposes and essentially modifies her attack on the art of acting, and, as a consequence, saves both her and her profession from the immorality and damnation that she describes. This ingenious folding of both Johan Ludvig Heiberg and Martensen into her discourse and her deliberate way of allowing them to override her own conclusion—that acting is immoral—gives her the double benefit of voicing her indignation at her fellow actors while making sure that others, her husband and Martensen, testify to the superior morality of the chosen few. She, indirectly, and without the sin of self-praise, is placed at the epitome of the ethical, far from the immoral, and consequently she serves not only the theater, but also the church and the state.

If redemption is what Mrs. Heiberg ultimately wants, we can see how she tries at all levels to facilitate this. In one of her last stage directions, of Henrik Ibsen's *The Pretenders* from 1864, she asked permission from Ibsen to change the last line, where Skule Baardssøn is called "God's stepson on earth, that is the riddle concerning him" to "now Skule Baardssøn returns home from his journey regretful of his waywardness on earth."[1] Ibsen, as always, infatuated with Mrs. Heiberg, granted permission for this change. It is tempting to see her retrospective religious and ethical critique of acting as a way to redeem her own imagined "waywardness" into the pleasures of performing.

But to her readers, particularly at the moment of the publication in 1891-92, the question of redemption took a different form and became a question of accountability. Because they perceived what Wayne Booth in

---

[1] Ibid., p. 274.

another context has called "powerful violations of generic expectations," they reacted with distrust. Booth has shown how we essentially "read-with" a text because of our genre expectation:

> we never question—if we go on reading at all—the terms of the contract clearly specified by the work's emphasis on its own genre. We rely—even the least sophisticated *and* the most critically up-to-date among us rely— on our past experience of genres, slotting in the new work until and unless we bump into powerful violations of generic expectations.[1]

The violation that Mrs. Heiberg's readers experienced had to do with expectations of authenticity and verifiability. Frustrated by overt and easily identifiable misinformation, or half-truths, her realization of self, became, to her readers, ethically suspect.

In many ways, her readers (both then and now) read the autobiography as a novel, waiting for the moment where the protagonist, Mrs. Heiberg, comes to some form of realization of self, or as Kirmmse phrased it "an aesthetic analogue to the ethical acquisition of the self."[2] Yet her writing was marked by anxiety of an ethical nature that transcended the standard conflict between the "real" and the "ideal."

In the end, Mrs. Heiberg's treatise can be seen as a poetics of performance, one that aims to correct what Friedrich Schiller had sorrowfully articulated, "for the mimic artist the future binds no wreaths."[3] In her own way she binds a memory wreath for her art form, albeit one with thorns.

---

[1] Wayne C. Booth, "The Ethics of Forms: Taking Flight with *The Wings of the Dove*," in *Understanding Narrative*, p. 103.

[2] Kirmmse, *Kierkegaard in Golden Age Denmark*, p. 330.

[3] Johanne Luise Heiberg, *Et liv genoplevet i erindringen*, vol. 4, p. 80.

Index of Persons

Index of Subjects

acting, 14, 15, 230, 241-54.
aesthetics, 1, 2, 4, 5, 10-13, 17, 18,
   21, 22, 26, 29, 39, 42, 47, 49-56,
   58, 61-63, 65, 71, 72, 85-88, 94,
   99, 104, 106, 108, 110, 111, 113,
   118-121, 124, 125, 127, 134-139,
   145, 147, 149, 153, 154, 160,
   165-167, 169, 170, 172, 173, 176,
   182, 183, 221, 242-251, 254.
art, death of, 58, 61.
autonomy, 148.

Bakkehus, 18, 19.
ballet, 124, 126, 180, 195-198, 205,
   208, 219-221.
Berlingske Tidende, 68, 118.
Biedermeier, 11, 35, 47, 51, 52, 78,
   197, 213, 221, 240.

Christianity, 25, 26, 37, 40, 149, 237.
comedy, 249, 250.
communication, indirect, 242, 244.
Copenhagen Flying Post, see Heiberg,
   Johan Ludvig, "*Kjøbenhavns
   Flyvende Post.*"
Corsair, The, 35.

criticism,
   aesthetic, 18, 22.
   dramatic, 7, 17, 18.
   literary, 36.

demonic, 79, 84, 207.
Den Frisindede, 142.

Enlightenment, 17, 38, 73, 199.
eros, 14, 213.
eroticism, 200, 207-209, 239.
ethics, 13, 14, 241-254.

Fædrelandet, 49, 68.
fairy tales, 31, 92, 132.
faith, 25, 40.
folklore, 77, 147.
folk songs, 69, 70, 73, 94.
folk tales, 74, 77, 91.
freedom, 83, 84, 126, 156-158.
French Revolution (1789), 48, 56, 67,
   75, 98.

genre, 1, 11, 12, 18, 28, 29, 31, 37, 39,
   72, 73, 89, 91, 94, 117, 118, 121-
   129, 131, 133, 135, 138, 140,

Previously Published Titles in the Series
Danish Golden Age Studies

Volume 1
K. Brian Soderquist, *The Isolated Self: Truth and Untruth in Søren Kierkegaard's On the Concept of Irony* (2007). Hardback. viii+247pp. ISBN 978-87-635-3090-3.

Volume 2
Robert Leslie Horn, *Positivity and Dialectic: A Study of the Theological Method of Hans Lassen Martensen* (2007). Hardback. xviii+246pp. ISBN 978-87-635-3089-7.

Volume 3
Jon Stewart, *A History of Hegelianism in Golden Age Denmark*
Tome I: *The Heiberg Period: 1824-1836* (2007). Hardback. xxi+629pp. ISBN 978-87-635-3086-6.
Tome II: *The Martensen Period: 1837-1842* (2007). Hardback. xx+775pp. ISBN 978-87-635-3101-6.

Volume 4
Curtis L. Thompson, *Following the Cultured Public's Chosen One: Why Martensen Mattered to Kierkegaard* (2008). Hardback. xvi+216pp. ISBN 978-87-635-1097-4.

Volume 5
Jon Stewart (editor), *Johan Ludvig Heiberg: Philosopher, Littérateur, Dramaturge, and Political Thinker* (2008). Hardback. xxii+548pp. ISBN 978-87-635-1096-7.

Volume 6
Jon Stewart (editor), Hans *Lassen Martensen: Theologian, Philosopher and Social Critic* (2011). Hardback. xv+351pp. ISBN 978-87-635-3169-6.

Museum Tusculanum Press
University of Copenhagen, Birketinget 6, DK-2300 Copenhagen S.
Tel. +45 35 32 91 09. Fax +45 35 32 91 13. E-mail: info@mtp.dk. www.mtp.dk.

Previously Published Titles in the Series
Texts from Golden Age Denmark

Volume 1
Heiberg's On the Significance of Philosophy for the Present Age and Other Texts, trans.
and ed. by Jon Stewart (2005). Hardback. xxii+46pp. ISBN 978-87-635-3084-2.

Volume 2
Heiberg's Speculative Logic and Other Texts, trans. and ed. by Jon Stewart (2006).
Hardback. xviii+387pp. ISBN 978-87-635-3091-0.

Volume 3
Heiberg's Introductory Lecture to the Logic Course and Other Texts, trans. and ed. by
Jon Stewart (2007). Hardback. xvii+33pp. ISBN 978-87-635-3085-9.

Volume 4
Heiberg's Contingency Regarded from the Point of View of Logic and Other Texts, trans.
and ed. by Jon Stewart (2008). Hardback. vxi+457pp. ISBN 978-87-635-1099-8.

Volume 5
Mynster's "Rationalism, Supernaturalism" and the Debate about Mediation, trans.
and ed. by Jon Stewart (2009). Hardback. vxi+683pp. ISBN 978-87-635-3096-5.

Volume 6
Heiberg's Perseus and Other Texts, trans. and ed. by Jon Stewart (2011). Hardback.
xiii+406pp. ISBN 978-87-635-3170-2.

Museum Tusculanum Press
University of Copenhagen, Birketinget 6, DK-2300 Copenhagen S.
Tel. +45 35 32 91 09. Fax +45 35 32 91 13. E-mail: info@mtp.dk. www.mtp.dk.

W0008252